S0-AVQ-604

Mining, the Environment, and Indigenous Development Conflicts

WITHDRAWN

X̱wi7x̱wa Library

Mining,

the Environment,

and

Indigenous Development Conflicts

Saleem H. Ali

The University of Arizona Press

Tucson

The University of Arizona Press
© 2003 The Arizona Board of Regents
All rights reserved

First paperback printing 2009
ISBN 978–0-8165-2879-0 (pbk. : alk. paper)

Library of Congress Cataloging-in-Publication Data
Ali, Saleem H. (Saleem Hassan), 1973–
Mining, the environment, and indigenous development conflicts /
Saleem H. Ali.
p. cm.
Includes bibliographical references and index.
ISBN 0-8165-2312-6 (alk. paper)
1. Indians of North America—Land tenure. 2. Indians of North
America—Claims. 3. Indians of North America—Civil rights.
4. Mineral rights—North America. 5. Mining claims—North America.
6. Environmental ethics—North America. 7. Business ethics—North
America. 8. Environmental policy—North America. 9. North
America—Environmental conditions. I. Title.
E98.L3A35   2003
333.2—dc21   2003008311

Publication of this book is made possible in part by the proceeds of a
permanent endowment created with the assistance of a Challenge Grant
from the National Endowment for the Humanities, a federal agency.

Manufactured in the United States of America on acid-free, archival-
quality paper containing a minimum of 30% post-consumer waste and
processed chlorine free.

14   13   12   11   10   09   7   6   5   4   3   2

With profound love

and gratitude to my mother,

Parveen S. Ali,

who taught me the virtue of principled confrontation,

and to my father,

Shaukat Ali,

from whom I learned the value of

pragmatic conciliation.

Like the miner's canary, the Indian marks the shift from fresh air to poison gas in our political atmosphere; and our treatment of Indians, even more than our treatment of other minorities, marks the rise and fall of our democratic faith.

—Felix Cohen, *Handbook of American Indian Law,* 1945

Contents

Figures

Tables

Preface

Five years have passed since this book was published, and it is gratifying for me as an author to see a paperback edition coming out as a mark of success for this modest academic treatise. This was my first book, and I did not expect it to gain such wide traction in academic and policy circles. However, given the immediacy of nonrenewable resource extraction, the book gained an audience in environmental studies and beyond. It was also useful to doctoral students as an example of how to conduct comparative case analysis research and transform a dissertation into a book. Much has changed since the case analysis was conducted in terms of the specifics of the projects. Ownership of some of the mining projects discussed have changed. Inco's Voissey's Bay project is now part of the Brazilian mining giant Vale Corporation. Peabody Coal's operations are in abeyance due to the closure of the Mojave Power station due to environmental violations. The Navajo tribe has now opened a casino on the reservation as an alternative development path to mining after many years of resisting gambling. Despite these specific developments, the basic arguments of the book about environmental conflict resolution between mining interests, environmentalists, and indigenous people remain unchanged.

This book asks the question: Why do indigenous communities support environmental causes in certain cases of mining development and not in others, when technical indicators of environmental impact may in fact be comparable? The empirical research question I am trying to address is: When does environmental resistance arise in native communities in the United States and Canada that are faced with the prospect of mining development? Native people in the United States and Canada have endured widespread environmental harm at the behest of mining ventures. During the past two decades, the enactment of environmental laws and the recognition of treaty violations by settler governments have collectively led to a politics of retribution in both countries. However, conflicts surrounding mining development and indigenous people continue to challenge policy-makers on both sides of the border. I use qualitative social science research techniques such as deviant case analysis, process tracing, congruence procedures, and counterfactual analysis to study four instances of mining development (cases involving both the prevalence and non-prevalence of environmental resistance in each of the two countries).

After using a process of elimination procedure in my initial scoping analysis for the case studies, I test process-oriented hypotheses anchored in theories of negotiation involving social movements and linkage politics. My study reveals that contrary to common belief, neither scientific studies (technical impact) and economic considerations nor external influence of civic society adequately explain the emergence or prevalence of resistance. Instead, the negotiation process (particularly the way in which issues are linked), strategic alliance formation, and the articulation of sovereignty are the key determinants of environmental resistance in indigenous communities. I conclude with some lessons for both the United States and Canada in terms of public policy and negotiation processes that can be most conducive to environmentally responsible and effective planning of mining ventures on or near indigenous land.

This book had its genesis as a doctoral dissertation in the Department of Urban Studies and Planning at the Massachusetts Institute of Technology. The challenge I embraced in researching this topic was to provide a balanced perspective on highly divisive development concerns, while also providing a fresh prescriptive analysis that would not alienate any communities of interest. The literature on mining and environmental conflicts is relatively limited and tends to be polarized by strongly entrenched normative positions. As a student of environmental planning, my objective is to seek a viable development trajectory both in biophysical and social terms. However, in order to do so, we must try to understand the underpinnings of existing conflicts that defy conventional technocratic explanations. This book is a modest attempt toward this goal.

For fledgling academics such as myself, the first book is a truly daunting deed—it is our first dive into deep discourse and data, beyond the relatively shallow surf of term papers and PowerPoint presentations. Thus, such a task must be approached with humility and an explicit recognition of all those who have offered support and guidance along the way. I would like to express my foremost gratitude to my dissertation committee comprising Professor Lawrence Susskind (MIT), Professor Joseph Kalt (Harvard), and Professor Paul Carlile (MIT), for their guidance and support. Larry Susskind, in particular, has been a mentor throughout my stay at MIT and an exemplary advisor. The faculty at MIT's Department of Urban Studies and Planning at Harvard's Kennedy School, where I did much of my coursework leading up to the dissertation, were a continuous source of inspiration.

My special thanks to all those individuals in the public and private sectors who agreed to be interviewed, particularly the tribal representatives from across the United States and Canada who were willing to talk candidly and discuss sensitive strategic issues with an itinerant researcher. Funding for travel to the case study sites was provided by MIT's Laboratory for Energy and the Environment and the Martin Sustainability Fellowship. Dr. Joanne Kauffman was particularly kind in arranging for funds in this regard. Institutional encouragement from my various employers—Brown University, Industrial Economics Inc., and the University of Vermont—allowed me to pursue this project to its completion. Constructive criticism from four anonymous reviewers and the patience of the editors and production staff at the University of Arizona Press, particularly Yvonne Reineke and Chris Szuter, were immeasurably helpful.

Professional support from one's colleagues is of course critically important but must also be supplemented with extended family support at home for an all-consuming endeavor such as a book to be completed. My parents, Dr. Shaukat Ali and Dr. Parveen Ali, to whom this book is dedicated, have been a comforting presence throughout my academic life and have always given me complete freedom to choose my career trajectory. My sisters Farzana and Irfana and their families continued to reassure me across the miles through phone conversations and frequent visits. Our sons Shahmir and Shahroze, despite being a delightful distraction, provided me with an incentive to finish quickly so that I could spend more time with them. Most intimately, my wife Maria showed patience with my schedule in ways which only truest love can instill.

Introduction

Minerals are a pivotal natural resource for native communities on both sides of the U.S.-Canadian border and hence an extremely important political concern. In the United States when tribally owned lands are considered together with lands owned by individual tribal members, Indians possess approximately 30 percent of the coal found west of the Mississippi, 50 percent of potential uranium reserves, and 20 percent of known natural gas and oil reserves (Fixico 1998). An inventory of on-reserve mineral potential prepared by the Canadian Department of Indian Affairs and Northern Development (DIAND) in 1990 recorded 3,276 "mineral occurrences" on the 2,267 First Nation reserves in Canada. Of these, 770 reserves were identified with precious and base metal potential. A meaningful number of reserves, 184, were classed as "of significant interest" — in other words, warranting further examination.[1]

However, many of the property rights and environmental jurisdiction concerns over these deposits are entangled in lawsuits and land claim conflicts. While providing a key source of revenues for many tribes, minerals are also the locus of immense environmental dissent within communities. There is thus a need for a study of this kind because of a wide-ranging problem of mineral development, specifically on native land, in an effort to constructively resolve environmental conflicts surrounding mineral development.

Modern society relies fundamentally on mining as a primary source of raw material and fuel for production at all levels of industry. Mining companies are thus powerful entities that can wield considerable influence with government and the population at large. They also have the resources to bring a sudden surge of development in otherwise remote and impoverished parts of the world that are sometimes inhabited by indigenous tribal populations.

Environmental resistance to mining is certainly amplified by the fact that it is a nonrenewable extractive enterprise. It thus forces us to frame the problem in the most extreme context and thus provides an unambiguous arena in which to explore resource conflicts that may not have simple win-win outcomes. Like most environmental concerns, there is often a stark difference between actual environmental impact and perceived impact—though policy decisions may not necessarily reflect this distinction. In the case of mining on Indian land, perceptions regarding current mining ventures may be largely linked to some of the historical impacts of mining that were all too real.

For example, of the 150 Navajo uranium miners who worked at the Kerr-McGee uranium mine in Shiprock, New Mexico, until 1970, 133 died of lung cancer or various forms of fibrosis by 1980. Yet, such historical harms do not necessarily translate into contemporary resistance either. There is a belief in many tribal establishments that technological advance and regulatory stringency can collectively allow for mining to be a means of sustainable development. This is most clearly manifest in the highly demanded programs of the Bureau of Indian Affairs (BIA) and the Department of Indian Affairs and Northern Development (DIAND) for mineral assessments on tribal land.

However, excessive involvement by the federal government is also resented by most native communities. European colonial repression of indigenous communities in the New Worlds of America and Australia was particularly severe and persistent. Unlike regions such as India or most of Africa, the settlers in America and Australia have become a permanent and overwhelming majority of the population, often displacing the indigenous peoples from their environment and instituting resource-intensive enterprises, such as mining, in their place. Environmental groups in Australia and the Americas have thus felt a particular degree of contrition toward the native cause.

The past few decades, particularly since the United Nations' involvement in indigenous peoples' issues, have brought forth a need for atonement in these countries. This is exemplified by the numerous initiatives to publicly apologize for the injustices of the past. Canada has been particularly strident in this regard through the publication of *Gathering Strength*, its plan for indigenous renewal in which the Canadian government recognized the legacy of injustices and officially apologized for the abuse of indigenous children in the residential system, committing $350 million to healing centers to deal with the effects of this abuse. The plan explicitly spells out a sense of contrition: "Sadly our history with respect to the treatment of indigenous people is not something in which we can take pride. . . . We must recognize the impact of these actions on the once self-sustaining nations that were disaggregated, disrupted, limited or even destroyed. . . . We must acknowledge that the result of these actions was the erosion of the political, economic and social systems of indigenous people and nations" (Canada 1997a).

New Zealand has followed a similar path vis-à-vis an apology and statement of reconciliation. In the United States and Australia, a public apology has not yet been issued, but the policies have moved strongly in the direction of undoing the injustices of the past through native title settlement in Australia and various monetary settlements and self-determination regulation in the United States.[2]

This sense of retribution is similar to the congruent need for remediation efforts in the environmental realm, as exemplified by laws such as the Superfund legislation in the United States. The common theme is clearly to undo the wrongs of the past — whether that is pollution of ecosystems or racial discrimination of native populations. There has thus been a confluence of interests between the indigenous rights movement and the environmental movement at some junctures of political lobbying, which may eclipse the latent conflicts in interest between the two movements at other levels of analysis. The common perception is that the native people of the world are inherently environmentalists because for so long they have led relatively sustainable lifestyles. The Web sites and published literature of environmental organizations tend to emphasize the linkage between a pristine environment and a peaceful and contented indigenous population, and they often highlight the lobbying efforts of the organization in preserving indigenous aspirations. However, a closer analysis reveals that there are in fact many points of disagreement between the two groups, and alliances that form are often opportunistic and may even be mutually destructive — they clearly live in a contested field (Ali 1999).[3]

The relationship between cooperative behavior and dependency interests me greatly, and the way in which many environmental accords tend to be brandished as success stories deserves greater attention. Too often we do not fully understand the dynamics of the agreements and the terms by which they are reached, and destructive policies can often result from such efforts.[4] In the context of Native American communities, this dialectic is further complicated by a history of paternalistic behavior on the part of the government as well.

The framework of parenthood has often been invoked to describe the European immigrant's attitudes toward Indians. However, this imposed parental care has been greatly resented by Indians. For example, in 1916 Carlos Montezuma, an Apache chief (and a medical doctor by training) raised the voice of dissent in the most unambiguous words and specifically targeted the Bureau of Indian Affairs in a speech entitled "Let My People Go." Montezuma stated that "the BIA's guiding policy that the Indian must be cared for like a child has directly encouraged dependency" (Iverson 1982, 25). To continue the metaphor of the parent, there comes a time when the child grows up and the parent must let go—hence, planned obsolescence is implied by this analogy.[5]

There are also two underlying observations in this research. The first is that when one talks to tribes on either side of the border regarding government involvement, the tribe members frequently express dissatisfaction with their own system and feel that their counterparts on the other side of the border are better off (Nichols 1998).[6] Is this mutual dissatisfaction merely an exemplar of the grass being greener on the other side, or is there a more complex dynamic at play? Secondly, although Canada and the United States have both faced very similar situations with regard to these conflicts, there has been little or no attempt to draw lessons from the experiences of the other on these issues. Furthermore, the linkage of environmental concerns to native demands for sovereignty is increasingly prevalent but has not been well studied.[7] While the literature of linkage politics demonstrates the connections between national and international policies,[8] very little has been done to show the connection between tribal politics and national politics, particularly in the area of environmental policy.

While this study aims to present many complex problems with multiple causality, the design of the research and the selection of cases aims to present a clear picture of how environmental resistance movements evolve; how they can, in turn, be agents of change; and how they may affect the development trajectory of native communities. I have tried to avoid any value judgments about the specific projects reviewed and have not posited any normative view about mining per se. Instead, my analysis focuses on the primacy of the process by which an outcome is achieved.

Abbreviations

BATNA	Best Alternative to a Negotiated Agreement
BIA	Bureau of Indian Affairs
CERT	Council of Energy Resource Tribes
DIAND	Department of Indian Affairs and Northern Development
EIS	Environmental Impact Statement
ENGO	Environmental Nongovernmental Organization
EPA	Environmental Protection Agency
HPL	Hopi Partitioned Land
IBA	Impact Benefit Agreement
IBLA	Interior Board of Land Appeals (U.S.)
ICMM	International Council on Metals and Mining
LIA	Labrador Inuit Association
MMSD	Mining Minerals and Sustainable Development
MOU	Memorandum of Understanding
MTN	Midwest Treaty Network
NAGPRA	Native American Graves Protection and Repatriation Act
NGO	Nongovernmental Organization
NMC	Nicolet Minerals Company
NRTEE	National Round Table on the Environment and the Economy
OSM	Office of Surface Mining Control and Reclamation
RCRA	Resource Conservation and Recovery Act
SISIS	Settlers in Support of Indigenous Sovereignty
SMCRA	Surface Mining Control and Reclamation Act
SME	State Mining Enterprises
VBNC	Voisey's Bay Nickel Company Ltd.

Part I

Communities of Interest and Emergent Conflict

Chapter 1

Mining on Indigenous Lands

The North American Experience

Perhaps the most valuable attribute of social science research lies in its ability to understand complex phenomena in human societies—to explicate situations whose dynamics cannot be replicated in vitro. This chapter aims to describe the phenomenon I am trying to understand in some detail so that the rest of the book can be contextualized. By understanding the scope and scale of the phenomenon I can move with trepidation toward more generally applicable theories as the story unfolds.

In this chapter I will endeavor to show that environmental resistance to mining activity on indigenous land is a phenomenon that merits in-depth research, particularly from a planning perspective. Since this research is a study of conflict, it is essential to gain close familiarity with the categories of stakeholders. This chapter also serves to introduce one of the main stakeholders in the conflicts that I am studying—indigenous groups. They are truly the key protagonists in this book—indeed it is the unique policy challenges that are presented by indigenous people and their predicament in settler-dominated countries that have motivated this study. To summarize the way various stakeholders in such conflicts can be envisaged, figure 1.1 attempts to present them as a Venn diagram. It is important to note that the representation of bargaining power in this diagram reflects the more prevalent "environmental justice" worldview that envisages governments and corporations to be much more powerful than indigenous communities and environmentalists. However, this differential of power will itself be a subject of much debate throughout the book.

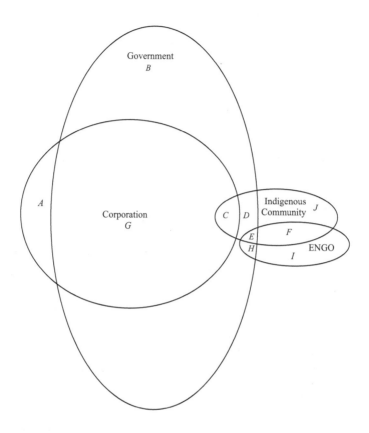

Figure 1.1
Loci of interest for various stakeholders. Size of ellipses
indicates the relative bargaining power of each group.

Indigenous Experiences with Mining in
North America

Many books on the history of mining in North America begin with a section on the first mystery miners—usually there is a description of how
Native American tribes, particularly in the Southwest of the continent,
may have discovered the usefulness of metallic elements several centuries
before the advent of the Europeans. There are numerous ancient abandoned mine sites in the Southwest that have spawned much debate among
historians. The Spanish chronicler Farfan de los Godos reported as early
as 1598 that he had been given a piece of pulverized ore by an Indian, who
later showed him a small primitive mine site in the mountains of what

Table 1.1

Explication of Loci in Venn Diagrams

Venn Diagram Regions	Context of the Conflict
A	Corporate interest only: maximizing profits from operations outside the country
B	Government interest only: policies of importance to constituencies outside the dispute
C	Common interests between community and corporation: employment and labor benefits. A portion of the community feels the compensation offered by the company is adequate. Potential for splinter group within community
D	Common interests between the government and the community only (excluding corporate or ENGO interest): welfare benefits, political representation
E	Common interests among ENGO, government, and community (excluding corporate interest): environmental protection through state-level economic analysis
F	Common interest between ENGO and community (excluding government or corporate interest): environmental protection based on normative concerns (value-based)
G	Common interests between corporation and government: strategic economic development concerns for the state, exogenous to the region
H	Common interests between ENGO and government (excluding community and corporation): other environmental lobbying efforts in which the ENGO is involved outside this conflict area (but within the country), which the government endorses
I	ENGO interest only: Based on a broader vision of the ENGO's charter; accountability to international headquarters and to the resolution of other disputes outside the country
J	Indigenous community's interest only: issues of cultural significance

Note: There is no region of common interest between most ENGOs and corporations. However, this may vary depending on the environmental group. As a general policy, ENGOs have refused to take corporate funding in their activities since the landmark decision of the Environmental Defense Fund to refuse funding from McDonalds Corporation for a study it conducted on packing material used by the company.

Government clearly has many levels and bureaucratic agencies that can act as sub-stakeholders. However, in this diagram, government is shown as an overarching entity for simplicity—different competing institutions within various levels of government can be visualized within the overlapping regions with other stakeholders.

is now eastern Arizona. There is considerable debate about the veracity of such accounts, but the consensus is that Indians probably did not use metals for tools and implements; rather, the ore was used as a source of pigment for body adornment and ornaments.[1] The association of indigenous people with mining activity in the presettlement era is thus somewhat obtuse, and clearly the extent of mining at that time was at a very small scale.

Mining does, however, play a pivotal role in the history of Indian-settler relations. Celebrated historian Frederick Jackson Turner noted in 1920 that the settlement of North America seemed to follow a rhythmic pattern. First came the mountain man into the wilderness hoping to make a fortune trapping and trading furs; then came the miners in search of a proverbial El Dorado. They were followed by cattlemen who grazed their herds on open range. Finally came the farmers who fenced the land and ended frontier life for good (Turner [1920] 1998). While revisionist historians such as Hine and Faragher (1999) have largely deconstructed Turner's frontier theories of western expansion, the reality of mining booms and the influx of settlement they brought remains beyond reproach (Hine and Faragher 1999; Limerick 1999).

Lucrative prospects for mining drew more and more settlers toward Indian lands in Appalachia, the Southwest, and the extreme Northwest (Alaska and the Yukon). The promise of mineral wealth provided a great impetus for European settlers to encroach upon Indian lands as early as the seventeenth century. While the fur trade involved reciprocal arrangements between Indians and Europeans and revolved around a commodity with which the Indians were familiar, mining activity occurred on a much more ad hoc basis and involved a commodity with which many Indians were not as familiar. Therefore, mining activity was regarded with far more suspicion in the eyes of many tribes during the early years of the frontier expansion.

The history of European colonization of native lands is beyond the scope of this book and has been addressed by a wide body of literature (see, for example, Debo 1970; Fleet 1997; Nichols 1998). Nevertheless, it is important to have some historical background to inform our discussion, since many arguments presented by resistance movements on native land are predicated on perceptions of history.

The profound demographic effect of European settlement should not be understated. There is considerable disagreement about the population of native societies in North America prior to settlement. However, even conservative estimates of native depopulation caused by disease, warfare, and overwork are staggering. For example, the population of Indians in Puerto Rico in 1508 by Spanish estimates of the time was 200,000. Within three years, the population was estimated at less than 20,000 (quoted in Champagne 1996, ix).[2] While the extent of such demographic change may vary from region to region, there is no doubt that the native population generally diminished in all areas where contact occurred. The perception of this change persists in the memories of many Native American activists to this day, and thus genocide is a frequent refrain in native discourse, as exemplified by the recent publication of Ward Churchill's *A Little Matter of Genocide: Holocaust and Denial in the Americas, 1492 to the Present*.[3] A more relevant variation of this term is *ecocide*, a term first used as the title of a book published in 1970 on the ecological impacts of wars in Indochina (Weisberg 1970). Since then it has been used to describe colonialism in the Americas by numerous native writers (see Grinde and Johansen 1999).[4]

It may be useful for our purposes to divide the period of Settler-Indian relations in North America into three segments—this broad delineation holds true for relations in both the United States and in Canada.

First was the wave of expansion from the sixteenth century to the end of the eighteenth century, which involved a series of battles and treaties between natives and Europeans. This was the time when many Indians were displaced from their lands because of the need for settlers to acquire land for either mining or agricultural activity. The second wave involved the development of institutions to effectively manage the Indians by relegating them to reservations or reserves within circumspect boundaries.

Initially, Native Americans were relegated to these lands because the lands were thought to be unproductive. As a recent review of a book on Indian mineral resources points out, "It is no small irony that after Native Americans had been forced onto reservations on land that nobody wanted, a wealth of natural resources would be discovered under those lands."[5]

When minerals were indeed discovered, there was a wave of policy initiatives to facilitate the development of mines on native lands through a rather ad hoc mixture of land appropriation, population displacement, and side payments that were anything but fair. In 1882, oil was discovered in the Oklahoma territory, which subsequently led to the Indian Mineral-Leasing Act of 1891. In Canada, mineral resources were included in treaty negotiations between tribes and the Canadian government as early as 1876, when Treaty 6 was signed. In this document indigenous people agreed to share topsoil "to the depth of a plough" (meaning six inches deep).[6]

Currently, North America is at the third stage of settler-native relations, wherein the political system has reached a level of maturity to preclude overt manipulation of Native American rights. However, there is a continuing sense of distrust among tribes about the terms of resource development on their land, and there is a congruent sense of resentment among many nonnatives about the special status of natives. Natural resource policy is a key issue in this larger conflict, since through the vicissitudes of history many tribes have large resource endowments, spawning a subsequent desire for resource exploitation on their land. Tables 1.2, 1.3, and 1.4 show the scale and scope of mineral deposits and mining activity on native land in the United States and Canada.

One of the puzzles that is evident from these tables is the enormous disparity between solid mineral potential on Canadian reserves and actual mining activity on the reserves. There are basically no large metallic or coal mining ventures on reserves themselves, despite the geologic potential for economically feasible extraction. Most of the mining on the reserves is of sand and gravel, which is qualitatively quite different from metallic mining or even coal mining. The Canadian case studies in this book involve land located in predominantly indigenous areas but that is not reserve land as such. However, the Saskatchewan case study encompasses the Fond du Lac band, which is the only metallic mineral *exploration* on reserve land. There are also certain treaty obligations with regard to mineral extractions that necessitate consultation with indigenous groups regardless of whether the deposit is on reserve land itself. From a comparative perspective, the research presented here attempts to tease out the differences in how resistance emerges in these two settings.

It is clear from the data presented here that solid mineral activity is an issue of great salience to Native Americans on both sides of the border. In the United States, tribes have had more experience with metallic mining on their land when compared to their Canadian counterparts. However, the huge mineral potential of Canadian reserves, and even more so the potential for further mineral activity as land claims are settled in British Columbia and Newfoundland, is immense.

While the specific nature of mining activity in terms of land tenure and legal regime may have been different on both sides of the border, the environmental impact of mining on native communities has been considerably serious for all. Apart from these mines there are several other proposed

Table 1.2

Indian Tribes in the United States with Mineral Activity

Reservation (Tribe)	Energy Mineral Potential	Trust Acreage (Percent Allotted)	Resident Indian Population	Government
Blackfeet (Blackfeet)	Coal, oil, gas	937,701 (68)	7,000	IRA
Crow (Crow)	Coal, oil, gas	1,516,005 (73)	5,500	Non-IRA constitution
Fort Berthold (Mandan, Hidatsa, Arikara)	Coal, oil, gas	419,198 (83)	3,100	IRA
Fort Peck (Assiniboine and Sioux)	Coal, oil, gas	904,683 (57)	5,200	Non-IRA constitution
Hopi (Hopi)	Coal, oil, gas	1,561,213 (0)	9,000	IRA
Jicarilla Apache	Coal, oil, gas	823,580 (0)	2,500	IRA
Laguna Pueblo (Keresan)	Uranium, coal	461,099 (0)	6,700	IRA
NANA Corp., Alaska	Zinc, copper	Nontrust, Alaskan corporation lease		Alaskan
Navajo (Dineh)	Coal, uranium, oil, gas	436,947 (27)	170,000	—
Northern Cheyenne (Cheyenne)	Coal, oil		3,300	IRA
Osage (Osage)	Oil, gas	168,794 (100)	6,200	—
Southern Ute	Coal, oil, gas	309,970 (1)	1,200	IRA
Spokane	Uranium	130,180 (9)	2,100	—
Uintah and Ouray (Ute)	Coal, oil, gas, shale	10,231,556 (1)	2,500	IRA
Ute Mountain Ute (Ute)	Coal, oil, gas, uranium	597,288 (1)	1,700	IRA
Wind River (Arapaho and Shoshone)	Coal, oil, gas, uranium	1,887,262 (5)	5,500	—

Source: Based on data presented in Ambler 1990 and BIA 2000.

Table 1.3
Canadian First Nation Reserves with Mineral Activity

Band Name	Province	Material Extracted	Population on Reserves	Area (hectares)
Big River	Saskatchewan	Sand, gravel	1,638	12,129
Blood	Alberta	Sand, gravel	7,442	134,293
Cheam	British Columbia	Sand, gravel	180	458
Clearwater River Déné	Saskatchewan	Sand, gravel	535	9,510
Cowichan	British Columbia	Sand, gravel	1,850	2,254
Cree (Bigstone)	Alberta	Sand, gravel	1,864	21,014
English River	Saskatchewan	Sand, gravel	595	13,100
Fond du Lac	Saskatchewan	Metallic Exploration	805	15,520
Joseph Bighead	Saskatchewan	Sand, gravel	462	4,700
Kamloops	British Columbia	Sand, gravel	—	—
Kwakiutl	British Columbia	Sand, gravel	326	420
Lac La Ronge	Saskatchewan	Sand, gravel	4,195	43,294
Matsqui	British Columbia	Sand, gravel	83	165
Montreal Lake	Saskatchewan	Sand, gravel	1,592	8,270
Pavilion	British Columbia	Limestone	165	2,126
Penticton	British Columbia	Sand, gravel	496	18,532
Peter Ballantine Cree Nation	Saskatchewan	Sand, gravel	3,157	15,067
Saik'uz First Nation	British Columbia	Sand, gravel	540	2,578
Saulteaux	Saskatchewan	Sand, gravel	482	11,820
Six Nations of the Grand River	Ontario	Gypsum	8,323	18,265
Skyway	British Columbia	Sand, gravel	52	680

Source: Personal communication with Jean-Louis Causse and Douglas Paget of the Canadian Department of Indian Affairs and Northern Development, Ottawa, September 2002.

ventures located on or near native land in the United States and Canada (see table 1.4).

Is This an Environmental Justice Issue?

An argument can also be made that the large preponderance of mining activity on native land, particularly uranium mining, was a manifestation

Table 1.4

Mining and Remediation Projects in Native Communities

Mining Project and Area	Tribe or Band Affected	Status
Carlotta and Gentry metal mines, Arizona	White Mountain Apache Tribe	Proposal for an open pit copper mine by Canadian mining company Cambior, near the reservation
Coeur d'Alene mines, Idaho	Coeur d'Alene	Department of Justice lawsuit against Asarco mining and area near the reservation has been declared a Superfund site
Colville, Washington	Colville	Tribe passed referendum opposing mining by Battle Mountain Gold and Santa Fe Pacific
Crandon mine	Mole Lake Chippewa, Menominee	BHP Billiton has purchased Rio Algom, which purchased the property from Exxon, but there is currently a moratorium on mining in Wisconsin
Crescent Valley, Nevada	Western Shoshone	Oro Nevada Resources has begun exploration work despite tribal requests to stay clear of the area
Crownpoint uranium mine, New Mexico	Navajo	Proposal for several uranium mines using in situ leaching process; EIS process is under way
Dawn uranium mine	Spokane	Under reclamation negotiations
Diavik diamond mine, Northwest Territories, Canada	Dogrib, Yellow-knives Déné, North Slave Métis, Lutsel K'e Déné, Kitikmeot Inuit	Diamond mine located in area of land claims being settled; participation agreements have been signed with each of the five affected Aboriginal groups; production was projected to commence in first quarter of 2003
Ekati (BHP Billiton) mine, NWT, Canada	Dogrib, Yellow-knives Déné, North Slave Metis, Lutsel K'e Déné, Kitikmeot Inuit	Impact and Benefit Agreements have been signed with each of the five affected Aboriginal groups. Production began in October 1998

Table 1.4

Continued

Mining Project and Area	Tribe or Band Affected	Status
Musselwhite gold mine— Placer Dome/TVX/ Normandy Americas, Inc., Ontario, Canada	Cat Lake FN, North Caribou Lake FN, King-fisher Lake FN, Wunnumin Lake FN, Shibogama FN Council, Windigo FN Council	One IBA has been signed and subsequently renegotiated between the affected First Nations (FN) and the companies; production began in 1997
Picuris project near Taos, New Mexico	Picuris Pueblo	Summo, a Canadian mining company, is conducting exploratory work adjacent to the reservation
Raglan mine, Quebec, Canada	Makivik Corporation	Nickel and copper project commenced in 1998 after an agreement was signed
Snap Lake diamond project (De Beers), Northwest Territories, Canada	Dogrib Treaty 11 Tribal Council, North Slave Métis Alliance	De Beers announced that it has signed MOUs with both of these groups to sign participation agreements in anticipation of the opening of an underground diamond mine as early as 2006; the company also plans to negotiate with the Akaitcho and Yellowknives Déné

Note: Based on various personal communications with the BIA and DIAND, as well as a memorandum, *Mining and Sacred Sites*, published by the Mineral Policy Center in Washington, D.C., in 1999. This list includes projects that are not necessarily on native land but are in close proximity to native areas and have thus required consultation or negotiations with the communities.

of environmental injustice. The preponderance of mining, according to this hypothesis, was not an accident of geology but rather a deliberate attempt by the mining industry to locate mines in areas where there would be minimal resistance on grounds of environmental and occupational harm. However, geological data does not support this idea. Extractable minerals are generally so few and far between that mining companies are seldom in a position to pick and choose deposits. For example, figure 1.2 shows the geologic potential for minerals in North America. Many of the mineralized areas happen to be in mountainous or rough terrain—areas that are often not ideal for urban establishments but where tribal communities have flourished because of relatively abundant water, game, and timber.

The historical record shows that in the early days of frontier expansion the decision to mine was determined totally by the perceived potential of minerals on land and quite irrespective of its prior occupancy (hence the term *mining rush*). Over time, the presence of natives on the land, environmental issues, and other regulatory regimes began to sink in as factors in decision making on the part of prospectors—but their inclusion was apparently more a cause for pause. Part of the purpose of this study is to understand the factors that contribute to the decision-making process within mining companies. What role do environmental regulations, indigenous rights concerns, and other regulatory forces play in the decision-making process of mining developers?

Too often scholars of Native American environmental concerns have fallen to the temptation of lumping together such issues as nuclear waste sites and mining development—perhaps this has been caused by the presence of uranium in both issues. However, the siting of nuclear waste sites is far less determinate by geological indicators than is the siting of a mine—the potential choices for possible waste repositories from a purely physical science perspective are far more numerous. For example, it was primarily social factors that ended up narrowing the list to nine sites in the case of the Department of Energy's plans for a waste depository in 1983.[7] Therefore, environmental justice arguments hold more credence in such cases than they do in the case of mining development.

Nevertheless, the subsequent compliance with various environmental laws and human rights issues post facto of a mine's establishment may well be viewed through an environmental justice lens. A comparison of environmental compliance and occupational health concerns on mines that are located on native versus nonnative land is thus quite reasonable. While such questions are not the focus of this research per se, the emergence of resistance may be motivated by at least a perception of such environmental injustice and hence will be discussed where it is evident in the case analysis. It is important to keep in mind at the outset these various distinctions and subtleties regarding environmental justice to avoid confounding issues.

Environmental justice is, however, becoming an expansive academic concept and acquiring a cache similar to sustainable development. Sus-

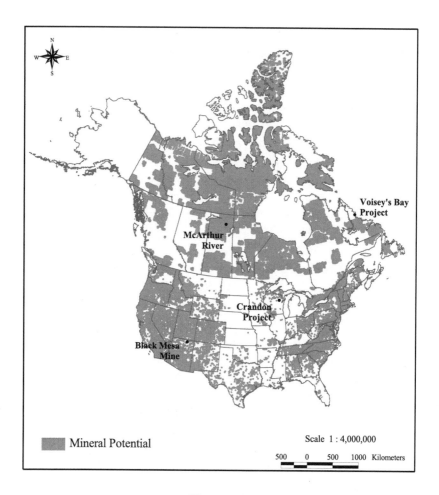

Figure 1.2
Case study sites and mineral resource potential based on geological composition in the contiguous United States and Canada. (Map by Steven DeRoy; based on data from the U.S. Dept. of the Interior, Bureau of Indian Affairs, Mineral Resource Data System; and Statistics Canada)

tainability and environmental justice are by no means synonymous concepts. Andrew Dobson (1999a, 1999b) is among the few political theorists to tackle the confluence and divergence of these two concepts. As he insightfully observes in his work *Justice and the Environment*, the key common ground lies in the common preoccupation that both concepts have with the distribution of "benefits and burdens" (Dobson 1999a, 73).[8] However, even with his neat typology of comparing the two concepts, he encounters the following problem: "The framework for the exploration of the relationship between environmental sustainability and social justice would have been neater than it turns out to be if it had been possible to demarcate distinct conceptions of social justice in the same way as I was able to do for the conceptions of environmental sustainability" (Dobson 1999a, 84).

As we shall see (particularly in chapters 6 and 7), much of the disconnect between native groups and environmental groups arises because of an inability to judge this disjuncture.

Mining and Sustainable Development

Retrieving rocks and minerals from the earth's crust changes the most basic structure of an ecosystem by disrupting the substrate on which life may develop. The environmentally deleterious effects of mining were noticed as early as 1556, when Georgius Agricola wrote his seminal text on mining, *De re metallica*: "The strongest argument of the detractors [of mining] is that the fields are devastated by mining operations. . . . When ores are washed, the water which has been used poisons the brooks and streams. Therefore the inhabitants of these regions, on account of the devastation of their fields, woods, groves, brooks and rivers find great difficulty in producing the necessities of life" (quoted in Eggert 1994, 1).

Enormous quantities of waste material are generated since minerals are generally a rare appendage to huge quantities of worthless sediment. Underground mining often involves rock dewatering and the lowering of piezometric head. This may in turn lead to compaction of sand and clay, alteration in rock mass, and the development of major jointing and surface subsidence. Mining activities are also likely to cause extensive chemical pollution and sedimentation in river channels because detergents and petroleum-powered machinery are often used in the mining processes. Dredge mining, a process in which unconsolidated mineral-rich sedimentary material is removed by suction from a water-covered area, is extremely deleterious for wetland areas.

Water within a mine has been traditionally considered a hindrance to mining; hence, draining programs from the mining site have caused major disruptions in groundwater regimes. The direction of groundwater movements may easily change due to mining, thus leading to disruptions in recharge regimes and the drying up of certain springs. There may also be a rise in groundwater in certain mining areas where geotechnological methods are used. Contamination of springs due to seepage of mine wastes may exacerbate the problem of water quality. Highly mineralized water may be very damaging to the organisms residing in rivers, not to mention the deleterious effects on humans.

> Mining activities generally change siltation rates in river systems and turbidity measures that may cause serious damage to fisheries. The excavation sites left by mining operations can fill with water and be a haven for mosquitoes and other undesirable pests. This has been a particular problem in the Brazilian mining region, where reported malaria cases increased from 52,469 in 1970 to 577,520 in 1989. (Hester and Harrison 1994, 12)

There is considerable variation in the environmental impact of different kinds of mining activities (see fig. 1.3). For example, in underground copper, gold, silver, and uranium mines in North America, the ratio of ore to overburden plus waste rock is on the order of 0.1:1 to 0.3:1, whereas for surface mines (often referring to coal), the ratios range from 0.5:1 to 0.1:1 (Eggert 1994, 8).[9] However, in other areas underground mining presents greater challenges, particularly in the areas of groundwater contamination, seismic disturbance, and occupational health. Overall, solid mineral mining presents different mitigation challenges, depending on the method employed, but collectively environmental concerns surrounding mining development of metallic minerals and coal are significant regardless of the mining method. Tables 1.5 and 1.6 highlight some of the key impacts and mitigation measures in the mining industry.

Waste generation is probably the most widely publicized mining problem — and deservedly so. Mining and beneficiation generate two billion tons of solid waste a year in the United States, representing about 40 percent of the country's total solid waste. However, these numbers can be deceptive. Interestingly enough, the total hazardous waste, which is classified as a subset of solid waste, is only 270 million tons. Unfortunately, there is no comprehensive data available on what percentage of hazardous waste actually comes from mining. Nevertheless, hazardous or not, the solid waste generated is still an immense challenge to dispose of, and the Environmental Protection Agency (EPA) has had a lot of difficulty classifying the waste under the Resource Conservation and Recovery Act (RCRA)

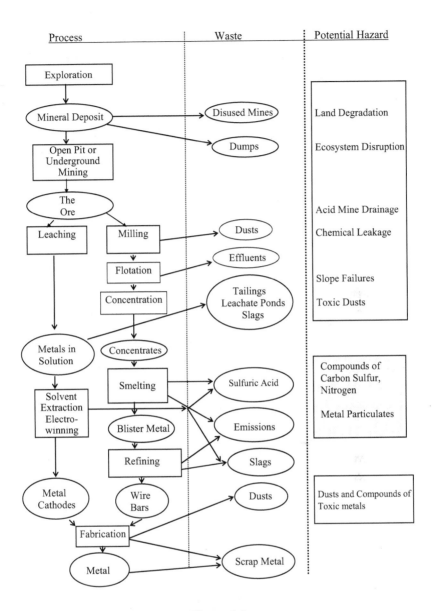

Figure 1.3

Mining and its environmental impact.

(Adapted from Warhurst and Noronha 1999)

Table 1.5

Environmental Effects of Various Methods of Mineral Extraction

Mining Method	Environmental Advantages	Environmental Disadvantages
Underground		
Open stopping	Less waste rock than with surface mining	High subsidence potential oxidation of exposed materials
Filled stopping	Lower risk of subsidence; disposes of some waste material	Possibility of oxidation and combustion of backfill; slurry drainage and water disposal aquifer impact
Surface		
Open pit	Accessibility and lower worker risk than underground	Waste rock and dust; noise; mine drainage; ore oxidation
Alluvial	Relatively easy to control damage although rarely done	High potential for particulate emissions to atmosphere and hydrosphere; surface disturbance
Non-entry		
Auguer	Minimum surface disturbance and low worker risk	Low extraction efficiency
In situ leaching	Reduction of solid wastes, mill tailings, surface disturbance and worker risk	Requires disposal of large amounts of soluble salts, possible groundwater contamination and surface subsidence
In situ utilization	Minimal surface disturbance, worker risk and solid residuals	Difficulty in containing and controlling underground process; high potential for underground contamination and explosions

Source: After Ripley et al. 1996.

of 1976.[10] In 1980 Congress passed the Bevill Amendment, which excluded the solid waste from mining, milling, and processing of minerals from regulation under Subtitle C of RCRA (which deals with hazardous waste). Subsequently the EPA prepared a report on the impact of mining wastes on the environment and differentiated between extraction and beneficiation wastes on the one hand and mineral processing wastes on the other.

Table 1.6

Abatement Procedures for Some Environmental Effects
of Mineral Exploitation

Effect	Traditional Abatement	Advanced Abatement
Surface disturbance and waste dumps	Reclamation, backfilling and slope engineering	Greater use of waste material for mine backfilling, roads, construction
	Physical stabilization: covering with inert material such as slag, soil, concrete	Greater use of non-entry methods of mining and alternative methods of disposal
	Chemical stabilization: spraying with oil-resin emulsion; vegetative stabilization	Better waste-dump siting
Hydrospheric effluents (water pollution)	Settling ponds, recycling, lime neutralization	Use of wet drilling or enclosure and dust collection, more recycling
	Chemical treatment: neutralization, coagulation, precipitation, oxidation, reduction, oil exchange	Biological polishing
	Chemical stabilization: spraying with oil-resin emulsion; vegetative stabilization	Better waste-dump siting

Source: After Ripley et al. 1996.

The report concluded that while some mineral processing waste met the criteria for Subtitle C hazardous classification, most exploration and beneficiation wastes did not. Therefore, the agency decided to regulate mining wastes under Subtitle D of RCRA (nonhazardous wastes), with the caveat that federal oversight and enforcement would be required (even though they are not stipulated in the statute).

This decision was challenged in court by the Environmental Defense Fund, and in 1988 the U.S. Court of Appeals ruled against the agency insofar that the exemption of all mining wastes from Subtitle C was too broad. Therefore the EPA issued two final rules in 1990 under which most were made subject to Subtitle C. Nevertheless, the rules also identified twenty mineral processing wastes whose impact would be studied further before a classification was made. These wastes included muds from bauxite refining, residue from chrome roasting, slag and tailings from primary copper processing, wastewater from magnesium processing, and slag from lead and zinc production. In 1991, the agency determined all twenty of these wastes to be nonhazardous. Two of them, phosphogypsum and process wastewater from phosphoric acid production, are now regulated under the Toxic Substances Control Act, while the other contentious wastes are now regulated under Subtitle D. This example illustrates the complexity involved in regulating only one aspect of the environmental impact of mining.

While mining clearly has had a deleterious impact on the environment, it has also had a profoundly positive impact on the development of industrial establishments and our modern way of living. In the words of one eminent historian of mining:

> Without mining—from coal to iron to gold—the United States could not have emerged as a world power by the turn of the century, nor could it have successfully launched its international career in the twentieth century. The Carnegies and Rockefellers, giants of the age, would have faced a hard go of it without the labor and sweat of thousands of now nameless men digging in the bowels of the earth, blasting and hauling mineral out of dark caverns far underground in now forgotten mines and mining districts scattered throughout the country. (Smith 1986, 2)

Mining of metals can also be defended on the grounds that metals are recyclable and hence, even though the extraction from the earth is non-renewable, the material itself is more worthwhile than a nonrecyclable substitute such as plastic. However, this argument ignores the fact that metals can also be oxidized and decay into forms that are not economically reusable. Perhaps more research on this issue is needed from an industrial ecology perspective (Ayres and Simonis 1994). However, this pessimistic outcome is by no means inevitable. There are some minerals, such as aluminum, iron, and silicon that are abundant in the earth's crust beyond projectable levels of utilization by humankind, and these minerals can conceivably serve as substitutes for less abundant materials. For example, more than 8 percent of the earth's crust consists of aluminum, the most abundant metal; iron takes second place at 5 percent. Modern technology has already led to the substitution of fiber optics (produced from sand) for copper, and ceramic materials (produced from clay) for iron and other metals. Materials technology has been advancing very rapidly in response to supply limitations signaled by rising prices for individual minerals. Moreover, the potential for recycling and conservation of less abundant minerals is enormous. The late economist Julian Simon extended this reasoning perhaps too optimistically to declare that even with the finite resources of minerals at our disposal, we can still say that the supply is infinite because we do not know the full potential of reserves and how they can be utilized. He compared the situation to a straight line segment that has a finite length but an infinite number of points contained within it (Simon 1999).

My aim in this section has been to present the significance of mining as an industry and also its environmental impact from a technical perspective. Clearly, there are many underlying issues of what certain human societies value about the environment, which often cause resistance to mining. Those issues are equally important but more difficult to measure and hence will be addressed on a case-by-case basis in part 2.

But the question still remains: Is mining compatible with sustainable development?[11] The answer must take two parts. First, there is no doubt that mining under present technological conditions does have a certain degree of permanent impact on a region. Second, mining involves extraction of nonrenewable resources. By these measures, the answer at one level is no, mining is not sustainable. However, while the landscape may be permanently changed by mining in certain ways, this does not necessarily mean that communities cannot thrive if the project is appropriately planned. Mining can therefore be a prelude to sustainable development if we are willing to absorb a certain degree of permanent impact. The key then is to be able to use mining as an entry point toward a more stable industrial or service-based economy that is not inherently obsolescent. Much of this book is about how communities, companies, and the government can move in a partnership to achieve this goal of a sustainable livelihood for a community with minimal environmental impact.

It is important to appreciate that mineral activity evokes a strong sense of ambivalence among tribes, as it does among society in general. Nevertheless, tribes are eager to at least explore options with mineral resources. The requests for mineral assessments to the Bureau of Indian Affairs' (BIA's) mineral resources department are staggering. In 1999, there were more than fifty tribes who applied for mineral assessments.[12] The BIA has had to initiate a screening process to determine which tribes are most deserving based on various geologic and economic indictors. Only about one-third of the tribes who apply are accepted for an assessment—such is the scale of the interest in mineral ventures.

In Canada, mineral potential studies have already been carried out for most reserves and are available. While the enthusiasm for mineral development in First Nations in Canada has not been as strong as in the United States, all First Nation bands clearly want to keep their options open. Mineral rights are a salient theme in treaty negotiations in British Columbia and Labrador and were a major demand by the Inuit in the Nunavut agreement, which has led to the establishment of the largest indigenous territory within Canada and the largest area governed by indigenous people in the world.

Mining is thus a very real option for tribes in the United States and Canada and poses important questions about viable trajectories for development of indigenous communities.

Chapter 2

The Resistance Brokers

Environmental NGOs and Mining

A revelatory metaphor for environmental resistance in the context of indigenous movements was offered by the president of the Innu Nation, Peter Penatshiu, in Labrador, Canada, when I interviewed him about the Voisey's Bay nickel mine: "We think of it [the mining negotiations] as an elastic — how much can we stretch it without letting it snap."[1] This insight is reminiscent of Piven and Cloward's classic work on social movements among the poor, in which they stated that "occasions when protest is possible among the poor, the forms that it must take, and the impact it can have are all delimited by the social structure in ways which usually diminish its extent and diminish its force" (Piven and Cloward 1979, 3).

Resistance in such movements can be tacit — manifest as intransigence at the negotiating table — or overt — involving public protests and civil disobedience. The form that the resistance may take depends on the opportunities and the dynamics of control that are exercised by other stakeholders in the process. According to Tilly, "far from the image we sometimes hold of mindless crowds, people tend to act within known limits, to innovate at the margins of existing forms, and to miss many opportunities available to them in principle" (Tilly 1978, 390). As shown in part 2, the perception of the other's control is critically important to the emergence of resistance against mining.

Within an environmental context, agricultural sociologist Nancy Lee Peluso has developed a theory of community resistance that is predicated on the work of the Tillys and political scientist James Scott (1985). In her detailed ethnographic study of resistance to forestry in Java, Peluso claims that the "repertoire of resistance" is embedded within — indeed it is a product of—"specific historical and environmental circumstances. The forms that resistance takes depend on the nature and generality of the complaint and the kinds of 'weapons' (social, political, or broadly defined technological) at the disposal of the resisters" (Peluso 1992, 13). The weapons at the disposal of indigenous communities are often quite different from those at the disposal of environmental nongovernmental organizations (ENGOS), who are usually the popularizers of resistance. However, not only are the weapons different, the consequences of resistance failure are also different—hence determining the form resistance may take. To return to President Penatshiu's metaphor, the effect of snapping an elastic is quite different for certain NGOS and communities depending on which side they are on. In the language of negotiation, one might say that the best alternative to a negotiated agreement (BATNA) is usually much better for ENGOS than it is for indigenous communities. In other words, native communities have much more at stake in the negotiations and are often more dependent on the outcome than the NGOS.

Before locating the place of ENGOS in the context of such conflicts, it is important to keep in mind a unique characteristic of environmental movements, which can often be misinterpreted. Anthropologist William Fisher highlighted this feature in his study of the resistance of the Kayapo Indians to hydroelectric development in the Amazon: "One of the unique features of environmentalism as an ideology is the indeterminate quality of environmental concerns as a social issue. In the abstract, there is no constituency that is uniquely or exclusively positioned to benefit from environmental quality, although there are pressing immediate interests at stake in any particular case" (Fisher 1994, 228).

I disagree with Fisher in his claim that there is an absence of exclusive environmental benefits in certain constituencies, since there are indeed instances of exclusive environmental benefit accruing to one party, usually by not having a particular industrial facility located in a particular place (leading the way to the infamous not-in-my-backyard, or NIMBY, syndrome). However, Fisher's insight regarding "the indeterminate quality of environmental concerns as a social issue" is compelling. He concludes, and I concur, that "the implications and agenda of environmentalism at any point need to be analyzed as a social product" (229). The term *social product* refers to the nexus of interactions between values and needs that collectively comprise notions of environmentalism in communities. In analyzing environmental resistance at the community level, we must not lose sight of the structural links that such movements have to other polities and systems of economic and social relations.

NGOs in Theory and Practice

The Greco-Roman tradition of jurisprudence, which forms the basis of most Western political economies, broadly delineates public and private domains of interest. Individual enterprise and rights are generally termed private, whereas collective goods and services fall in the public domain. The evolution of the modern nation-state has caused the public sector to take the form of large institutional structures that often alienate the citizenry. Somewhat ironically, the same seems to have happened with the private sector as well, where individual enterprise has given rise to large organizational structures that rival nation-states. Indeed, the contemporary multinational corporation certainly has the size and scope of many public entities. Though collective action on the part of private actors has been a primordial feature of almost all societies, the institutional polarization of public and private domains — and perhaps public alienation from both — has stimulated the emergence of a third sector. This third sector, or "civil society," manifests itself most prominently as nongovernmental organizations.[2] NGOs can be thought of as buffers between the classically defined public and private domains.[3]

Christopher Hood (1984) has constructed a typology of what he refers to as "paragovernmental organizations," reminding us that the nonchalance with which the acronym "GO" is used in various forms often detracts from appreciating the menagerie of highly varied organizations that actually fall under this rubric. Indeed, in Hood's analysis several paragovernmental organizations are created by the government itself and are used for policy purposes. However, I am more interested in environmental organizations, which, according to Hood's typology, would fall under "private or independent, bottom-up organizations" (Hood 1984, fig. 1).[4] As will be shown, the significance of this sector is acute when dealing with disenfranchised communities and efforts to empower such groups to assert what they perceive to be their environmental rights.

The idea of mediating or buffering institutions should not be confused with mediation, where an external, and usually neutral, party helps to resolve a dispute.[5] Though ENGOs may play the role of mediators in rare instances, the context of this research involves ENGOs that are by no means neutral and which mediate only in the most contorted sense of the word—organizations that stand between the individual and the larger institution of public life. These larger institutions of public life may also involve economically private entities such as corporations. Individuals with shared perspectives on a certain issue may also comprise a community that normatively assume the same domain as the classical conception of private, since the devolution of government authority may not be sensitive enough to account for their collective will. Once again the issue of scale in government institutions is the key factor in necessitating the involvement of ENGOs.

The value of natural resources in monetary terms is often at odds with their intrinsic worth to certain communities. In most modern economies, the primary agent of change in a resource-rich ecosystem is usually a profit-driven entity such as a private corporation for which ecological considerations are mere economic externalities. The inertial forces in the same system are often indigenous groups, and nonprofit organizations and individual activists, for whom environmental change is unusually traumatic. The government is an ambivalent player in most of these disputes, owing allegiance to all sides—a circumstance that must not be confused with neutrality. Whereas neutrality implies indifference to outcome, allegiance to all sides indicates a desired optimal outcome.

The involvement of ENGOs in these kinds of situations depends largely on the actual charter of such organizations and their adherents. Social movement theorists divide ENGO activism into two broad categories: consensus movements and conflict movements.[6] This delineation is defined by most theorists in terms of what the majority of the surrounding community believes about a particular issue. If the majority concurs with the objectives of the movement, then it is termed *consensus* (an example is Mothers Against Drunk Driving, or MADD), whereas if the movement represents the points of view of a minority within the community, then it is termed a *conflict movement*. The Green Party presidential candidacy of Ralph Nader (whose running mate, Winona LaDuke, is, incidentally, Native American) may be called a conflict movement at one level, since he would garner a small minority of the vote. However, when specific issues are brought to the fore (such as unequal income distribution), environmentalists argue that his positions are espoused by a majority of the population. Environmental movements, as manifest in NGO activity, depending on the issue and the locus of analysis can fall into either of the two categories.

There is considerable disagreement in the literature about the efficacy of this distinction. Instead of joining this debate, my aim is to focus on the commonality in the way these movements succeed or fail in achieving their initial objectives. I am also interested in how conflict movements can be transformed into consensus movements and whether such transformations can achieve the initial aims of the movement without necessarily compromising the principles on which the movement was galvanized.

While conventional social movements have attempted to alter the state, contemporary social movements often serve as countervailing forces to the state, motivated by issues of identity and embracing more than economic considerations (Tinker 1996). This is particularly true with certain ENGOs that operate in *developed* countries where the basic necessities of life are rarely placed on the bargaining table. My choice of case studies in two high-income developed countries is thus more than a mere coincidence.

Since my focus is on the process by which resistance is galvanized, I would also like to distinguish between confrontational and collaborative approaches to hammering out differences. Some environmental conflicts are by their very nature intractable and not conducive to negotiations. Indeed, many ENGOs find themselves in this situation vis-à-vis environmental disputes because disagreements are so often framed in win-lose terms. In such cases legal recourse is often seen as the only alternative. However, we can also reframe these conflicts by taking the perspective of constructive confrontation (Burgess and Burgess 1995). This approach realizes the limitations of mediation and negotiation but attempts to look at ways in which a mediator can attempt to optimize benefits by reducing conflict and creating forums for dialogue and problem solving that seek to maximize joint gains (Susskind and Cruikshank 1987).

Internal Disputes and Conflicts within ENGOs

Disputes are an essential part of organizational life and often the way by which creativity is exercised. However, it is important that people who are part of the same organization live up to Martin Luther King's celebrated aphorism: "disagree without being violently disagreeable." At this juncture, it may be useful to differentiate *dispute* and *conflict*—the former implying an episodic disagreement; the latter referring to a more protracted and perhaps systemic divergence of views, which may be tacit or active (Kolb and Bartunek 1992).

The sociological roots of organizational theory, particularly the writings of Max Weber ([1924] 1947), depict disputes and conflicts as an inevitable consequence of hierarchy. Management theorists, on the other hand, think of disputes as correctable failures of management. Barnard (1938) summed up conflict as a "melancholy failure of leadership," while March and Simon (1993) briefly describe disputes as basically an "interpersonal problem." Both these literatures frame internal disputes within organizations as pathologies, and not much effort has been made to focus on structural issues.

Disputes within organizations are often latent; hence, the research methods needed to study them must often be quite subtle. Dalton (1950) pioneered the use of intensive participant observation (in four organizations over a ten-year period) to study organizational behavior. He concluded that "conflict fluctuates around some balance of the constructive and destructive," caused by "active seeking nature of man, his ancient and obvious tendency to twist the world to his interests" (quoted in W. R. Scott 1998, 76). Implicit in these theories is that individuals within an organization have divergent goals and that this can often lead to disputes.

However, in my discussion of nongovernmental organizations, particularly ENGOs, there is often a normative metagoal that may challenge the applicability of conventional organizational models to such entities. Research on organizational behavior and internal disputes within NGOs is still inchoate.[7] Most of the literature on NGOs tends to focus on their external involvement with political establishments and development as manifestations of "civic society" (Wapner 1996; Tinker 1996). However, anyone who has seen the massive nine-hundred-page book *The Gulliver File* will undoubtedly concur that antimining activism is a global social movement (Moody 1992). The book lists mining projects and their parent companies around the world in alphabetical order and gives background history and environmental impact information (albeit from a particular activist perspective) about each project. The somewhat ambiguous title refers to a speech made by Charles Barbour, the erstwhile president of the American Mining Congress, who referred to antimining activists in the following terms: "Like Gulliver, the mining industry is a robust giant held down by a million silk strings."[8] Barbour estimated that ENGOs had added an extra fifteen cents to the cost of producing every pound of refined metal in the United States (Moody 1992, 9).

The Gulliver File was the product of collaborative efforts among some ninety groups around the world working on antimining activism. These groups take the form of NGOs, largely funded through private contributions from interested donors. They are opposed to mining not only because of its immediate ecological impact but also because it encourages the use of nonrenewable resources, and in the case of uranium mining, it adds to the risk of nuclear weapons proliferation.

There is also a critical element of anticorporatism in this movement: an overt rebellion against what is perceived to be capitalistic aggrandizement of wealth and resources. The introduction to *The Gulliver File* states: "It is not that this huge sector—with such vast tangential and peripheral operations—is entirely inimical to human needs or unhearing of human demands. Rather the truth is that—by being organized primarily along corporate lines, with decisions taken according to an industrialist, as opposed to conservationist, or rural-revitalisation, agenda—mining cannot support its own best intentions, nor fulfill its most sustainable expectations."

This perception dovetails with the literature on corporate power that is increasingly becoming popular, perhaps best exemplified by David Korten's book *When Corporations Rule the World* (1996). The corporate structure of the mining sector will be further discussed in the next chapter. However, for the purposes of understanding the antimining movement it is sufficient to recognize that the concentration of wealth, and resulting power, is itself a cause for resistance by many NGOs.

When I asked Pratap Chatterjee, activist and former employee of the Berkeley-based antimining NGO Project Underground, for any examples of socially responsible mining companies, he responded by saying: "We don't really give examples of 'good' companies if only because sometimes these companies turn out to be hypocrites and liars."[9] This strong sense of distrust of the corporate world permeates many antimining NGOs. It is also a distrust that is shared by many in the native rights movement. However, as we shall see, constructive alliances cannot be built simply on mutual mistrust of a third party. The relationship between ENGOs such as Chatterjee's and native peoples has a rich history steeped in controversy.

The Native/Environmental Debate

The relationship between indigenous societies and nature has been a source of debate and wonder in academic discourse at least since Rousseau's use of the celebrated metaphor of "the noble savage" in his *Social Contract* (1762). Anthropologists and historians alike have struggled with an understanding of how Native Americans interacted with the environment before the advent of European settlement. It is thus no wonder that ENGOs are often largely uninformed about native aspirations regarding environmental conservation.

While it is true that ecosystem disturbance was greatly accelerated after the advent of European settlement, historical native practices of wildlife management are widely debated. For example, the extinction of 73 percent of large mammal species in North America some eleven thousand years ago was coincident with a wave of ancestral Indians across the Bering land bridge. By eight thousand years ago, 80 percent of the large mammal genera in South America were also extinct (Ridley 1996). The Pleistocene overkill, as it is sometimes called, has been used by revisionist historians to argue against the presumption of a native environmental ethic. However, these extinctions could indeed have been caused by numerous other factors such as climate change.

A slightly more convincing, though acerbic, argument in this vein is presented by Calvin Martin in his landmark study of the fur trade between Native Americans and the Europeans. Given the extent of Indian involvement in hunting and trapping animals for the Hudson's Bay Company, Martin (1978, 187–88) concludes: "Even if we absolve him of his ambiguous culpability in certain episodes of despoliation, invoking instead his pristine sentiments toward Nature, the Indian still remains a misfit guru. There can be no salvation in the Indian's traditional conception of Nature for the troubled environmentalist."

However, native scholars (Weaver 1996, 6) have argued that Martin's own data illustrate the fact that "beyond economic dislocations creating incentives to participate in the trade, native destruction of animal populations was a means for them to come to terms with epizootics and their potential impact upon humans."

Detractors of native environmentalism also cite the academic manipulation of Native American discourse by Western scholars in the late nineteenth and early twentieth century. The much-celebrated speech that is attributed to Chief Seattle is often shown as an example of how European scholars concocted stories about native environmentalism. The speech that continues to grace many walls and texts, and has been quoted most recently by an environmental scholar of no less eminence than Jane Goodall (1999) or political celebrities such as Al Gore (1992), is now believed to have been drafted by ABC screenwriter Ted Perry in 1971.[10]

Historians such as Sam Gill and John Bierhorst have also questioned the now widely accepted concept of native association with Mother Earth as a theological concept. Gill concludes that, "while I have been able to find a number of tribal traditions that make references to the earth in personal and kinship terms, there is an absence in the vast literature on Native American tribes of any identification of the earth or a spiritual personification of the earth as a major goddess . . . she has become so only in the twentieth century."

Bierhorst goes a step further and contends that Mother Earth is little more than a form of political expediency. This point of view is not held just by historians. Indeed, even certain radical environmentalists have notably extricated themselves from native causes on these grounds. The founder of Earth First!, David Foreman, has pronounced native people a "threat to the habitat" (Churchill 1992, 195–96).

However, native scholarship has countered these claims with numerous other citations and oral histories. Vine Deloria has traced references to an ecologically sensitive theology among natives as far back as 1776, before the times of "corruptibility" of manuscripts that Bierhorst, Gill, and their colleagues have referred to.[11]

The Cherokee writer and scholar Jace Weaver (1996, xvi) has summed up the debate eloquently:

> We are not Moses coming down from Sinai with the Ten Commandments of environmental protection. Indians have been stereotyped far too long by the environmental movement as those with the mystical, ancient wisdom that alone can save the planet. Rather we presented and represented the honest and extremely difficult struggles of indigenous peoples to meet ecological challenges confronting them. Though traditional knowledge and ways play an important part in these battles, so do all the tools of technology, modern modes of communication, and the simple investment of time and sweat.

An appreciation of the salience of this debate is critically important as we try to understand the dynamics of environmental resistance to mining on indigenous land. An interesting European comparison to the ostensibly ambivalent environmentalism of certain native communities is presented by David Rothenberg in his essay on Norwegian environmentalism. On the one hand, Norway is the land of Gro Harlem Brundtland, the famed leader of the World Commission on Sustainable Development, and the home of Arne Naess, the founder of the deep ecology movement, but, on the other hand, Norwegians are adamant about their whaling traditions and mainstream environmentalists (or *miljomennesker*) are often dismissed as urban elite (Rothenberg 1995).

There are indeed voices on either side of the political spectrum. Native people, like all communities, have disagreement and dissent regarding the primacy of environmental concerns. However, the discourse of native environmentalism assumes a certain homogeneity—any deviation from which is perceived to be a sign of Western adulteration—from both sides of the debate.

Native environmentalism is nevertheless a very real contemporary phenomenon. It is not necessarily embedded in Western environmentalism and has found its own voice in the writings of activists such as Harvard-educated Winona LaDuke (Anishnaabeg), who was Ralph Nader's running mate in the Green Party's presidential campaign in 1996 and 2000. Native organizations such as the Indigenous Environmental Network or Honor the Earth have a sizable following. What remains to be understood is why such groups have selective success in mobilizing resistance, while in other cases they are largely ignored.

The Greening of Red Sovereignty?

"The tribes possess a tenacity—a tenacity stronger than all the technology and guile levied against it, a tenacity that will not, will not ever, let go. If that tenacity is the secret, then the secret inside it is the core value that creates the tenacity: a reverence—think that word through—for the land, for a particular place" (Wilkinson 1999, 20). This quotation from *Fire on the Plateau* (Wilkinson 1999) reflects the strength of conviction that many scholars have about the strong association native people have with the land. However, while such feelings are certainly true and important, there is also a particular tendency to go the next step and assume that this attachment to the land translates into an irrevocable attachment to environmentalism. Another example of this tendency is the frequent quotation from the Apache language that the word for "self" and "earth" is the same. However, a closer examination of the linguistic and locational ethos of the Apache reveals that this similitude does not have environmentalist implications. Basso (1996) in his detailed study of the Apache entitled *Wisdom*

Sits in Places reveals that in fact the Apache sense of place has much more to do with moral attachments to particular sites rather than a more holistic view of sanctity for land as envisaged by environmentalists.

It is an amazing irony of history that the current rights to self-determination and sovereignty that are being won by indigenous people at the international level are themselves being made possible because human rights issues have trumped the sovereignty of conventional nation-states. In this section, I will try to answer the related question of whether environmental issues have trumped the notions of sovereignty among native people.

This is a particularly sensitive area for discussion among native peoples, as was recently manifest in the outcry against Sheppard Krech's book *The Ecological Indian: Myth and History* (1999). Krech is not denying that natives have a particular respect for nature but rather that their actions were often not congruent with the Western notion of conservation attributed to Gifford Pinchot or Aldo Leopold and certainly not the kind of preservation ethic articulated by John Muir.

Much of Krech's argument was caricatured by both sides of the political spectrum. The negative reaction from native peoples occurred because, much to the dismay of Professor Krech, the book was appropriated by right wing activists who thought it was a vindication of their beliefs that Indians did not deserve special treatment.[12] Hence, many tribes felt that it may be a threat to their assertion of sovereignty in much the same way as the issue of "who were the first Americans" issue has been perceived vis-à-vis the Kennewick Man controversy (see chap. 4).

Some of the disconnect between native and nonnative allegiance to the environment may be also be the result of a fundamental misunderstanding about contending views of sovereignty and subsistence. Chamberlain (in Asch 1997, 12) draws our attention to this gap between indigenous and nonindigenous understandings of the terms:

Sovereignty, for example, is understood on the one hand as underwriting political and constitutional power. In the case of the Americas, this power was historically realized by both European and indigenous nations in the circumstances of contact, including contact before Columbus, was then qualified after European settlement by peace treaties and land cession agreements. On the other hand, sovereignty is affirmed as the inviolable expression of a people's collective identity transcending particulars of time and place and the irrelevant polemic of treaties. It does not need anyone else's validation, indigenous or non-indigenous; and it is inextinguishable, like an individual's conscience.

Therefore, in the words of one tribal leader from the Lac Courte Oreilles band of Chippewa from Wisconsin (before a congressional hearing in 1998): "We define and accept sovereignty as 'Spiritual Sovereignty.' We do not accept the assertion that sovereignty had its origins in the political ideologies of medieval European nations. We believe and accept that we practiced spiritual sovereignty long before the arrival of Europeans on this American continent . . . sovereignty cannot be given or bestowed from one nation to another" (U.S. Senate 1998, 168).

The various uses of the Maori words *kawanatanga* (which roughly means governance) and *rangatiratanga* (which roughly means chieftainship) to deal with questions of sovereignty in New Zealand's Waitangi Treaty highlights this from another perspective. *Kawanatanga* in the treaty as well as in modern Maori reconciliation documents refers to the allowance of governance at the state level given to the settler government of New Zealand, whereas *rangatiratanga* refers to self-determination and is derived from the word for "chieftain"—hence having ultimate authority.[13] The relationship is thus different from one between a state and federal government—since in this case it is the native populace that believes in its ultimate authority—even if it does not have control.

The same dilemma in an environmental context is even more obvious with the word *subsistence*. It is on the one hand a diminishing term, the minimum necessary for survival, and yet a term used routinely by indigenous peoples to refer to all that is essential to their well-being, including their attachment (spiritual as well as material) to their homeland. This latter conception is not properly acknowledged—indeed, often is not even recognized—by an instrumental understanding of the term, which is common in many nonindigenous societies, where relentlessly utilitarian habits often inhibit a better appreciation of what is meant when traditional indigenous people talk about subsistence that is about "shaping their lives according to patterns of sufficiency rather than of surplus."[14] For example, subsistence has been at the core of Alaska's native advocacy efforts since 1989, when the Alaska Supreme Court declared that a "subsistence priority" for natives was "unconstitutional" (Alaska 1998).

Given this dialectic between contested views of sovereignty and subsistence, how do environmental concerns figure into the debate? To answer this question, the divergent notions of cultural determinism versus environmental determinism must be addressed. The distinction between these two contending views of the world is critically important in understanding the emergence of resistance and also alliances between natives and environmentalists. If it is assumed, for analytical purposes, that environments shape cultures, the possibility of asking how cultures shape environments is effectively precluded. Many of the arguments about the preservation of ecosystems to preserve indigenous cultures, and the use of the term *ecocide*, emanate from this belief. However, environmental determinism in its extreme form is incompatible with the environmentalist concern to protect the environment through human effort. The assumption that human activities are somehow caused by environmental factors, that the environment is the prime mover in human affairs, implies that human beings are helpless in the face of natural forces, in much the same way that some religious doctrines imply that we are helpless in the face of supernatural forces. As Kay Milton (1996) points out, such a view "induces a rationality of fatalism, in which planning is redundant and in which outcomes, good or bad, are simply to be enjoyed or endured but never achieved." Moreover, in the context of indigenous peoples, Milton goes on to argue that

> environmentalists fail, as anthropologists used to, to distinguish between culture and the things people do. The actual impacts of nonindustrial societies on their environments depend on how they use those environments to meet their need. . . . Without distinguishing between what people think, feel and know about the world (culture) and the things they do, it is easy to make the mistake of assuming that societies which have little impact on their environment must necessarily have environmentally benign cultures. (Milton 1996, 56)

On the other hand, the cultural determinist model is incompatible with environmental activism, which depends on the recognition of an independent reality that can be modified by human actions. Activism depends on the assumption that the environment exists independently of our thoughts and therefore presents a real threat to the physical state of the earth and its inhabitants. Thus, neither the view that environments determine cultures nor the view that cultures determine environments offers a useful means of advocating the environmentalist/native alliances at this level. On the other hand, both the recognition that environmental knowledge varies among cultures and the description and analysis of such diversity are important resources in the quest for environmental protection and improvement.

To bring forth a more dynamic approach to understanding human interactions with the environment and to give further scientific credibility to his work, anthropologist William Fisher uses the ideas of evolutionary biologists Levins and Lewontin (1985) concerning the relationship between organisms and the environment. Their work attempts to explain why the environment cannot be treated as a preexistent "thing" standing on its own: "To describe an environment as 'rich,' 'lush,' 'forbidding,' or, perhaps even 'complex' involves the fallacy that an environment is simply 'there,' confronting beings that attempt to survive within it. This imperative to explicitly link description of the environment with specific activities of organisms is associated with a view of evolution and ecology that reintegrates the organism and environment as processes actively creating one another" (W. H. Fisher 1996, 21).

The key word here is *processes*. Environmental interactions for native people, as revealed in the case analyses, are all about processes by which communities can be sustained. At present, sustenance is synonymous with sovereignty, though at some points in native history sustenance was synonymous with conservation or perhaps even preservation. Native societies, like all societies, have undoubtedly changed through their interactions with the settlers in a way that is not assimilative but truly adaptive in its form. In his more recent works, Fisher continues his analysis of the Xikrin Kayapó of Brazil and their adaptive resistance to resource ventures. He sums up his findings as follows: "The indigenous forms that develop do not conform to an inexorable logic of either the market or tradition but are actively created through transforming techniques and organizational forms valued by Indians themselves. Subsistence and organization are never imposed from without in any mechanical sense; as indigenous creations, they have their own dynamic tendencies and contradictions which must be analyzed."[15]

Thus, native people who are willing to have nuclear waste on their reservations (which can be articulated as an environmental justice question) should not necessarily be considered a sign of desperation on the part of the tribe or as a "sovereignty of convenience" on the part of the federal government.[16] Rather, it should be seen as a self-conscious (and, perhaps, misplaced) attempt to invigorate self-determination, absent other avenues to do so.

Chapter 3

Mining Companies and Management Dilemmas

The Cost of Business

Since the 1999 protests against the World Trade Organization and the 2000 protests against the World Bank and the International Monetary Fund, corporations worldwide have been increasingly on the defensive about their relentless pursuit of profit. While capitalism has clearly triumphed over communism at a global economic scale, there is a feeling in many underprivileged communities that corporations are assuming the erstwhile role of centralized power structures that were the bane of irresponsible communism (Korten 1996; Mitchell 2001). Much of the discontentment with corporations is premised on the environmental and human rights records of companies. The argument is often made that the modern corporation, and indeed the greater neoclassical economic framework, regards environmental and human rights concerns as externalities that should be addressed only as a means to an end—the end being profitability (Houck and Williams 1996). Mining companies, in particular, because of their operations in remote underdeveloped areas and their relative secrecy of operations, are regarded with much suspicion by those who oppose corporate power.

Why Are Mining Firms Targeted by Activists?

Whether or not environmental and human rights concerns should be means to an end or ends in themselves is a timeless normative debate. However, the consequences of corporate behavior can, and should, be evaluated on their own merits without any insinuation of motives. Thus, my aim in this chapter is not to paint mining companies as antagonists, but rather to present them as stakeholders with their own set of constraints and embedded values.

That being said, the historical conduct of mining companies on a global scale must be recognized, and the injustices perpetrated by some mining firms that have led to their contemporary caricature must not be denied. Perhaps the most persistent negative image of mining companies emanates from the narratives of mining life in South Africa, where the institution of apartheid was all too often used to the benefit of mining companies and vice versa.[1] Some of the management strategies of large multinational mining companies, most of which have had at least some operations in Africa, were quite secretive. In the words of one De Beers executive, "We stride across Africa in a very satisfactory way in all sorts of strange places. Part of the secret is we respect confidences. We don't talk much" (Kanfer 1993, 7).

While many of the misgivings about secrecy and human rights violations pertaining to mining companies have diminished since the end of apartheid, there are still recurring examples of some ventures that are notably disturbing — though multinational mining companies are not always involved in these cases. The civil war in Sierra Leone, for example, is largely a resource war between the democratic government and the rebels who control much of the diamond mining in the east part of the country. The same is largely true of the strife in the Democratic Republic of Congo, with its diamond and cobalt mines, and continuing civil strife in Angola (one of the most resource-rich countries in the world).

Even the recent war in Kosovo has been described by a notable *New York Times* reporter as being largely about mineral resources surrounding the Stari Trg mining complex (Hedges 1998). According to the mine's director, Novak Bjelic, "the war in Kosovo is about the mines, nothing else. This is Serbia's Kuwait." Greece's support for the Serbian government may also be predicated on a half-billion-dollar five-year mining contract. In May 1998, Mytilinaios SA signed a five-year contract, worth $519 million, with the state-owned RMHK Trepca and the Serbian agency of foreign trade, in which Mytilinaios agreed to forward one-third of the mineral production in the international market and also upgrade mining equipment and facilities.[2]

In other cases, activists argue that civil strife may be suppressed by rogue governments. Since mineral resources are a direct source of economic gain for governments, there is a perceived collusion between companies and public authorities and a perpetuation of the Old World colonial infrastructure. Perhaps the starkest example of the perpetuation of colonial control over mining is the continuation of French rule over the island of New Caledonia in the South Pacific, despite vociferous protests and rebellions by the Kanak indigenous population. New Caledonia has among the largest concentration of nickel reserves in the world and has still not been granted independence, probably for this reason, though a referendum is scheduled for 2014 (O'Neill 2000).

There are also some mining companies with particularly troubling environmental and human rights records, such as Freeport McMoRan, a New Orleans–based company, which has been the subject of lawsuits because of its impact on the lives of the Amungme tribe in Irian Jaya, Indonesia. While the citizen-action lawsuits against the company have been dismissed in the United States (most recently on appeal in March 2000), the firm continues to be under fire from environmentalists and human rights activists. The firm's controversial involvement with the Indonesian military in suppressing rebellion was even profiled as a full-page story in the *Wall Street Journal* (Waldman 1998).[3]

With such stories making their way to the front pages of business newspapers, it is not surprising that mining companies are regarded with suspicion by many social observers and the general public. In fact, a 1997 survey conducted by Praeger for the *Engineering and Mining Journal* found mining to be the least favored industry by the American public—even less favored than the much reviled tobacco industry.

Apart from the specific case histories of firms, there is also a general feeling in the activist community that mining is inherently unsustainable. Large-scale gold and diamond mining in particular are targeted by activists because most of these minerals are used for jewelry and are thus considered a dispensable industry.[4]

The aim of this chapter is to understand the systemic issues that may lead to such perceptions. Following is a closer look at the organizational and economic dimensions of the mining industry and how they explain the behavior of such firms in environmental negotiations with communities.

The Anatomy of a Modern Mining Firm

In 1847, a twelve-year-old Scottish immigrant named Andrew Carnegie earned $1.20 a week working in a Pittsburgh cotton mill. Half a century later, he received $250 million from the sale of his steel firm to J. P. Morgan and others who were forming U.S. Steel. That firm, known as Big Steel, was the world's first billion-dollar company.[5] The success of the Carnegies and other major industrial families are emblematic of the concomitant success of mining and mineral processing companies following the industrial revolution.

Ownership and control of world mining is heavily concentrated in a small number of multinational mining firms (most of which are privately owned) and in state mining enterprises (SMEs). There are thousands of small, privately owned mining firms in developed countries and in some of the major Latin American mining countries. However, small mines produce less than 25 percent of world output, and their activities tend to be concentrated in gold, silver, diamonds, and other precious stones and in types of mining where economies of scale are less important. While the primary cases studied in this book involve large multinational companies, the lessons learned are equally applicable to smaller firms and ventures.[6] An exception to this may be the subsistence-level gold panning operations that are common in South America.[7]

The growth of SMEs has affected the competitive structure of the world mining industry in three important ways. First, cost elements of SMEs differ from those of privately owned mining firms. Second, the objectives and considerations governing investment decisions of SMEs differ from those of private enterprises. Third, production and marketing strategies of state enterprises tend to be less sensitive to cyclical declines in market demand and price than is the case with privately owned mines. Investment decisions by SMEs are often made on the basis of relative profit-earning opportunities.

SMEs tend to be insensitive to price declines in their production and market strategies for two reasons. First, labor costs in developing countries are more a fixed cost because of termination of pay regulations and government policies to maintain employment. Second, state enterprises generally seek to maintain exchange earnings in the face of low prices despite the fact that their current receipts may not cover total foreign exchange and domestic currency costs. Therefore, private industry groups contend that the existence of a large segment of the world mining industry in which investment and production/marketing decisions are made more on the basis of government policy than on the basis of private profit maximization has made investment decision-making in the private mining industry exceedingly difficult. Comparative cost advantage and projections of world demand and supply balance no longer serve as reasonably reliable guides for decisions to invest in capacity.

In most countries outside the United States and Canada, mining industries have been recipients of a variety of government subsidies, and domestic markets have been protected by import restrictions. However, the United States has low tariffs and no quota restrictions on primary metals. The U.S. mining industry argues that subsidies on foreign production plus the importance of a strong domestic industry for national defense reasons justify government measures to assist the domestic industry. But the U.S. mining industry has had much less success in lobbying for import controls on minerals than have the more labor-intensive industries such as textiles.

Disputes between developed and developing nations on mining have also played themselves out at the level of treaty making. The negotiation of the Law of the Sea Treaty brought into conflict the positions of the United States and certain other developed countries with those of Third World countries regarding the control of exploration and development of manganese nodules on the ocean floors (see Sebenius 1990). The international community agreed in principle that the manganese nodules were not located on land and thus were a "common heritage of mankind." However, consortia of mining enterprises in the United States and other developed country mining enterprises had spent hundreds of millions of dollars investigating this source of minerals for eventual development by multinational mining companies and thus wanted flexible royalty arrangements. Developing countries insisted that these resources belong to all countries and that exploitation should be governed by an international organization. Also, there was considerable danger that trade in nonferrous metals might become subject to the kind of market-sharing arrangements that had characterized trade in steel products. Eventually, the International Seabed Authority was established to oversee exploration activities and special allowances were provided to pioneer investors—countries that had already invested resources in seabed exploration.

Risk Management in the Mining Industry

Mining projects are among the most risky industrial enterprises. They involve large capital investment at the outset and yet there can be little or no guarantee of profits even in the short term. While geological prediction based on empirical core studies and remote testing procedures are

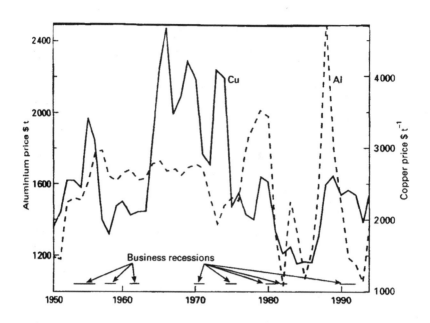

Figure 3.1
Price fluctuations in the mineral sector, 1950–1990.
(Adapted from Evans 1997)

becoming increasingly reliable, the actual grade and extent of an ore deposit is often not fully recognizable until mining commences. Moreover, the international mineral market system is highly capricious in terms of price fluctuations, and this can greatly affect the profitability of a particular mining venture (see fig. 3.1). According to Mikesell and Whitney (1987), the business strategies of mining firms are governed by five key considerations.

First, mining location is determined by geology, which often means that in order to be profitable the firm must be willing and able to have a presence in various and often remote parts of the world. This may explain why mining firms were the first modern nonfinancial multinationals.

Second, modern mining is highly capital intensive and requires a long gestation period following the initial investment before the product can be produced and sold. This influences the way new ventures are financed and explains why most large mining corporations initiated early in the century were financed by investment houses willing to provide large amounts of venture capital.

A third feature is that most minerals (especially metals) are more or less homogeneous products, sold in world markets at prices determined on commodity exchanges, as contrasted with differentiated manufactured products. This means that reducing or limiting costs by introducing better technology and profitability in mining depends on improving management rather than consumer choice. Marketing and developing new products play a lesser role in traditional metals than in manufacturing. An exception is the development of new metals and alloys and their industrial applications, a specialization of the materials industry into which some mining firms have entered in recent years.

A fourth characteristic of mining is that every ore body is a depleting resource, the output of which tends to decline over time. Therefore, mining firms must continually discover or acquire new ore bodies to maintain a relatively stable output over time. Due to uncertainties in exploration, geographical location of mines may be more a matter of taking advantage of opportunities than of conscious planning. Since exploration is usually not undertaken for only one mineral, product diversification or concentration may also be more a consequence of discovery than planning.

The bottom line in considering these characteristics is that mining is an unusually high-risk industry that has thus necessitated very elaborate means of risk management. Following are some of the ways the industry has tried to manage risk.

Horizontal Integration

Mining companies most commonly try to manage risk through horizontal integration, organizational devolution, and intra-industry alliances. Seldom does one come across a mine that is wholly owned and operated by one company. Almost all large mining ventures involve more than one company and constitute a joint venture. There are sometimes arrangements for royalty proportions and joint liability among firms. For tax purposes and logistical ease, most mine sites have a local management company that is then owned by a set of larger multinational mining firms.

Horizontal integration has been the traditional strategy for the growth of mining firms. It utilizes the professional skills and managerial experience of the firm and complements its need to acquire and develop new ore bodies as existing ones are depleted. Horizontal integration in mining may take place in several ways. The mining firm may undertake exploration to find additional reserves. Alternatively, companies may acquire ore bodies—or the right to develop ore bodies—that have been more or less fully explored or even partially developed by others. However, the geologists of the firm acquiring an ore body are likely to undertake considerable exploratory work on their own in order to verify the data of others.

Vertical Integration

The degree to which a mining firm is vertically integrated depends in part on the volume of mine production and in part on the availability of financing. Integration of a copper mine into smelting and refining requires a large volume of concentrates (refined ore) and a substantial capital investment. The degree of vertical integration is also determined by business strategy. Having a smelter near a mine saves transportation costs and avoids the possibility of a shortage of smelter capacity, which is usually accompanied by high fees for custom smelting or lower prices for concentrates if sold to smelters. Locating a refinery near a mine is not important for saving transportation cost, since the metal content of blister metal (crude product) produced by a smelter is usually comparable to that for refined metal. It is frequently more important for a refinery to be near the market for the product than near the mine.

Interlocks

There are also several interlocks between mining companies and other investment agents and nonmining multinationals that can make a final difference. A primary interlock between a pair of corporations occurs when someone holds a seat on the board of both corporations. A secondary interlock occurs when two directors of two companies both hold seats on the board of a third company. Antitrust law prohibits primary interlocks between competitor companies. However, secondary interlocks are common and are an important means of networking among mining companies. Such interlocks are also criticized by activists, who contend that they can lead to cartel formation and monopolistic behavior as well as the formation of an elitist corporate class.[8]

The empirical evidence regarding the effect of interlocks on corporate behavior is highly varied. A recent large-scale study of interlocks conducted by Pamela Haunschild and Christine Beckman (1998) at Stanford Business School revealed that the impact of interlocks on corporate decision making is largely determined by the flow of alternative information sources. The study revealed that interlocks matter much more so for firms that get large amounts of business press coverage and for medium-sized firms—much of the mining industry falls into this category. The prevalence of interlocks is an important component of the analysis vis-à-vis perceptions of corporate power among indigenous communities in part 2.

Planning for Mines in Remote Areas

In much of the public policy literature the concern with firm regulation tends to revolve around the notion of monopoly power. While mining firms in some cases have been accused of monopoly, particularly the diamond mining and processing firm De Beers, the most significant issue that concerns mining projects in remote areas is not monopoly power but *monopsony* power. While the former refers to a market that is dominated by one *seller*, the latter refers to a market situation where one *buyer* is dominant. In remote areas, mining companies are often the sole source of income for communities and hence have monopsony power over labor.

Ever since Joan Robinson (1969) first introduced the concept of monopsony in economic literature, it has been viewed with skepticism by economists and is usually relegated to a sidebar in economic textbooks. However, recent research has revealed that monopsony may be far more prevalent than previously thought (see Blair and Harrison 1993). It is, however, important to differentiate between monopsony arising because the supply of labor to each firm is relatively inelastic and monopsony caused by employers acting in concert or colluding. In the case of mining firms, either or both models could be operating. However, the inelasticity of labor as a result of limited alternatives is more plausible.

Figure 3.2 shows various economic implications of monopsony power and how it can be manifest. A monopsony would want to choose the most profitable point on the labor supply curve. Given the marginal cost of labor being higher than the labor supply curve in remote areas, the monopsonist would arrive at the most profitable decision shown as L^*, whereas under perfect competition, the firm would hire and pay wages at point Lc (where the value of the marginal product of labor equals the wage). Thus, a monopsonist hires less labor and at a lower wage than a competitive firm.

The most comprehensive econometric study testing the monopsony hypothesis in the mining sector has been conducted by Boal (1995), in which coal-mining data (1897–1932) from West Virginia was studied. Boal's study used Bertrand and Cournot coefficients methodology along-

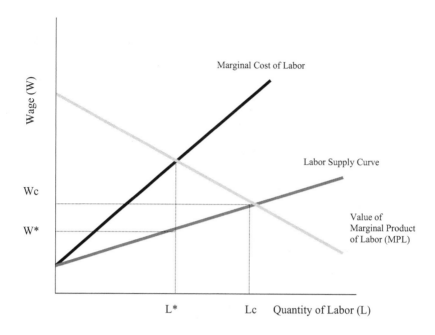

Figure 3.2
Monopsonistic competition.

side the Lerner index to study the potential for monopsony power using wage and labor supply data.[9] The study does not test whether this power was actually exercised — thus it does not measure the actual gap between the marginal revenue product and the wages. Based on his model, Boal concludes that monopsony power in coal mining during this time existed only at a short-term level and was sharply attenuated if employers "considered the future" — that is, if they foresaw the effect of current wages and employment levels on their own future labor supply. In the long run, given discount rates being used by the employers in decision making, there was no significant evidence for monopsony power of the mining companies. However, these results are by no means translatable to most cases of mining in remote areas. Indeed, in a subsequent review article, Boal and Ransom (1997) have acknowledged that "monopsonistic exploitation" deserves further study.

Economic theory and some empirical evidence thus suggests that mining companies operating in remote areas may have a significant monopsonistic power, though this is by no means the end of the story. Companies are becoming increasingly aware of the political reality of operating in remote areas and of certain ethical and regulatory obligations to the communities concerned. Community relations consultants, many of whom are anthropologists, are often hired by companies to formulate community relations programs.

Many large mining companies now have environmental health and safety reports that highlight the ways impact is being mitigated. While some of these programs are voluntary, most of the efforts that have been made in this regard have been spurred by governments—who, as shown in the next chapter, are stakeholders in their own right.

Industry Responses to Environmental and Community Concerns

While industry's perception of risk is largely figured in economic terms, there is, of course, another very real risk associated with mining ventures —environmental harm. Environmental impact assessment is now considered a routine procedure, with specialized consultants having emerged for this very purpose. However, only a few decades ago, mining agreements did not have any provision for environmental considerations. Perhaps the first book to focus on the negotiation process involved in mineral agreements, particularly in developing countries, was written by two professors at Harvard, David Smith (Law School) and Louis Wells (Business School). This book aimed to give advice to governments of developing countries and corporations operating there about reaching agreements that would be mutually advantageous. Their intention was to bring "an element of realism to a subject that had long been clouded by mythology and misunderstanding" (Smith and Wells 1975, 2). However, this entire treatise, despite its merits, made absolutely no mention of environmental concerns and how they might figure in these negotiations.

Another study, conducted by a Nevada consulting firm in 1987, listed a series of factors responsible for "unsuccessful" mining ventures (table 3.1). Here, too, environmental factors were not listed—though the results of this study would most likely be quite different if it were conducted today.

More recently, a study conducted by Roderick Eggert (1994) for the Washington-based think tank Resources for the Future determined that environmental regulation does not play a significant part in the investment strategies of international mining firms. Mining, like other natural

Table 3.1

Sources of Problems in Unsuccessful Mining Ventures

Problem Category	Percentage of Mines with Problems
Ore reserves	23
Construction sequence and cost	29
Mine plan	19
Milling	36
Processing	42
Operation management	23
Market analysis	33

Source: Whitney and Whitney Inc., Reno, Nev., quoted in Mikesell and Whitney 1987.

resource-based industries, does not have as much discretion when it comes to selecting investment areas, and perhaps it is for this reason as well that the industry is particularly resolute in pushing certain mining projects even in the wake of community resistance.

While the aforementioned data illustrate that environmental and community issues may not necessarily affect project selection, they do not suggest the same for project implementation. Indeed, environmental concerns and community issues are all too often a major impediment to implementation of mining projects. Environmental concerns are becoming an increasingly important cost consideration for mining companies and have led to the formation of inter-industry collaboration on environmental initiatives. The Ottawa-based International Council on Metals and the Environment is an example of such an initiative, though this organization is also being transformed to become the International Council on Mining and Metals.

To highlight its commitment to environmental issues at the 2002 World Summit on Sustainable Development (WSSD) in Johannesburg, the mining industry and the World Business Council on Sustainable Development also conducted a major self-evaluation of its practices through the Global Mining Initiative (GMI). The GMI commissioned the Mining Minerals and Sustainable Development project (IIED 2002), which was undertaken by the London-based International Institute for Environment and Development. As an outcome of the MMSD initiative, the mining industry has established a permanent International Council on Metals and Mining (ICMM) to be headquartered in London. The ICMM charter contains management principles in four key areas: environmental stewardship, product stewardship, community responsibility, and general corporate responsibilities. As stated earlier, the organization thus expands on an earlier industry organization known as the International Council on Mining and the Environment, which was based in Ottawa. The key difference between the organizations is intended to be in management personnel and the level of independence they will be given to undertake research and provide recommendations. The ICMM was initially led by Jay Hair, a former head of the National Wildlife Federation. For the industry, it is a major cultural shift to allow someone from the nonprofit sector to lead a major industry organization. However, it was also perceived by critics as an attempt at co-optation of more malleable activists. Dr. Hair passed away soon after this appointment, and ICMM is still recovering from this shock.

Because of the centrality of industry funding of projects such as MMSD, many NGOs have boycotted forums organized under these initiatives and dismissed the effort as "greenwash."[10] Critics of the industry have argued much of the work in this regard has been reactive and the industry has been quite resentful of regulatory pressure. Mining companies and industry groups believe strongly that the use of minerals is a part of modern living and often use advertisements to show that any challenge to them is a challenge to the modern way of life. A graphic from the Mineral Information Institute in their latest advertising campaign in 2000 illustrates this belief (fig. 3.3). This advertisement highlights the continuing perception in industry that they are involved in a truly noble endeavor. The nonrenewability of mineral extraction is still largely a nonissue for the metal mining industry, unlike other sectors such as energy minerals, where companies such as BP are trying to reinvent themselves as energy service companies and not just mineral extractors (thus opening doors to renewable resource management). Often the argument is made that because of their durability, metals are highly recyclable and hence renewable, while the energy and means required to attain this renewability are often downplayed.

Such exchanges between industry and communities have led activists such as Al Gedicks (1998, 2000) to posit that apart from the firms' business strategies, the industry also has a set of strategies for overcoming local resistance, which follows an activist agenda as well.

The NGOs that boycotted the initiative wrote an open letter to the industry indicating their reasons for making this decision and largely predicated their resistance on the perception that the outcome of the process

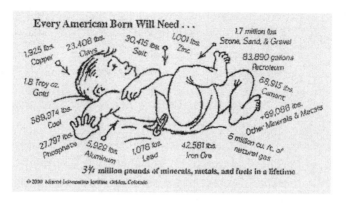

Figure 3.3
An example of mining industry advertising. (Reprinted by permission of Mining Information Institute, Golden, Colorado; copyright 2000)

had been predetermined by the funders by characterizing mining as sustainable under mildly mitigating circumstances. Some of the NGOs that have resisted this effort have an uncompromising normative stance with regard to mining as being inherently unsustainable and thus would label any attempt at defining sustainable mining as greenwash. There are others, however, who had direct process-oriented concerns about the initiative and were able to get some specific workshops organized, such as those on the rights of indigenous people in mining areas, and subsequently joined the initiative.

Most of the groups that boycotted the main MMSD initiative did, however, attend the culminating conference in Toronto in May of 2002. While their presentations were not conciliatory by any means, there was at least an engagement of stakeholders during this four-day event. Another remarkable feature of the MMSD initiative was the advent of numerous mirror events and conferences that boycotting groups organized. This was similar to the World Social Forum, which some NGOs organized in 2001 to mirror the World Economic Forum. However, the NGO conferences during the MMSD process were by invitation only and largely excluded any industry stakeholders. They were mainly strategic events to plan for responding to MMSD rather than democratic engagement of issues. The argument presented to justify such lack of transparency on the part of the NGOs is generally the overwhelming power differential believed to exist between the corporate sector and civil society.

My aim is not to be judgmental one way or the other, but rather to understand how the various characteristics of stakeholders and their manifest behavior in negotiations influence the emergence of resistance.

Chapter 4

The Embedded Stakeholder

Governmental Strata in the United States and Canada

Almost two centuries ago, Duc De Levis, a little-known French political philosopher, wrote that "to govern is to make choices," a simple message that is still relevant and compelling. While democratic governments are, in some ways, a mediating force for conflicting interests in a polity, they must inevitably make choices and hence become embedded stakeholders. They are embedded because they express interests of their own, but they do it in less visible ways than other stakeholders and have divided loyalties.

Democracy has clearly emerged as the penultimate form of government in the absence of any alternative. Much of my analysis in this chapter will acknowledge the primacy of democratic processes in contemporary times. However, given the diverse cultural traditions of native governance from the Iroquois confederacy to the Apache chiefdoms, it is important to evaluate native perceptions of Western governance and its applicability to various social concerns.

This chapter lays the conceptual groundwork for part 2 of the book by placing much of the stakeholder debate in the context of planning discourse. The eclectic attributes of the issue can often detract from cogent analysis; therefore, it is important to realize that the ultimate goal of this book is to help stakeholders in *planning* for development projects in remote communities in an environmentally sound and economically efficient way.

The recognition of a need to plan, particularly at a state level, has of late been a source of much debate in the literature on sustainable development.[1] While there continues to be much dissent about the definition of sustainability and about the appropriate role of government in this context, there is increasing agreement that sustainability can only be achieved by focusing on the future and relating that to the present.[2] Since planning is inherently a futuristic discipline, it provides a means by which governments can work toward sustainability. Whether we like it or not, governments do engage in planning at some scale, and the ways in which they do so have important implications for the kinds of environmental conflicts discussed here.

In their compendium on planning sustainability, Kenny and Meadowcroft build on the work of political theorists (exemplified in Skocpol, Evans, and Rueshmeyer 1985) by suggesting the following: "One of the principal implications of planning in liberal democratic contexts concerns the setting of 'meta-social objectives' by the state, or the steering of economic life to meet pre-determined social goals. The state thus looks like one of the most likely candidates for an agency which may oversee the shift to a (more) sustainable society" (Kenny and Meadowcroft 1999, 4). The challenge at hand, therefore, is to understand the current structure and operation of government institutions and to see how improvements can be made in the existing framework.

Delineating Federal, Provincial/State, and Tribal Jurisdiction

To borrow a much-celebrated phrase from Thomas Schelling, micromotives and macrobehavior are emblematic of the essential tension between various tiers of government—from local to provincial/state to federal. The situation with regard to tribal governance adds a somewhat perplexing layer of authority since tribes are highly diffuse and quite local in their geography, yet their aspirations for governance are those of a nation-state. The situation is perhaps reminiscent of the United Arab Emirates in the Middle East or the Swiss Confederation in Europe. However, the situation with regard to Native Americans is complicated by the fact that tribes are all too often competing with states or provinces for localized jurisdiction and authority—thus there are two parallel tracks vying for decision-making power with overlapping geographies. It is therefore not surprising to find lawsuits brought by states or provinces against tribes, and vice versa, in federal courts.

This triangulation of power is prevalent in both the United States and Canada. There are clearly some notable differences in the way the power is wielded in both countries, but in general there has been dissatisfaction on both sides of the border about the way in which nonnative governmental policies have affected tribal populations. In an interview, Native American scholar and activist Ward Churchill described the difference between Canadian and American approaches to indigenous issues: "The U.S. approach was to concentrate large numbers of people on fewer reservations. The Canadian approach was to fragment the population into numerous small reserves."[3]

Organizational Jurisdiction for Indian Mineral Development in the United States

Apart from instances of state-tribal compacts, much of the regulatory oversight pertaining to Native American trust lands in the United States and Indian affairs in general is relegated to the federal government. A notable exception to this rule is the state of Alaska, whose native population (12 percent of the total population—the largest statewide percentage in the union) chose to adopt a corporate system of land administration. Here too there is an exception vis-à-vis the Annette Island band in southeastern Alaska, which chose to remain under federal trust obligations and hence under the jurisdiction of the Bureau of Indian Affairs.

A somewhat remarkable feature of the U.S. federal government structure is that diverse issues such as mining, native rights, and environmental protection largely fall under the umbrella of one cabinet-level department—the Department of the Interior. The emergence of the department in its current form is a manifestation of the U.S. government's fascination with the Western frontier that has evolved from notions of conquest to conservation. Figure 4.1 shows the organizational structure of the Department of the Interior with special reference to offices that are of relevance to mineral development on Indian land. Apart from the Department of the Interior, there are a few other governmental agencies that are important in terms of governmental involvement in specific situations and concerning certain issues. A more complete picture of federal agency involvement is thus offered in table 4.1. Unlike most governmental structures, U.S. cabinet-level departments are extensions of the executive branch and are insulated from the legislative branch of government by the constitutional provision that bars federal government appointees from being part of the legislature.

Among these various organizations, the one that has the most overarching authority over Indian development efforts at present is the BIA. The

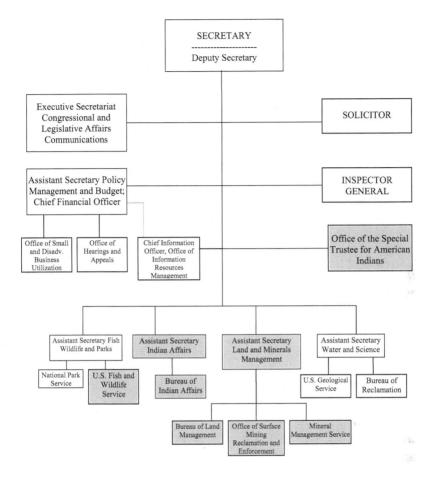

Figure 4.1
An organizational diagram of the Department of the
Interior, highlighting offices relevant to Indians.

BIA is a public organization with a chamelionic history of organizational
dynamics that actually predates the formation of the Department of the
Interior. Steeped in a history of colonial subjugation, the bureau is currently the federal agency with primary responsibility for administering
and managing 56.2 million acres of land held in trust by the United States
for the Indians. The stated mission of the agency in 1998 was to "enhance
the quality of life, to promote economic opportunity, and to carry out the
responsibility to protect and improve the trust assets of American Indi-

Table 4.1

U.S. Government Agencies of Relevance to Indian Mineral Development

Government Agency	Task
Bureau of Indian Affairs	Leasing arrangements
Bureau of Land Management	Preparation and review of mining plan
Environmental Protection Agency	Compliance with environmental standards; review of EIS
Minerals Management Service	Royalty arrangements
Office of Surface Mining Control and Reclamation	Regulatory jurisdiction over coal mining
U.S. Army Corps of Engineers	Wetland protection
U.S. Fish and Wildlife Service	Endangered species protection

ans, Indian Tribes and Alaskan natives. We will accomplish this through the delivery of quality services, maintaining government-to-government relationships within the spirit of Indian self-determination."[4]

The BIA has often been termed "a government in miniature," and in its various incarnations it has been a manifestation of various theoretical models of organizational behavior. By combining various federal, state, and local functions, this organization has an unusual set of goals and thus presents many challenges to effective management. As a trustee of Native American interests, the BIA also has a set of duties that are usually found in the private sector. Cultural factors take on a new and more profound meaning in this organization that is supposed to act as a buffer between disparate civilizations.

Congress always intended for BIA to be a transient and ephemeral agency. It was meant to serve a purpose and then write its own dissolution—thus it was an exercise in planned obsolescence. As Steven Novak states in his important paper on the topic: "Once natives had taken up their yeoman farms, they would be absorbed into white society, regain their independence and allow the transitional government programs to end. The BIA was meant to be short-lived. . . . The BIA was meant to dissolve once the natives regained their 'independence' and government officials always dreamed that it was near its end" (Novak 1990, 640). In 1913, the secretary of the interior said, "the Indian Bureau should be a vanishing bureau." Congressman George Schwabe, one of the architects of the termination policy, promised in 1946 "to get rid of the Indian Bureau as fast as possible." However, none of these plans for obsolescence have come to pass. The bureau is still alive and well, and even though reforms are being considered at this time, there is no sign of dissolution of the organization.

There will be even more challenges for the bureau as tribes gain additional legal autonomy and economic development. Several tribes are now drafting their own regulations, and the question of sovereignty reigns supreme. Will the BIA's role ever become peripheral? The reason why obsolescence is not given much attention in organizational discourse is perhaps because most organizations strive to prevent their demise no matter how clear their goals of dissolution. Without another recourse of employment or empowerment, the individuals that make up the organization struggle to keep it alive—hence there is seldom any planned obsolescence from within an organization. The way in which Indians have been given preferential hiring is an example of this process. While this led to a form of captive bureaucracy, it helped to preserve the organization. Many scholars of Indian history have argued that the BIA's Indian employees are victims of co-optation by the system. They are labeled collaborationists and "Uncle Tomahawks" and have to endure considerable censure at the hands of their own kin.

However, Novak has argued that the opposite is closer to the truth. Indians employed by the BIA have been activists for native rights and are beginning to apply their lessons from working at the BIA to tribal government. While preferential hiring has created a form of Indian dependence on the BIA, the long-term effect of this policy on the future of the organization remains unclear. It is notably in sharp contrast to the Canadian Department of Indian Affairs and Northern Development, which has less than 20 percent native employees in its workforce.[5]

In 1995, the U.S. Senate held hearings on reforming and downsizing the BIA. Republican Sen. John McCain of Arizona, the chairman of the Senate Committee on Indian Affairs, lambasted the BIA on several fronts: "As a financial manager, the BIA has failed miserably . . . as the trustee responsible for education of Indian children the BIA has been shamefully neglectful . . . [the failings of the BIA] brings new meaning to the phrase 'a parade of horribles.' " Most of the Indian representatives agreed that the BIA should be downsized and more authority given to tribal governments, but there was no talk of obsolescence. The restructuring of the bureau is currently being undertaken. It is clear that there will be some reduction in personnel and that more authority will be devolved to tribal governments, but the organization will still remain alive and will perhaps rise from its ashes with renewed vigor and vitality.

Organizational Jurisdiction for First Nations Mineral Development in Canada

Canada's federalist structure gives considerably more authority to the provinces than the American model — partly because of the Francophone demands for autonomy in Quebec. Therefore, even with regard to indigenous affairs, the provincial governments often have just as much, or perhaps more, involvement than federal authorities. Moreover, Canada has much unfinished business vis-à-vis treaty settlement with certain indigenous groups in British Columbia and Newfoundland. Categorizing indigenous people into full-blooded Indians and métis (mixed blood), and on-reserve and off-reserve, has added yet another dimension to the policy-making process.[6]

There is also considerably more formality in terms of how mineral rights are exercised in Canada than in the United States. For a First Nation to initiate mineral activity on its reserve, it must first surrender its mineral interests to Her Majesty, since the head of state is the only sovereign entity under British legal tradition. Mineral rights can then be negotiated for sale to third parties for the purposes of mineral exploration or development. A surrender means a First Nation surrenders its mineral interest so that the minister can deal with that interest, as consented to by the First Nation. This interest can include the exploration, development, and sale of metallic minerals.

The Canadian counterpart of the BIA is DIAND. While DIAND has similar roots to the BIA, initially being an extension of the military apparatus, the current structure and jurisdiction of DIAND is quite different from the BIA. The current department was created in 1966 by an act of Parliament and is a decidedly ancillary organization. Initially, DIAND was involved with directly providing services such as education, housing, road maintenance, and water/sewer systems to First Nations. However, in its present mission statement, the department acknowledges that it is "becoming much more of an advisory, funding, and supportive agency in its relations with First Nations, Inuit and northerners."[7]

Table 4.2 shows the various Canadian government departments and agencies that have relevance to mineral development. A notable difference between this table and the corollary U.S. table (4.1), is the presence

Table 4.2

Canadian Federal Organizations of Relevance to
Indigenous Mineral Development

Federal Government Agency	Task
Atomic Energy Control Board	Jurisdiction over uranium mining
Canadian Environmental Assessment Agency	Facilitating environmental assessments (process oriented)
Canadian Heritage	Promoting cultural diversity
Canadian Human Rights Commission	Preventing discrimination and referring grievances to a tribunal
Environment Canada	Compliance with various environmental regulations
Indian and Northern Affairs	Advisory body to assist in indigenous development
Indian Claims Commission	Hold public inquiries regarding land claims
Industry Canada — Indigenous Business Canada	Promote First Nation business enterprises
National Roundtable on the Environment and the Economy	Think tank on policy reform
Natural Resources Canada — Minerals and Metals Sector	The regulation of natural resource development and research
Western Economic Diversification Canada	To promote development in under-developed parts of Western Canada

of a separate cultural heritage organization in the Canadian government. The United States has generally been averse to institutionalizing cultural issues at the governmental level—which lends credence to the proverbial "melting pot" (U.S.) versus "salad bowl" (Canadian) divergence of policy making. Canada also has a more decentralized structure for its departments, with thirty-seven cabinet members as compared to fourteen in the United States; though, unlike their American counterparts, the Canadian cabinet members (following British tradition) may be part of the legislative branch of government as well and are therefore referred to as ministers.

In addition to the federal agencies mentioned above, there are several provincial agencies in each province that can often be actively involved in mineral issues, given the greater devolution of authority to provinces in Canada. In Canada the unique issues surrounding mining development on indigenous land have led the National Round Table on the Environment and the Economy (NRTEE), an independent federal agency, to launch a task force on indigenous communities and nonrenewable resource development, which published a report and recommendations on the issues at hand.[8]

Comparative Organizational Analysis

The changes in public organization have been studied in considerable detail by Denhardt (1993) using the classification scheme of Burrell and Morgan in their important work, *Sociological Paradigms in Organizational Analysis*. A refined version of this scheme is shown in figure 4.2, with my addition of two stages of BIA and DIAND development on the planar axes. The original diagram was meant to be used for positive categorization of social theories and the assumptions on which they are based. However, these quadrants are also representative of the change in government allegiance to particular kinds of sociological paradigms that led to the changes in organizational behavior. This may still beg the question of why the governments changed their outlook on Indian policy, but the focus here is more on the consequences of that change than on the causes of the policy change—a task admirably tackled by numerous historians.[9]

However, the earlier years of the BIA, probably up to the middle of this century, are shown by the circle marked "BIA 1." The subsequent changes and the future trajectory of the BIA is congruent with the second circle, "BIA 2."

The DIAND has a much more diffuse history since it has had several different organizational incarnations and did not exist as a unified entity until 1969 (DIAND 1 in fig. 4.2). However, even during this relatively brief duration, DIAND has clearly moved to the left of the horizontal axis in figure 4.2. It was not meant to be a regulatory organization and is thus situated in the northeast quadrant.

While this diagram may seem somewhat contrived, it allows us to conceptualize the two dimensions on which theories of public organization can be arrayed. The horizontal spectrum focuses on theorizing and ranges from the objective existence of society as posited by sociologists such as Durkheim (1949) to the subjective realm of institutional anthropology. The second, vertical dimension focuses on assumptions about the nature of society as manifest in the order-conflict debate. The BIA has clearly

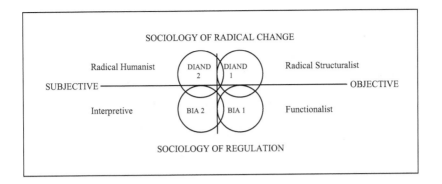

Figure 4.2
Paradigms in organizational analysis as applied to public organizations.

moved more from the functionalist quadrant with an emphasis on regulatory control to a more humanist and interpretive organizational domain.

Many of the changes that have occurred toward a less regulated and more culturally sensitive role of government in native America are directly related to a sense of contrition that has emerged in North America following the civil rights movement in the 1960s. The government has come to symbolize a timeless connection with the past for many indigenous communities, and the predominantly white governments of the United States and Canada have recognized that they must try to atone for the injustices of their forefathers. As we shall see, this has spawned a series of revisionist attacks on tribal institutions and the questionability of the politics of retribution.

Land and Water Claims

At the heart of any political debate in the Greco-Roman system is the question of property, particularly physical property, most notably manifest as claims to land and water and the resources therein. Who owns as well as controls land and water is a critically important issue for tribes and indeed for governance. Much of the contrition voiced by both the U.S. and Canadian governments with regard to the mistreatment of natives during the past is now being articulated through natural resource settlements in various forms. These are in turn tightly tied to the concept of sovereignty.

At this point, the important issue is that land claims, particularly in

Canada, are being thought of as a means of atoning for past injustices. The most remarkable development in this regard has been the creation of the territory of Nunavut in 1999, which is a hybrid of a territory and a province when it comes to the governance rights accorded to it (see appendix 1).[10]

While the formal treaty-making process has ended in the United States, there continues to be a cavalcade of congressional requests for tribal recognition and land settlement, particularly following the Indian Gaming Act of 1988. This in turn has led to strong resentment toward native sovereignty, particularly in states where casinos are otherwise banned or restricted. The enormous success of the Mashantucket Pequot tribe in Connecticut has led to a backlash from many circles whose members have even gone so far as to challenge the Indian credentials of the tribe itself.[11] This is posing yet another challenge for government institutions that are trying to implement a politics of retribution.

At this point it may be instructive to consider the lament against the Pequot and how it relates to native politics in general. While it may be true that the Pequot tribe in its current form does not have as much native pedigree as some other tribes, that does not necessarily mean that they are being deceitful. Native people were historically forced to assimilate and were made to feel shameful of their lineage; thus it is not surprising that some of them claimed to be white at some points in their lives. This reality in fact adds to the tragedy of native persecution. Moreover, on a factual basis, the descendents of the Pequot tribe, and some others, started to seek government recognition long before the casino was even an idea.

What is most troubling to native leaders is that there is an emerging cadre of politicians, such as former Washington Sen. Slade Gorton, who are suggesting a reversal of governmental policy toward Native Americans in terms of compensation for past injustices. As Gorton warns in a recent interview, "making a case out of what happened to your grandfather is not the best way to decide public policy" (quoted in Thomas 2000, 237). However, one may contend that Senator Gorton and his supporters are missing the point. It is easy to say, "Well, we were not the ones persecuting them then," but the whole point is that there were clear violations of treaties and other agreements by settler governments that are meant to be valid for time immemorial unless otherwise stated. Native activists further argue that even if there were no treaties (as is the case in British Columbia or Australia), there should still be a recognition of past injustices—isn't that what Western notions of timeless truth are all about?

A related trend in revisionist thought about native policy is the use of archeology to question the primacy of native settlement in North America. The discovery of a skull in the Columbia River valley that is morphologically dissimilar to most native skeletal remains has brought this debate to light. However, much of the revisionist arguments are moot here as well since the native claims to land and water rights are predicated on treaty violations and not on who was here first. Nevertheless, there is no doubt that the Indians were here before the current European immigrants. The Viking visits a thousand years ago did not lead to permanent settlements, as documented in their own narratives, and even so, they came long after the ancestors of the current native people of the Americas. The likely explanation for the archaeological mystery is that Asian ethnic groups who were related to the Ainu in Japan came to the Americas at some point in history as well. Their skeletal morphology is different from the predominant Mongoloid descendents that comprise a majority of current Native populations in the Americas.[12]

New Zealand offers an important comparison in this regard. The Maoris are known to have come to the two islands only a few hundred years before the Europeans (probably in the thirteenth century). Indeed, it is also believed that the Maoris annihilated and cannibalized the preexisting Polynesian inhabitants of New Zealand. Nevertheless, New Zealanders have recognized that such a history does not in any way diminish the treaty obligations that European settlers accepted upon their signing of the treaty of Waitangi and subsequent commitments.

Interestingly enough, land and water rights were often taken from Indians even in the name of environmental conservation. Mark David Spence (1999) has documented the removal of Indians from present-day Yosemite, Yellowstone, and Glacier National Parks in his book *Dispossessing the Wilderness*. The Chapleau Crown Game Preserve in Ontario was created in 1925 under a similar approach. The same sort of arguments that led to the removal of Indians from national park areas are now also being used in controversies surrounding hunting and fishing rights for tribes. These will come to light in the discussion in part 2 of the case of native-nonnative alliances in Wisconsin. Canadian natives are confronted with similar challenges as well by groups such as the Ontario Federation of Anglers and Hunters, who have a powerful lobbying presence in Ottawa. Ultimately, such instances of backlash toward natives are rooted in deep misperceptions of the "other."

The Ambivalence of Courts and Parliaments

Much of the debate over land rights, and the interpretation of the ever-elusive concepts of trust and sovereignty, have been played out in the courts and halls of legislatures in both the United States and Canada. The vicissitudes of native policy and legal wrangling in both the United States and Canada are too great to be discussed in any detail here. However, there are some landmark cases and some important statutes that have defined and redefined the meaning and relevant interpretation of native rights.

Statutory Comparison

In both the United States and Canada governments have tried to wrestle with competing notions of how to reconcile the somewhat paradoxical and sui generis status of native people as politically independent and yet economically dependent entities by enacting laws that have followed a kind of cyclical pattern during the past century. There have been waves of assimilative policies, such as the two termination episodes in the United States and the Canadian White Paper of 1969, followed by a resurgence of Indian self-determination programs, initially enunciated in the United States under the Indian Reorganization Act of 1938, followed by the Indian Self-Determination and Education Assistance Act (1975), and enunciated in Canada under the Indian Act, first enacted in 1876 and most recently revised in 1985. Attempts at privatization of Indian interests in the United States, such as the Dawes Allotment Act of 1887 or the Alaska Native Claims Settlement Act of 1971 have been important aberrations in U.S. Indian policy that do not have a Canadian corollary. Finally, a steady equilibrium appears to be developing in Indian policy on both sides of the border—at least, a legal framework for how to proceed and resolve the vestigial problems of colonialism appears to be emerging. This equilibrium in both Canada and the United States is predicated on a paramount recognition of native sovereignty.

Mineral rights are an important legal manifestation of sovereignty for native people. During the early part of this century, as U.S. Congress tried to come to terms with the various competing demands on Indian trust lands, there was a move toward separate leasing policy for Indian reservations, which culminated in the passage of the Omnibus Indian Mineral Leasing Act of 1938. For nearly fifty years this law was the only touchstone for mineral leases on Indian land alongside other leasing demands.

In the early eighties, there was a federal U.S. inquiry into the theft of Indian oil, as well as the misappropriation of royalties, prompted by whistle-blowing of audit findings by a Cherokee U.S. Geological Survey worker named Chuck Thomas. This was an unusual situation where states and tribes were both on the same side of the fence in their outrage. To states and tribes, oil and gas revenues were of vital importance. The states received 50 percent of the royalties from federal leases within their boundaries, except for Alaska, which received 90 percent. The Indians received all of the royalties from Indian leases. In 1982, the peak year, the Indians earned $198 million in royalties from oil and gas production. As a result of the subsequent commission and inquiry, the secretary of the interior created the Minerals Management Service in January 1982. By the end of that year Congress also passed the Federal Oil and Gas Royalty Management Act to implement other recommendations of the commission. Around the same time the Indian Minerals Development Act was also passed (Ambler 1990).

While the 1982 Indian Mineral Development Act was a turning point for Indian self-determination insofar that it gave tribes the right to directly negotiate contracts, it also added a distinct element of risk. The 1938 Omnibus Indian Mineral Leasing Act had required competitive lease sales to protect tribes from abuses prevalent at the time. Now the tribes were on their own. An example of the advantages of government oversight in mineral leases was apparent in 1976, when Secretary of the Interior Cecil Andrus refused to approve the Burnham mine lease until it had been renegotiated by the Navajo Tribal Council. After the lease was finally approved, the newly created federal Office of Surface Mining (OSM) took an additional fifteen months to approve the mine plan. Marcus Wiley, consolidation mine superintendent, later said, "If they [the Navajos] had been sovereign, we would have been in business three years sooner." Yet both federal delays seemed well justified. Later, the Navajo chairman praised the Department of the Interior for its role in improving the lease terms. The OSM delay stemmed from serious doubts that the Burnham site, which received fewer than six inches of rain a year, could be reclaimed. When OSM finally issued the permit, it included several rigorous stipulations (Fixico 1998; Ambler 1990). However, trust responsibility with proper accountability can be also a major hindrance to tribal development, as exemplified by the ongoing *Cobell* v. *Norton* case regarding the mismanagement of Indian accounts in the United States.

As many tribes are often quick to point out—it is often better to make your own mistakes and learn from them rather than to follow others. In the words of the oft-quoted jurist and scholar of Native American law Felix Cohen, self-determination must be redefined: "Not all who speak of self-government mean the same thing by the term. Therefore let me say at the outset that by self-government I mean that form of government in which decisions are made not by the people who are wisest, or best, or closest to some throne in Washington or in Heaven, but rather by the people who are most directly affected by the decisions."

The year 1982 was momentous in Canadian legal history as well—the Constitution of Canada was revised and approved with specific provisions for indigenous people. While the Constitution of the United States contains only oblique references to Indians in terms of commerce and tax exemption (art. 1, sec. 2, 7), the Constitution of Canada in its present form has a separate segment (pt. 2) allocated to indigenous rights that affirms the preexisting treaty rights of First Nations.

While such rights are clearly outlined in the Canadian constitution, the body of Canadian law pertaining to First Nations is not nearly as rich as in the United States. The key statute is the Indian Act, which was initially promulgated in 1876 but which has been revised several times since then (most recently in 1985). Apart from this law there is a Federal Indian Oil and Gas Act (1974) that was enacted to deal with the growing oil industry in Alberta. The act stipulates that "all oil and gas obtained from Indian lands after April 22, 1977 is subject to the payment to Her Majesty in right of Canada, in trust for the Indian bands concerned, of the royalties prescribed from time to time by the regulations." At the same time, the statute states that "nothing in this Act shall be deemed to abrogate the rights of Indian people or preclude them from negotiating for oil and gas benefits in those areas in which land claims have not been settled."

There are also many areas where Canadian laws are more restrictive of native enterprises as compared to their U.S. counterparts. In the United States, the more expansive interpretation of tribal sovereignty as a policy-making measure following the Nixon administration (and then reinforced by Reagan) immunizes certain forms of gaming operations from state legislation, although they are subject to a generally permissive act of Congress, and may require state compacts for larger ventures. Canada regulates gambling through the Criminal Code, and the courts have not recognized any exemption from the relevant provisions on the basis of self-government. Thus, gambling is illegal in Canada unless a license is obtained from the provincial government, which is "a permitted inter-delegation of powers."

In Ontario, the Chippewa of Rama have secured a license for a casino from the provincial government on the basis that revenues will be shared with other First Nations. There are also two current developments of on-reserve charitable gaming facilities: these are effectively rented out to li-censed charities to conduct bingo and casino nights onsite. There is no indication that governments will soon encourage or permit on-reserve gaming in Canada to the extent that industry has taken root in the United States.[13]

Canada's Indian policy received a considerable jolt in 1990 when a group of Mohawk Indians took arms to oppose the construction of a golf course near their Kahnesetake reservation in Oka, Quebec. There was a seventy-eight-day standoff between law enforcement authorities, includ-ing 3,700 troops, and sixty-three Mohawk warriors, which ultimately led to a disarming of the Mohawks. However, during the confrontation, one police officer was killed and the country was suddenly given a rude awaken-ing regarding the immediacy of indigenous issues. This incident galva-nized the government to renew a process of reconciliation, which led to the formation of the Royal Commission on Indigenous People in 1991. The commission published a four-thousand-page report in 1997 that cost more than $55 million to prepare (Switzer 1998).

Legislating a respect for the spiritual beliefs of indigenous peoples is also a particularly sensitive issue that American lawmakers first confronted by passing the Native American Religious Freedom Act of 1974, which was subsequently revised in 1994 to make a special exception for the use of potentially narcotic substances (for example, peyote was allowed for native ceremonial purposes). Even so, several Navajo families brought forth a complaint regarding religious intolerance to the UN Commission on Human Rights in 1997. The following year Abdelfattah Amor, the UN special rapporteur on religious intolerance, visited Black Mesa and filed a report that was quite critical of the U.S. government (*Navajo-Hopi Ob-server*, 5 May 1999).

Since many native people also have a strong sense of ancestral linkage, the Native American Graves Protection and Repatriation Act (NAGPRA) was passed by Congress in 1990 to repatriate the remains of native people that had been acquired by museums and also to prevent desecration of any native burial sites that might subsequently be excavated. This law is currently being tested through various cases in which scientists and museum curators are battling the issue in the courts, most notably around the skeletal remains known as "Kennewick Man" found in the Columbia River basin (See Thomas 2000).[14] It is important to note that current reluctance of tribes to allow research on skeletal remains under the pretext of NAGPRA is only exacerbating the negative perception of tribal governments, and such entrenchment deserves review by tribal leadership. The recent court decision by the U.S. District Court in Oregon (31 August 2002) in favor of the scientists' right to study the remains of Kennewick Man affirms the general view in the legal establishment that NAGPRA should not be used to hamper scientific research. Similar laws do not exist in Canada, though considerable caution is exercised by the government in reviewing environmental assessments that include sites of spiritual significance to natives.

The conflict between mining interests and environmentalists is perhaps greater in the United States than in most other countries, largely because a high proportion of federally owned lands are areas where minerals tend to be found, and there is a strong public interest in wilderness preservation that has been growing throughout the twentieth century. As of 1979, the U.S. government controlled about 760 million acres (about half of it in Alaska), which is about one-third of the land in the United States. Approximately 42 percent of these acres have been completely withdrawn from mineral activity, another 16 percent are severely restricted, and 10 percent are moderately restricted (Mikesell and Whitney 1987, chap. 6).

Major areas at issue between environmentalists and mining interests are some 80 million acres designated as wilderness under the Wilderness Act of 1964, plus 174 million acres identified by the Bureau of Land Management as wilderness study areas that are being reviewed for possible inclusion as designated wilderness areas. Exploration and mining activities are not allowed or are severely restricted in wilderness areas and national parks. The U.S. mining industry favors elimination of such restrictions as well as limiting the acreage of new areas brought into the wilderness system.

While the U.S. government's anecdotal suggestion of declaring certain parts of the United States as "national sacrifice areas" for mineral development has been largely dismissed, there is still much room for reform. The basic elements of U.S. minerals policy historically can be seen in President Reagan's report on 5 April 1982 to Congress on the National Materials and

Minerals Program—a report requested by Congress in the National Materials and Minerals Policy, Research, and Development Act of 1980. In the report, which recognizes the role of minerals for both national production and national defense, the president stated that his administration was considering the feasibility of using Title III of the Defense Production of 1950 (as amended) for subsidizing the creation or expansion of capacity of minerals that cannot be profitably produced at current world prices. The United States encourages nonfuel mineral mining by means of tax incentives, the most important of which is percentage depletion. The depletion allowance (which is deducted for determining taxable income) is calculated on gross income at various percentages ranging from 15 percent for copper, iron ore, gold, and silver to 22 percent for lead, zinc, nickel, and tin. The allowance may not exceed 50 percent of net income, calculated without regard to depletion. Intangible costs of mining development can be expensed as well as exploration expenditures, up to a certain limit.

There is still much room for change in both legal systems and lessons to be gleaned from the legal history of both the United States and Canada. As native legal scholar Kathy Brock has stated in her recent comparison of indigenous policy on both sides of the border:

> Unlike Canada where Indian Legislation tends to be centralized and systematic, in the United States Indian legislation comprises over 5,000 federal statutes, 2,000 federal court opinions, and nearly 400 ratified treaties and agreements. Although Canadian policy is moving in this direction, it in no way approximates the sheer volume and complexity of the American case. This cumbersome attribute of the American model is worth noting and avoiding in the present era, which emphasizes objectives of government efficiency and responsiveness. (Thomas 2000, 344)

Comparison of Jurisprudence

In the United States the three case decisions enunciated by Justice John Marshall in the mid-nineteenth century (known as the Marshall Trilogy) are foremost in this regard and established the principle of "domestic dependent nations" and "trust responsibility."[15] The trust responsibility doctrine has evolved from one of a "guardian-ward" relationship (in Marshall's words) to a "trustee" relationship. The wording of a statement issued by the BIA describes the relationship as follows: "The Federal Government is a trustee of Indian property, it is not a guardian of individual Indians. The Secretary of the Interior is authorized by law, in many instances, to protect the interests of minors and incompetents, but this protection does not confer a guardian-ward relationship."[16] However, this may just be an issue of semantics, and the concept of trust continues to be widely debated in the literature (see Deloria 1985).

Another principle in American Indian law that is particularly important and perhaps less ambiguous is the concept of "reserved sovereignty," which was expressed in a 1905 Supreme Court decision, *United States v. Winans* (198 Sup. Ct. 662). The Court concluded in this case that, when signing a treaty with the government, the tribes reserved a right that was preexisting to the influx of settlement and noted "that a treaty was not a grant of rights to Indians, but a grant of rights from them — a reservation of those not granted."

Canadian legal history concerning indigenous people tends to begin with the Royal Proclamation of 1763, which is often called the Magna Carta of Indian rights in Canada. However, much of the case law that is relevant to contemporary times begins with the Supreme Court's decision in the *Calder* case (1973). The case concerned the claim of the Nishgaa people in British Columbia to the Nass River valley. The significance of this case lies in the legal recognition of indigenous title, even though the case itself did not resolve the Nishgaa claim (which was ultimately settled in 1998). This recognition has been present in American jurisprudence since at least 1905, in the aforementioned *Winans* decision. In New Zealand, Maori title to the land was recognized as early as the Treaty of Waitangi (albeit poorly and unjustly implemented). Surprisingly, Canada was rather late in this recognition, though not as late as Australia, which did not have a recognition of Aboriginal title in its legal history until 1993, in the *Mabo* decision. Unlike the United States, where court opinions tend to be highly nationalistic, the Canadian courts often refer to cases in other countries with similar legal history, and the *Mabo* decision, as well as numerous U.S. court decisions, are often cited in Canadian courts (see Asch 1997).

Another landmark Canadian case that subsequently led to a test that is often applied to the resolution of issues respecting ownership and jurisdiction of lands is the *Baker Lake* case. This case concerned a request by the Inuit of Baker Lake in the Northwest Territories to obtain an injunction to stop the exploration activities of certain mining interests, based on the view that such ventures would adversely affect indigenous rights to occupy the land for hunting caribou. Justice Patrick Mahoney denied the injunction on the grounds that mining activities were not interfering significantly with an indigenous right to occupy land to hunt caribou. Nevertheless, the decision was important insofar as Justice Mahoney established a set of guidelines to be used when considering indigenous title, which are the following:

1. They and their ancestors were members of an organized society.
2. The organized society occupied the species territory over which they assert the indigenous title.
3. The occupation was to the exclusion of other organized societies.
4. The occupation was an established fact at the time sovereignty was asserted by England.

Since then, the most significant and often-cited ruling is the *Delgamuukw* decision, in which the court made an expansive ruling allowing for oral histories as proof of indigenous title alongside looser definitions of historical occupancy. However, the court was quite divided in many aspects of the decision, and there is still a sense among indigenous communities that they will need to fight for their rights on a case-by-case basis. The same sentiment holds true for Native Americans in the United States. There is a strong belief among Native American lawyers, such as Prof. Robert Williams of the University of Arizona, that the Supreme Court decisions thus far are by no means indelible, and in recent years the Rhenquist court has given native leaders considerable cause for anxiety.[17]

Economic Development and Indigenous Rights

Carl Schurz, the U.S. secretary of the interior in 1881, once stated: "there is nothing more dangerous to an Indian reservation than a rich mine" (Ambler 1990, 32). This statement was a prelude to the appropriation of land by the U.S. government because of mineral potential. The taking of the Black Hills in South Dakota after Gen. George Custer's confirmation of gold deposits in the region is perhaps the most flagrant example of this move. Such practices were given an interesting "sympathetic" twist by Commissioner of Indian Affairs Francis Walker, who wrote: "It is the policy of the government to segregate such [mineral] lands from Indian reservations as far as may be consistent with the faith of the United States and throw them open to entry and settlement in order that the Indians may not be annoyed and distressed by the cupidity of miners and settlers who in large numbers, in spite of the efforts of the government to the contrary, flock to such regions of the country on the first report of the gold discovery" (Ambler 1990, 33).

While such statements can perhaps be considered a mark of the times, they also reflect a more lasting tension between the government's role as trustee for Indians and the land in general on the one hand and as an agent of economic development and prosperity on the other. Mining, in particular has been an industry that is considered with great respect by governments in both Canada and the United because it is also a source of handsome tax revenues and can bring about sudden surges of wealth within a short span of time—a phenomenon that can serve important political functions as well.

In the United States, one of the oldest laws that has still not been amended or replaced is the General Mining Law of 1872. Under this law, miners can still stake claims to an underground ore body by paying a one-hundred-dollar holding fee per year. Powerful lobbying efforts by some in the mining industry have prevented any reform of the law. The 104th Congress did pass legislation amending the mining law, but it was vetoed as part of a larger package. Former Secretary of Interior Bruce Babbit called the law "an obscene example of corporate welfare" (Watkins 2000, 81). Nevertheless, considering when it was enacted, there are some positive features of the law for tribes, which Marjane Ambler describes as follows:

> Although designed primarily to provide access, three positive aspects of the 1891 law should not be ignored: It provided for leasing rather than whole-scale cessions of mineral lands; it represented a significant departure from existing policy on public lands whereby prospectors who found minerals could obtain the ownership of the minerals and the surface land under claim/patent laws (with a few exceptions, Congress did not authorize leasing public energy minerals until 1920); and it required tribal consent. (Ambler 1990, 37)

Apart from this law, the only significant regulations that apply specifically to hard rock mining are the Section 3809 regulations (43 CFR) under the Federal Land Policy and Management Act of 1976. However, these regulations only apply to mining on federal land. The Bureau of Land Management is in charge of promulgating mining regulations under this act and is currently soliciting comments for proposed reviews to the existing regulation.

The only area of mining in the United States where specific organizational reform has taken place is coal mining. The Surface Mining Control and Reclamation Act (SMCRA) of 1979 was enacted initially to cover all aboveground mining activities, but its jurisdiction was largely limited by Congress to coal mining. The Office of Surface Mining Control and Reclamation is the federal agency that administers the provisions of the act. The work of OSM will be discussed in further detail in the analysis of the Navajo/Hopi coal mines.

In Canada the laws pertaining to mining have also had to acutely balance economic considerations. There is greater dependence on mineral revenues in Canada, particularly in regions such as the Northwest Territories, where mining is the lifeblood of the economy. Although industry has claimed that noncompetitive taxation levels are a significant disincentive for investment in Canada, NGO reports show real rates of taxation — which account for capital cost allowances, deferrals, credits, and tax holidays for new developments — make Canadian tax levels in the middle to low level on an international scale. In 1996, tax concessions were granted through accelerated write-offs of development expenses for mine expansions.

"Flow-through" shares are another example of taxpayer subsidies of the Canadian mineral exploration community. These shares allow investors to deduct exploration expenses and related depletion allowances against any income. According to the Environmental Mining Council of British Columbia, individual taxpayers seeking tax shelters have made extensive use of this program, representing more than $150 million of the exploration capital raised in 1996.

Finally, a range of concerns have been raised in regard to Canada's current taxation and subsidy policies that provide a variety of incentives for the capital intensive primary/extractive resource industries such as mining. These incentives, it is argued, are introducing market distortions and present biases against key elements of the sustainable economy growth, including recycled materials markets and the labor-intensive service sector.[18]

In July 1998, Natural Resources Canada launched a "Federally Initiated Review of Federal Environmental Regulations Affecting Mining in Canada," with reference to the recommendations for reform made by a Standing Committee of Natural Resources Canada. Of the fifty commitments identified in the government's responses to the recommendations of the standing committee, thirty-one (62 percent) have been implemented, and progress has been made on another sixteen (32 percent), for a total of 94 percent. Action on the remaining three commitments has either been delayed or postponed. A year after the signing of the government's response to the final report of the standing committee, forty-seven (94 percent) of the government's commitments have been, or are in the process of being, implemented.

Progress has been made in relation to the federal acts and regulations covered by the federal-provincial-territorial review — that is, the Canadian Environmental Assessment Act, the Fisheries Act, the Navigable Waters Protection Act, and the Metal Mining Liquid Effluent Regulations. However, as mentioned earlier, the high level of devolution concerning regulations to provinces necessitates a more in-depth discussion for each mine with reference to provincial regulations. This area of provincial regulations is covered in part 2.

Suffice it to say that nontribal government institutions in both Canada and the United States have had a daunting task before them to balance economic issues, environmental concerns, and native interests. While they may aspire to be neutral overarching authorities, they are inevitably stakeholders in the conflicts that may arise during mineral development ventures. However, they are embedded stakeholders with certain integral responsibilities that are incumbent upon them as democratic institutions.

Part II

Analyzing Resistance

Chapter 5

From Nain to Navajo

The Stories behind the Scenery

To fully appreciate the wellsprings of resistance, we must attempt to understand the stories and lifestyles of the people whose struggles are being described and analyzed. This chapter aims to narrate the stories of the communities who shared with me their trials and triumphs as mining ventures were proposed or developed amidst their land.

Mining in the Four Corners Region (Case U1)

The four corners region of the United States is perhaps more than an accident of geography. It is the terrestrial confluence of the most distant parts of each state (Colorado, Utah, Arizona, and New Mexico) that share this desolate yet spectacular terrain. With less than ten inches of precipitation per year, the area is a vast desert punctuated with occasional resilient bushes and cacti.

While the Hopi people lived in this area for centuries before European conquest, the Navajo moved to the region relatively recently (probably around the same time as the advent of Columbus in the late fifteenth century).[1] The Hopi are believed to be the descendents of the ancient Puebloans (of Mesa Verde fame), whereas the Navajo are Athabascan in origin and thus share much in common linguistically with their Déné relations in north-central Canada. Apart from linguistic differences, the two cultures are also quite different on other accounts. Many Hopi believe that the Navajo were invaders who drove their relations to the mesas where they currently reside. However, there is considerable disagreement among scholars about the historical antagonism between the two peoples.

Charles Wilkinson (1999), a former attorney for the Native American Rights Fund and a professor of law at the University of Colorado, has described the differences between the Hopi and the Navajo as follows:

> To be sure the historical antagonisms between the Hopi and the Navajo are sometimes exaggerated. Many Hopi and Navajo families have lived near each other in amity for generations. Yet the fact remains that these are two very different peoples. The Navajo are a herding and hunting tribe, assertive and aggressive, able to change in order to meet new circumstances, quick to move into new territory and defend it. The Hopi are farmers rooted in one place. Navajo see their tribal personality as firm and strong, the Hopi view theirs as peaceful. (Wilkinson 1999, 150)

Nevertheless, despite their differences, both communities share a similar environmental ethic as revealed in much of their oral histories and traditions. In the words of Hopi traditionalist Thomas Banyacya, who believes in greater solidarity with the Navajo, "We must not forget who we are. We are red men who live on our red land" (quoted in Benedek 1999, 9).

Unfortunately, Hopi-Navajo relations for much of the past century have been characterized in terms of territorial squabbles. The land dispute between the two tribes can be traced back to the late nineteenth century when the Hopi, who had initially not signed any treaty with the U.S. government, asked the federal government for exclusive land. They reported incursions by Navajo grazers on what they considered to be their ancestral lands.[2] The Navajo were much more numerous than the Hopis (currently there are more than 250,000 Navajos and fewer than 13,000 Hopis), and so the Hopi appeal was given a sympathetic ear by the authorities. Subsequently, President Chester Arthur created a reservation for the Hopi tribe by executive order in 1882. However, there was continuing competition for grazing land and water between the two tribes, and eventually the matter ended up in court in what was meant to be a "friendly litigation process" initiated in 1958 by Congressman Stewart Udall of Arizona, a great sympathizer of native causes.

The well-intentioned lawsuit, entitled *Healing* v. *Jones* (after the Hopi and Navajo tribal chairmen), was meant to be a formality for dispute resolution purposes, but as is often the case with legal challenges, it took on a life of its own. The court issued its ruling in 1962. The Hopi were given exclusive title to the surface and subsurface areas in District 6, which formed the central core of the reservation on the numbered mesas. However, the tribes have joint rights to surface and subsurface resources in the area demarcated in the 1882 executive order outside of District 6. The squabbles continued because of the ambiguity of the decision regarding the way in which the joint use area was to be administered. In 1974, Congress passed the Navajo-Hopi Settlement Act, which officially partitioned Hopi and Navajo lands and allowed for relocation arrangements to commence. While some people accepted the relocation package, many others resisted.

The situation continued to fester. Various legal challenges and counter-challenges were brought by both sides until the early nineties, when the Navajo and the Hopi were under the leadership of particularly agreeable presidents—Vernon Masayesva (Hopi) and Peterson Zah (Navajo).

There was an important utterance the Hopis had been waiting for more than a hundred years to hear, and Navajo Nation president Peterson Zah offered it to them as an apology during a speech before the Hopi tribal council in 1993. He said, "This is your land. I've got people living on it who are attached to it. They'd like to stay there. I'd like to see them accommodated." Former Hopi chairman Vernon Masayesva, a true statesman in his own right, described Zah's eloquent speech as follows: "So, basically, the Navajo president did the Hopi thing. Because that's how the Hopis were admitted into the villages. They asked permission. They didn't just say 'We're here, we're going to stay'" (Benedek 1999, 396).

According to Benedek (1999), "the federal government, including representatives from Interior and Justice, were also instrumental in keeping the negotiations going." The process also utilized the services of mediators appointed by the Ninth Circuit, including former Judge Harry McCue, who played an important role in ensuring that the negotiations went forward as the tribes wanted and without any judgmental pressure from the government. This effort culminated in the Accommodation Agreement signed into law by President Clinton in October 1996. While the land dispute was officially over as far as the negotiating parties were concerned, there were still some wrinkles that needed to be ironed out. As shall be shown in subsequent sections, mining was presented by some parties as the losing card.

Project History: A Tale of Uranium and Coal

During the past fifty years several mining companies have been involved in activities on Navajo and Hopi lands. Mining was aimed at extracting two different energy minerals—coal and uranium. Much of my analysis will focus on coal mining given its current significance. Nevertheless, it is important to keep the uranium mining issue in perspective, particularly when compared to the Saskatchewan uranium industry that is still quite alive.

Uranium Mining at Navajo

Uranium mining predates coal activity in the region and is now largely in a reclamation phase. Mining on Navajo lands started as early as 1918 in the Carrizo Mountain area, which is just about thirty miles west of Shiprock. At first, vanadium was the key metal mined and uranium was considered a byproduct.

In the early 1920s, the first uranium extraction began on Navajo land, when the U.S. government opened the area to exploration. These initial mining facilities ceased operation in 1923, when rich sources of cheap uranium were discovered in the Belgian Congo (formerly Zaire and now the Democratic Republic of Congo). More concerted efforts at uranium mining began in earnest in the Southwest United States after World War II, when atomic weapons were being developed. Escalation of the cold war between the United States and the Soviet Union sent workers to uranium mines for ore to process into nuclear weapons. More than fifteen thousand people have mined uranium or worked in ore processing mills in the Southwest since the 1940s. Some thirteen million tons of uranium ore was mined while the mines were in operation. The Vanadium Corporation of America and Kerr-McGee were the principal owners of these mines.

The Navajos were not the only tribe to endure uranium mining. The Laguna Pueblo first signed a lease in 1952 with Anaconda Copper, now the Anaconda Minerals Company, a division of Atlantic Richfield Company. By 1980, Jackpile was the largest open-pit uranium mine in the world. Combined Jackpile-Paguate pits encompassed 2,800 acres of the 461,098-acre reservation. When the mines closed down in 1982, one commentator said it would take 400 million tons of dirt to fill the pits—enough to cover the District of Columbia to a depth of forty-five feet (Ambler 1990, 210).

Once the dangers of uranium mining gradually became clear, a few Navajo began to ask for accountability from the government. Throughout the 1970s, a few people struggled both to put controls on operations in the mines and to help Navajo victims of radiation exposure find some compensation. In December 1978, one hundred Navajos, most of whom were allottees,[3] joined with Friends of the Earth to file suit against six federal agencies, demanding a regional study of the impacts of uranium mining. The federal court declined to issue an injunction, saying that it was questionable whether they wanted to continue their "pastoral way of life" when they could be miners or millworkers. The case was eventually rendered moot since the uranium activity at that time stopped due to a decline in uranium prices.

Even after the mining activities ceased at Navajo, the legacy of environmental harm continued. In the early morning hours of 16 July 1979—fourteen weeks after the accident at Three Mile Island—the worst fears of the community were realized when a tailing dam at Church Rock, New Mexico, burst, sending eleven hundred tons of radioactive mill wastes and ninety million gallons of contaminated liquid pouring toward Arizona—the largest accidental release of radioactive material in U.S. history. What made the Church Rock disaster especially tragic was that it could have been avoided. Soon after the spill, an angry U.S. representative, Morris Udall (D-Ariz.), told a congressional hearing that "at least three and possibly more Federal and state regulatory agencies had ample opportunity to conclude that such an accident was likely to occur."[4]

Needless to say, the remediation programs for the mines are still far from over. Harry Tome, a Dineh from Red Rock chapter, worked throughout the decade to bring relief to Navajo miners. Toward the end of the eighties, former U.S. Secretary of the Interior Stewart Udall intervened on his behalf. The result of this intervention was the Radiation Exposure Compensation Act, which was signed into law in 1990. The intent was to provide "compassionate payments" to victims of radiation exposure.

In February 2000, the Navajo Nation was presented the 1999 reclamation award from the Office of Surface Mining Control and Reclamation for its work in cleanup activities at uranium mines in the Monument Valley section of the reservation. There are some tentative plans for another uranium mine near Crownpoint, New Mexico, but the project has been stalled because of legal challenges and permitting woes. Interestingly enough, despite the historical legacy of uranium mining, on 19 January 2000, the Resources Committee of the Navajo Nation Council reversed the Nation's moratorium on uranium mining. While the 1983 moratorium was affirmed for open-pit and underground mining, the in-situ leaching of uranium is now "welcomed" (*Navajo-Hopi Observer*, 5 February 2000). However, the predominant form of mining in the region continues to be coal, and this is therefore the focus of my case analysis for this region.

Coal Mining at Navajo and Hopi

Coal mining in Navajo country commenced in 1963 with the opening of the Navajo mine in the eastern part of the reservation. However, much of my discussion will focus on the Black Mesa and Kayenta mines, which are in the western part of the reservation and are environmentally much more questionable and territorially more complex (and hence a likely flashpoint for resistance movements).[5]

In 1966, the Hopi and Navajo tribal councils signed mining leases with a consortium of twenty utilities that had designed a new coal-fired energy grid for the urban Southwest. The terms of this lease were highly unusual and gave unprecedented concessions to the coal company; for example, it allowed the company to have control of 40,000 acres of land, as compared to the limit of 2,560 acres in the federal regulations for Indian leasing. The royalty rate, which the two tribal councils split, was set at thirty cents per ton, at a time when the government royalty rate for coal extracted on public lands was $1.50 a ton. There were hardly any environmental safeguards and no provisions for renegotiation. The most problematic provision, however, was the allowance to Peabody to pump four thousand acre-feet (approximately a billion gallons) of water a year to run a coal slurry line that extends 273 miles from Black Mesa to the Mojave Generating station. The company was to pay the Hopi only $1.67 per acre-foot for the precious groundwater in this arid land, a number Colorado law professor Charles Wilkinson refers to as "laughable" (Wilkinson 1999, 301).

The lawyer representing the Hopis in this transaction was later accused of also working on behalf of Peabody Coal. John Boyden has been the subject of major posthumous investigations by such legal scholars as Wilkinson. In archives unearthed at Brigham Young University, Wilkinson found Boyden's correspondence with both parties. There was clear evidence that showed the lawyer had been hired contemporaneously by both the tribe and the mining company (Wilkinson 1999, chap. 7).[6] John Boyden remained the Hopi's lawyer for thirty years. Although he presented himself as a charitable lawyer working for the Hopi pro bono, his fees—paid by the government out of funds held in trust for the Hopi—totaled $2.7 million, a figure revealed only after a Freedom of Information Act suit filed by the Native American Rights Fund (Nies 1998). While this connection is troubling from an ethical standpoint, activists have used Boyden's incrimination as an indictment for the entire coal mining industry that is also somewhat problematic. A close observer of the Navajo-Hopi conflict, Emily Benedek comments on the activist's misrepresentation of the issue as follows: "There is no convincing evidence of a broad-based conspiracy behind the land dispute. The Hopis' unhappiness with the Navajo presence on the land is well-established in the historical record. It is more accurate to say that the energy interests provided the Hopi lawyer with an extremely powerful tool with which to bring attention to the problem, and ammunition with which to push for partition" (Benedek 1999, 139).

Until 1969, the coal around Black Mesa lay untouched, though writer Judith Nies observed the proximity of the coal to the surface was obvious to any passerby (Nies 1998). With a long-term value estimated as high as $100 billion, the coal lies completely under Indian reservation lands. The complex consists of two separate but adjacent operations—the Black Mesa mine and the Kayenta mine—and is operated by Peabody. Also included in the complex is the Mesa Preparation Plant, which is operated by the Black Mesa Pipeline, Inc. Mining at the Black Mesa/Kayenta complex has been in existence since 1970 and the complex currently produces about 12 million tons per year. The two mines cover 62,753 acres of Hopi and Navajo Tribal lands, of which 6,137 are Hopi surface ownership and 56,616 acres are Navajo surface ownership. As of 1 January 1999, there has been 17,158 acres disturbed, 65 acres on Hopi land and 17,093 acres on Navajo land.

Individual Navajo residents are not landowners, but instead have certain land use rights arising under the laws of the Navajo Nation. The U.S. Interior Board of Land Appeals (IBLA), in *Dineh Alliance and Maxine Kescoli v. The Office of Surface Mining and Peabody Western Coal Mining Company* (IBLA 96-294), has held that the consent of the individual land users residing on Indian lands is not required, as the tribes are the landowners for purposes of the SMCRA. If it became necessary, the Navajo Nation, by its power of eminent domain, has the authority to move these individual land users and require Peabody to provide compensation to these land users for the loss of their land use rights.[7]

The Navajo Nation has established policies and procedures that must be followed in all instances where the Navajo Nation exercises its power of eminent domain. There were eighty-two individual households within the Navajo Nation lands of the Black Mesa/Kayenta leasehold. To date, fifty-two households have been moved as a consequence of mining and an additional ten households will be relocated if mining operations continue. Peabody is responsible for compensating the families. Navajo land users have three options—they can be moved off of the reservation; they can be moved to another location on the reservation; or they can be moved within their customary use area as long as there is no coal beneath the area and it is two thousand feet from active mining. In order to deal with this issue the Navajo Nation established the Black Mesa Review Board in the Navajo Nation Code (2 NNC art. 5, Black Mesa Review Board) to act as a liaison between the people and Peabody. The purpose of the board is to provide compensation to Navajo families whose economic interests are adversely affected by the mine.

The lease for the mine was renegotiated in 1987 by the tribes and Peabody, and an environmental impact statement for the Black Mesa/Kayenta mine was completed in June 1990 through the federal Office of Surface Mining. The Environmental Impact Statement (EIS) took more than four years to complete. The EIS process included four public meetings held in the vicinity of the mine. This process resulted in 226 individuals submitting 1,035 separate comments that OSM responded to in the final EIS.

It is important to keep in mind that while historically the tribes did not have much leverage or information in making appropriate decisions, they did indeed have an opportunity in the 1987 renegotiation to veto the project, but they chose to go ahead with the renegotiated lease. According to some commentators, the EIS was inadequate and the Environmental Protection Agency was indeed quite "unsatisfied" with the quality of the study.[8] However, OSM argues that comments from EPA were in fact included in the revised EIS.[9] In any event, the renegotiated lease now gives Peabody permission to mine the coal until 2005, at which time the lease will again be negotiated.

Peabody Coal

Peabody Coal was founded in 1883 by the Chicago-based entrepreneur Francis Peabody and is now the world's largest coal company with 1999 annual revenues exceeding $2.3 billion. It is also a leading U.S. power marketer, fueling more than 9 percent of U.S. and 2.5 percent of the world's electricity. With high-grade properties in the United States and Australia, along with the nation's most productive mines, Peabody provides products and services to more than 180 power plants and forty industrial facilities in the United States, as well as customers in eighteen other countries. Currently Peabody is owned by Lehman Merchant Banking Partners, LLP, who bought it from the British-owned Hanson group in 1998 (Peabody Group Annual Report 1999). During 1999, Peabody's U.S. surface and underground mines reported a 4.31 average injury incidence rate, which is 39 percent better than the industry average.

The Mining Continues

Environmental activists from around the country have tried to conflate the mining at Black Mesa with the Navajo-Hopi land dispute. As early as the late seventies, Greenpeace and numerous other environmental groups were involved in fighting against mining on the pretext of supporting the Navajo residents on Hopi partitioned land. The area on most maps designated as "Big Mountain" is the focus of much of the resistance movement since this is the area where the few families who have not signed the accommodation agreement with the government reside. The details regarding the Big Mountain resistance will be discussed in much more detail later. Suffice it to say, resistance to coal mining continues to be marginalized by the tribal governments and by many indigenous environmental groups as well. For example, the Indigenous Environmental Network has distanced itself from this issue because of their belief that external nonnative environmental groups have caused divisions within the community.[10] Nevertheless, that is not to say that the tribes are satisfied with Peabody Coal's performance per se either.

In a rare show of unity on legal matters, the Navajo and Hopi tribes both filed lawsuits against Peabody in November 1999 seeking recovery of $600 million in damages from Peabody Western Coal Company for "unlawful acts defrauding [the tribes]." However, this lawsuit still does not detract the tribal governments from condemning the activists and rendering much of their activities futile.

Peabody contends that since mining operations began, the Black Mesa and Kayenta mines have injected more than $1.2 billion into Navajo and Hopi tribal economies in royalties, taxes, wages, and charitable contributions. Each year, Peabody Western provides the Navajo Nation and the Hopi tribe with more than $40 million in royalties and taxes generated from the mining operations. The complex employs approximately 750 Native Americans, representing 90 percent of the workforce, and additionally supports indirect employment in restaurants, hotels, and other American Indian employment industries. Royalties and taxes from coal mining provide about 80 percent of the Hopi general operating budget and about 60 percent of the Navajo general fund budget.

The Crandon Mine in Wisconsin (Case U2)

Family clans of Chippewa migrated from eastern Canada to Madeline Island in Lake Superior a thousand years ago, led by a vision that their journey would end in a land where the "food grows on water" (*manomin*, or wild rice). The Sokaogon band's journey ended in this area of abundant wild rice. Competition from the Sioux resulted in the Battle of Mole Lake in 1806. A marker stands on Highway 55 in the village of Mole Lake to mark the battleground where more than five hundred warriors were slain in fierce hand-to-hand battle. The Sokaogon Chippewa reorganized soon thereafter and currently constitute a small tribe of about eleven hundred individuals who occupy a reservation of about eighteen hundred acres.

The tribe is named Sokaogon, which means "post in the lake people," because of the spiritual significance of a post—possibly the remains of a petrified tree—that stood in Post Lake nearby. The lake and surrounding precincts are the last remaining ancient wild rice beds in the state of Wisconsin. The Sokaogon Ojibwa are also known as the Lost Tribe because the legal title to the twelve-square-mile reservation from the treaty of 1854 was lost in a shipwreck on Lake Superior. The band, under the leadership of Chief Willard Ackley, finally and after a long struggle, received federal recognition and reservation status in 1937. The Sokaogon (Mole Lake) band has access to three lakes either on or adjacent to the small reservation: Mole Lake, Bishop Lake, and Rice Lake, which lies at the headwaters of the Wolf River. The river is presently classified as a "Wild and Scenic River" by the Nature Conservancy and has thus become a cause célèbre for many Wisconsin environmentalists.

Project History

Mining is not a new industry in Wisconsin. As early as 1658, mining of lead ore commenced in the southwestern lead region, and French explorers mined lead throughout the eighteenth century. During this time Native Americans, particularly the Sauk and Fox, were also involved in mining around this area and in fact invented an innovative smelting process alongside the French.[11] The early miners shaped Wisconsin into a major producer of lead, zinc, and iron. In 1971, the Wisconsin legislature passed a bill designating galena—lead sulfide—as the official state mineral. Currently, more than ten thousand people in Wisconsin are employed in mining-related jobs.

The Crandon ore body (zinc, copper, and lead), discovered by Exxon in 1975, lies in Forest County, five miles south of the City of Crandon and two miles east of State Highway 55. The boundary of the mine site borders the Mole Lake Sokagoan Chippewa Reservation. The company submitted permit applications in the early 1980s but later withdrew them, citing depressed mineral prices. Crandon Mining Company (a partnership between Exxon Corporation subsidiaries and Rio Algom Ltd. subsidiaries) announced the intent to submit new mine permit applications in 1994. Since then, the Wisconsin Department of Natural Resources has been leading the state review of this project. The federal environmental impact review is being led by the Army Corps of Engineers. The corps is involved as the lead agency because of the mine's likely hydrological impact. In 1998, Rio Algom bought out Exxon's shares in the project and had sole control over the mining proposal, through its subsidiary Nicolet Minerals Company (NMC), which continues with the same name and management under BHP Billiton's ownership.

The area where the Crandon mine is planned lies in a relatively pristine part of the state. The largest industrial base in the vicinity is logging, and the town of Rhinelander, which is located some twenty miles from the mine site, is a major hub for the logging industry. Indeed, some of the native tribes, including the Menominee, have their own lumber companies as well.

Opposition to mining in Wisconsin emerged soon after Exxon first announced its discovery in 1976. The first voice of resistance was offered by the Chippewa community itself, which realized that the ore body lies in a 92,000-acre tract of land that the U.S. government had promised them in an 1854 treaty. It is important to note that nonnative groups became involved in this effort after the resistance voiced by the tribe itself. In 1975, Exxon gave a check of $20,000 to the Chippewan tribal chairperson for the rights to explore on the reservation itself. When the tribal council found out about this, they were outraged and the check was torn up at the council meeting.[12]

Following this episode the tribe has been quite resolute and united in its resistance to the project. According to historian and activist Zoltan Grossman, between 1986 and 1992 several important events took place in northern Wisconsin that led to the antimining movement gathering force.[13] First, a large movement against Chippewa treaty rights to spearfish garnered support from white sportfishermen in northern Wisconsin. Antitreaty groups appealed to environmentalists to stop spear fishing because of a fear that "the Indians would overfish," but their efforts were largely thwarted by a separate contingent of pro-treaty white groups that formed a coalition called the Midwest Treaty Network in 1989.

Mining activity in other parts of Wisconsin was increasing, but not without resistance. In the early 1990s, local environmentalists and the Lac du Flambeau Chippewa managed to stop the Canadian firm Noranda from opening the Lynne zinc-silver mine near the Willow Flowage in Oneida County. The only mine that did end up opening was Kennecott Corporation's Ladysmith copper-gold mine in Rusk County, next to the Flambeau River, partly because the mine was not as close to a reservation and the resistance movement was not as persistent. However, the opening of this mine did lead to greater pan-Wisconsin resolve to stop mining. It was during this time that Rusk County activist Evelyn Churchill proposed a moratorium on sulfide mining. In 1994, the Midwest Treaty Network sponsored a large rally in Madison and cosponsored (with the Indigenous Environmental Network) a Protect the Earth gathering that drew one thousand people to Mole Lake.

In 1995, the network initiated the Wolf Watershed Educational Project, which quickly mushroomed into a grassroots alliance of about thirty Native American, environmental, and sportfishing groups. They held monthly strategy meetings around the northern counties of the state. Out of those meetings came a spring 1996 speaking tour up the Wolf River, as well as the Wisconsin River, where Exxon was then proposing to dump its liquid mine wastes. The tour reached twenty-two communities and eleven hundred people and culminated with a rally of one thousand people in front of the company headquarters in Rhinelander (which was covered only by northern media). A 1997 tour around other parts of the state increased support for the moratorium bill that had by then been introduced in the legislature.

Gov. Tommy Thompson signed the Mining Moratorium Law (1997 Wisconsin Act 171) on Earth Day in April 1998. The moratorium law provides an additional requirement that a mining applicant must meet in order to receive a mining permit. In order to meet this new requirement, a mining company must submit data for a similar mine that has been closed for ten years without causing significant environmental pollution, and one that has *operated* for ten years without causing pollution. The candidate mines identified by the company must be located in sulfide ore bodies that, together with the host rock, have the potential to create acid runoff. The final decision about whether sites meet the requirements of the Mining Moratorium Law are made by the hearing examiner and are based on the record developed at the master hearing.

In the case of the Crandon site, however, the law itself was not enough to quell the urge to mine there. Indeed, only a year after the law was enacted, Rio Algom began a new effort to revitalize the Crandon project.

The Companies Involved

Nicolet Minerals Company (NMC), named after the famed Wisconsin explorer Jean Nicolet, was formed in January 1998 by Rio Algom—a Canadian mining and metals distribution company. As mentioned earlier, Rio Algom has been a part of the Crandon project since 1993. It became sole owner when it bought Exxon's share of the project in 1998 (though Exxon is still supposed to receive royalties from ore revenues). Rio Algom was bought by the South African mining giant Billiton in 2000, which was subsequently bought by the Australian mining conglomerate BHP in early 2002 to form BHP Billiton. The project is now under the ownership of BHP Billiton, though much of the research and the resistance struggle against the mine has occurred during the Rio Algom ownership and thus the following case analysis focuses on Rio Algom's involvement in the project.

Rio Algom, headquartered in Toronto, was all too often confused with its former parent company, Rio Tinto (one of the world's largest mining conglomerates). Rio Algom was a moderate-sized company with annual revenues of about $1.5 billion dollars and operations mostly in North and South America. The company had to contend with a legacy of old uranium mines that are currently under reclamation, most notably the Elliot Lake uranium complex in Ontario, which cost the company more than $74 million. While activist groups have criticized Rio Algom for its record, the company generally had a favorable regulatory compliance record. For example, the overall recordable case frequency during 1999 for lost-time injuries in mining operations was 1.06, whereas the Ontario mining industry average is 10.9.[14]

Development Plans and the Prevalence of Resistance

The Crandon mine site contains 55 million tons of ore, primarily zinc and copper, with small amounts of lead, silver, and gold. The ore body is about

4,900 feet long from east to west and about 100 feet wide from north to south. It begins about 200 feet below the surface and extends to a depth of about 2,200 feet. Rock containing metallic minerals sought by NMC (mainly zinc and copper, with lead and far smaller amounts of silver and gold) will be finely crushed and ground. The minerals will be separated from the rest of the ore by a process called flotation. Millions of tons of fine rock residue, called tailings, will remain for disposal.

Mine structures will occupy about 550 acres, including mainly forest and also smaller tracts of wetlands and open land. Major facilities on the surface will include the head frame, housing the opening to the main shaft, a mill for ore processing, a tailings management area, a water management and treatment system, offices, maintenance shops, storage buildings, and parking. The mine will produce about 5,500 tons of ore per day. Ore will be mined underground by blast-hole open stoping. To reach the ore, miners will construct three vertical shafts and a series of horizontal tunnels called drifts. Ore will be removed from rooms, called stopes, each 100 feet wide, 75 feet long, and upwards of 300 feet high. The ore will be hauled to an underground crusher, then hoisted to the surface for processing. Mined-out stopes will be backfilled with tailings mixed with cement (technical details concerning the environmental impact will be discussed in the next chapter).

According to Rio Algom, more than $20 million was spent on the environmental impact statement process for the mine site. Officials of NMC claim to have thus far met with more than ten thousand individuals for public comments.[15] In January 2000, the company also hired a former tribal president from the neighboring Hochunk Nation to act as a cultural consultant to the company and to mediate the deliberations between the community and the company.

However, the resistance continues to be resolute. Most recently, the native groups have employed an important regulatory strategy to block the project by promulgating their own highly stringent environmental standards. The state of Wisconsin has subsequently tried to sue the tribes for infringing on its authority. However, in a 28 April 1999 decision, the U.S. District Court dismissed a lawsuit by the state against the U.S. EPA and the Mole Lake Chippewa. The suit was an attempt to deny EPA's authority to grant treatment-as-state status to Mole Lake Reservation. The EPA originally granted this status to Mole Lake in 1995 to support Mole Lake's sovereign authority to set its own water quality standards under the federal Clean Water Act. Similar regulatory primacy has also been granted for air regulations to the Forest County Potawatomi. At the same time, the tribes have also become involved in nontribal local government bodies, such as town councils. The town of Nashville now has a Mole Lake member on the town board and has recently managed to rescind an earlier agreement between the mining company and the town. NMC sued the town for breach of contract and a decision was granted in favor of the mining company in September 2001 in which the contract was upheld. Even so, there is yet another court case pending that questions the jurisdiction of such local contracts.

With such an array of challenges, the prospects for the Crandon mine opening are indeed dim. The vice president for Environmental and Community Affairs at Rio Algom and now at BHP Billiton, Maxine Wiber, stated in an interview that the company was becoming "increasingly pessimistic" about the project going forward because of resistance.[16]

The Saskatchewan Uranium Mines (Case C1)

Chipewyan Inuit, Déné, and Cree bands comprise 80 percent of the thirty thousand inhabitants in the northern mining region of Saskatchewan, mostly centered around the shores of the numerous lakes that punctuate the landscape. Even these settlements were artificially created by the Europeans, since traditional societies here were hunter-gatherers that had territories but no permanent settlements. The European settlers often mistook this itinerant lifestyle as a mark of poverty, whereas the communities were quite contented. According to a native individual, "we didn't know that we were poor until we found a Canadian government official on our door with food supplies saying: you need help."[17] The cultural shift led to high unemployment and other social concerns in these communities. For example, the unemployment rate for indigenous communities in Saskatchewan is about 65 percent, whereas for nonindigenous communities it is around 30 percent.

By 1995, all the tribal bands in Saskatchewan had settled their land claims with the government and received compensation. Some of these claims covered land on mining leases as well. The policy of land entitlements was premised on a "willing buyer/willing seller" principle and was not based on traditional land associations. Some bands did indeed want to purchase lands that were under mineral exploration. However, in most of these cases the price being demanded was too high. An exploration area near Dawn Lake, owned by Cogema Resources, was the subject of a native acquisition request, but because of the high development costs and the existing investment of the companies, the band was not able to go through with the deal.

The development dichotomy is quite stark between northern and southern Saskatchewan. In contrast with common development discourse, the north in this case is the impoverished and underdeveloped region, while the south is considered the more affluent and developed part of the province. More than two-thirds of the residents of northern Saskatchewan claim indigenous ancestry. Surveys conducted by the company show that a majority of the people in the north supported uranium mining. An independent poll of 825 respondents in Saskatchewan, conducted in November 1999, revealed the following support ratios: 13 percent strongly supportive; 57 percent somewhat supportive; 10 percent somewhat unsupportive; 13 percent not supportive at all; 7 percent doesn't matter.[18]

Project History

Canada has a long and checkered history of uranium mining. Eldorado Nuclear (one of Cameco's precursor companies) was among the earliest mining entities to work with radioactive ores. Originally owned by the gold prospector Gilbert Labine, Eldorado began to prospect for pitchblende ore in 1929 and set up the Port Radium mine in the Northwest Territories (Canada's first uranium-producing operation) four years later.

When the demand for uranium increased during World War II, Eldorado became involved in further prospecting around Canada. According to the 1968 annual report of the company, "An urgent need for uranium in quantity arose with the inception in 1942 of the Manhattan Project, the joint British–United States–Canadian undertaking that eventually brought forth the atomic bomb. Canada's role was to supply uranium raw material . . . the amount of uranium provided by Eldorado for military purposes."

The government nationalized the company in 1944. A year after establishing the Atomic Energy Control Board the government lifted the private prospecting ban and offered incentives to private prospectors in 1946. This ushered in the "uranium rush," leading to more than ten thousand radioactive ore discoveries, most notably the deposits in the Athabasca region of Saskatchewan.

Saskatchewan has been called the "Saudi Arabia of the Uranium Industry." Collectively, the province contains the largest known reserves of uranium in the world, with more than five active mines within an area of about two hundred thousand square kilometers. Chipewyan Inuit, Déné, and Cree Nations comprise 80 percent of the thirty thousand inhabitants in this region, mostly centered around the shores of the numerous lakes that punctuate the landscape.

In the early eighties, Eldorado Nuclear entered into an agreement with the provincial government of Saskatchewan to begin mining activities in the vicinity of Wollaston Lake. The Saskatchewan Mineral Development Corporation was thus formed to organize the mining activities. The native communities of the region felt that their subsistence lifestyles of hunting and fishing would be threatened by water pollution from the mining development. Their opposition at that time was partly due to the past experience of affected communities in Uranium City.

In the late 1980s, the Saskatchewan government deregulated the uranium mining industry and largely divested its own interests to form a publicly traded company named Cameco. This would soon become the largest uranium mining company in the world, with control over two-thirds of the world's largest, high-grade uranium mines at Key Lake and Rabbit Lake in Saskatchewan. The best was yet to come. The McArthur River ore body was explored extensively in the early nineties after a governmental environmental review for underground exploration. The highest grade deposits (as much as 50 percent of uranium oxide U_3O_8) were discovered 550 meters beneath the surface soon thereafter.

The Environmental Impact Statement for the project was prepared in May 1995 and circulated for public comment. Cameco and its partners, Uranerz Exploration and Mining and Cogema Resources Inc., proposed to mine the ore body underground, crush and grind the ore and render it into a slurry suitable for pumping, thicken the slurry into a paste, and transport it eighty kilometers southwest to the Key Lake operation for milling. The wastes would be disposed at the existing Key Lake Deilmann tailings management facility. The environmental impact of this project would thus be spread across two sites, raising many concerns for environmental groups, most of which were based in southern Saskatchewan.

The federal and provincial government convened a panel to review uranium mining activities in Saskatchewan in 1991. This panel submitted comments on various proposals for mining and also held a protracted series of hearings in 1996 in which all the environmental groups participated actively. This was the main forum for informational exchange between ENGOs and native groups. The environmental groups in this case were mostly regional organizations such as the Inter-Church Uranium Committee and the Saskatchewan Environment Center. Greenpeace had been involved in lobbying efforts in the eighties but had since withdrawn for financial reasons. The panel itself comprised four members, a mining engineer, a biologist, an industrial hygienist, and the chief of the Prince Albert Grand Council, John Dantouze (Canadian Environmental Assessment Agency 1997).

In early 1996, the panel began to plan a series of hearings across Saskatchewan in order to have an organized means of public involvement in the process and to expedite the reports, which the panel was obliged to issue after almost five years of deliberations.

Cameco Corporation

The Canadian Mining and Energy Corporation, or Cameco, as it is termed today, was formed in 1988 as a result of restructuring the uranium mining sector in Canada. The company was formed primarily through a merger of Eldorado Nuclear (a Federal Crown Corporation) and the Saskatchewan Mining Development Corporation (a Provincial Crown Corporation).

When it was formed, Cameco was owned by the provincial and federal governments and headquartered in Saskatoon, Canada. However, in 1998 only 10 percent of the company was owned by the provincial government and 90 percent was owned by public shareholders. The company stock is traded on the New York and Toronto Stock Exchanges and has been the focus of research reports by Goldman Sachs and Bear Stearns, which have generally been quite positive about the community relations of the company.

With annual revenues of over $642 million in 1997, Cameco was considered the world's largest uranium mining company, accounting for one-quarter of both the Western world's uranium production and conversion capacity. The four largest uranium mines, which the company owned and operated, were in Saskatchewan, with two smaller operations in Wyoming and Nebraska. Processing centers for the uranium were located a couple of thousand miles away in Ontario. While the uranium sector of the company accounted for 95 percent of revenues in 1996, the company continued to expand its operations in the gold mining sector as well. It owned one-third of a gold mine in the central Asian republic of Kyrgyzstan and had a gold mine in central Saskatchewan at Contact Lake. Exploration projects were in progress in the United States, Canada, and Australia in an effort to target the growing Asian market for nuclear fuel.

The Mining Commences

The first good news for Cameco came on 28 February 1997, when the Environmental Review Panel recommended approval of the McArthur River project. While the panel's credibility had been somewhat damaged by the resignations of two prominent members, there was a general feeling that the communities had been engaged through other means that would not undermine the lack of representation from Chief Dantouze and Dr. Annalee Yassi.[19] The panel's approval for mining was, however, not universal. In fact, the Midwest satellite mine at McClean Lake (not a Cameco site) was opposed by the panel on environmental grounds.

The next approval came from the Saskatchewan government on 5 May 1997, followed by the federal approval for the project three days later. The final approval to commence construction was granted by the Atomic Energy Control Board of Canada on 25 August 1997.

On 31 January 1998, the Athabasca Working Group, a collective of native community organizations, announced that it had reached an agreement with Cameco as well. The agreement covered compensation/indemnification in the event of damage from project emissions, jobs, training and business, and approaches to benefit sharing.

On the political front, a planning meeting of chiefs and the premier of Saskatchewan Roy Romanow was held in July 1998. The northern leaders signed a memorandum of agreement supporting the long-term development planning goals of the government, including mining. The venue for the meeting, quite surprisingly to some, was Wollaston Lake, the same area that had been the site of major anti-uranium protests in the early eighties (Sinkewicz 1998).[20] Meanwhile, Vice Chief Dantouze had asked for some of the chiefs of northern bands to sign a letter asking for a moratorium on mining until revenue-sharing arrangements were negotiated. The chiefs who signed the letter were soon confronted by many of their constituents who were working in the mining industry. The leadership in Black Lake, Fond du Lac, and Wollaston Lake (three groups who had opposed mining) were subsequently defeated in elections or were forced to resign by the constituents.

The vice president for human resources at Cameco, Jamie McIntyre, reflecting on the experiences of negotiating with First Nations, summed up the company's perception of the issues as follows:

> On the political front we are still dealing with very high expectations. Expectations which we may never be able to live up to. . . . The journey which we have taken has taught us much about how to facilitate and encourage the flow of positive benefits to the people of the North. The traveling companions have not always got along during this journey and the road has not always been a smooth one. Probably the most important lesson we have learned is that we achieve our objectives most efficiently when we work in cooperation.[21]

Given that this was a high-grade uranium mining project, one might have expected there to be far greater resistance from indigenous communities—in fact, the resistance from indigenous groups was minimal and the resistance from environmentalists was not able to take root.

The Voisey's Bay Project in Labrador (Case C2)

The desolate icy coast of Labrador, which the explorer Jaques Cartier called "the land God gave to Cain," has surprisingly been inhabited for more than twelve thousand years. It is not entirely clear who the first inhabitants were, but at the time of European settlement two distinct indigenous groups inhabited the area—the Inuit (or Eskimo as they have sometimes been called)[22] and the Montagnais-Naskapi Indians (or Innu, as they are now known).

These two communities lived in relatively close proximity but pursued quite different lifestyles. In the words of Inuit mineral officer Chesley Anderson, "the Inuit were a sea people and the Innu were a land people," referring to the different sources of subsistence for the communities.[23] The staple diet of the Innu consisted of caribou, whereas for the Inuit it was fish. The two communities nevertheless had some measure of competition over resources and territory and were not natural allies. In many ways their situation was quite analogous to the Hopi and the Navajo, particularly since the Inuit had also been latecomers to the area (like the Navajo). Here, too, the communities were faced with resettlement under colonial rule. In Navajo country the missionaries were Mormons; in Labrador the missionaries were Catholic and Moravian (a Czech denomination).

During much of the nineteenth and early twentieth centuries the provincial and federal governments tried to concentrate the relatively no-madic communities of Innu and Inuit into permanent settlements, which have not been very successful, given the high rates of suicide, gasoline sniffing, and alcoholism within the communities. The two largest Innu settlements Sheshatshiu and Davis Inlet are more than 300 miles apart. The Inuit capital is located in the northernmost town of Labrador, Nain.

Newfoundland and Labrador also have a rather prolonged colonial his-tory, being the last regions in North America to relinquish separate do-minion status with the British Crown in 1949, when they became the last Canadian province. Interestingly enough, the Innu are among the few in-digenous communities in North America who thought of sovereignty in terms of a separate nation-state outside the Canadian union. This posi-tion was, however, abandoned in 1990 with the election of Peter Penatchiu, who moved the community toward negotiating a land claims agreement with the government.[24]

Nevertheless, the community has been particularly strident in opposing low-level flights at the NATO airbase at Goose Bay and also in its opposi-tion to the Voisey's Bay mining project and the expansion of the hydroelec-tric project on the Churchill River. The Inuit have been somewhat more conciliatory than the Innu, but they, too, have asserted their claims to the land quite vigorously.

The Innu call the land Nitassinan and the mine site area for the Voisey's Bay project is called Emish. They are among the few native communities in North America for whom English is still a second language. Not sur-prisingly, no treaties were signed between the settlers and the indigenous groups in this part of Canada. The Innu and the Inuit have overlapping land claims to much of northern Labrador. As will be shown, the linkage of land claims and environmental concerns is an important cornerstone of resistance formation in this case.

Project History

The proposed site for the nickel-copper-cobalt mine and mill develop-ment is located on the Labrador coast about thirty-five kilometers south-west of the Inuit capital of Nain and seventy-nine kilometers northwest of the Innu community of Davis Inlet. The massive sulfide deposit was dis-covered by the prospecting company Archean Resources Limited while under contract to Diamond Fields Resources Inc. of Vancouver in 1994. As the enormous size of the deposit became clear, Diamond Field Resources found itself in a major bidding war over the rights to mine the ores. Diamond Fields was a penny-stock company that suddenly found itself atop one of the major ore findings of the decade, with an estimated potential revenue of $25 billion. The company apparently was unaware that they had started drilling in a region with contested land claims by Innu and Inuit groups. The activity enraged both Innu and Inuits and a series of protests were held at the mine site, including a standoff in February 1995 in which the Royal Canadian Mounted Police had to be called.

The executives at Diamond Fields, which included the infamous investor and entrepreneur Robert Friedland,[25] clearly had little or no incentive to interact constructively with the native groups because their aim was mainly to sell the company to a larger mineral conglomerate. A bidding war was afoot in the background for the project. Toronto-based Inco Ltd. finally won the bidding over its rival Falconbridge, paying $4.3 billion for the rights to develop the deposit in 1996. Inco acquired the Voisey's Bay Nickel Company Ltd. (VBNC) of St. John's, Newfoundland, as a wholly owned subsidiary and continued exploration of the massive mineral deposit while pushing ahead with plans to develop a mine and mill operation at the site.

On 26 September 1996, VBNC formally announced its intent to file the project for environmental assessment under the Canadian Environmental Assessment Act. Inco was clearly much more professional about its dealings with native people than its predecessor, even though it did not have much experience in this regard. Subsequently, the Innu Nation, the Labrador Inuit Association, and the governments of Canada and Newfoundland successfully negotiated a memorandum of understanding (MOU) establishing a joint, four-party environmental assessment process for the project. The MOU draft was referred for public comment in November 1996, and it was formally signed by the parties in January 1997. This MOU is a first for environmental assessment in Canada. Instead of the federal minister making the final decision on the project, a panel would report to all four parties.

A five-person panel was appointed jointly by the four parties. According to the MOU, the panel had 120 days from their appointment (31 January 1997) to issue EIS guidelines to VBNC. During this 120-day period, the panel held scoping hearings in Nain, Utshimassit, Hopedale, Postvill, Rigolet, Cartwright, Sheshatshiu, Goose Bay, and St. John's. Following these hearings, the guidelines were released, which include recommendations about the application of the precautionary principle and sustainability assurance, as well as directing VBNC to incorporate traditional ecological knowledge into their EIS or to facilitate its presentation during the assessment process.

The VBNC released its EIS in December of 1997, and the public review of it concluded on 31 March 1998. Based on more than three hundred pages of public and regulatory agency comments submitted as part of the initial public review, the panel issued a deficiency statement on 1 May 1998. The panel concluded that the EIS did not meet the guidelines and asked the company to provide additional information on issues such as shipping routes, alternative production methods and rates of production, fisheries impacts, socioeconomic effects, and the impacts of the project on the endangered Harlequin duck.

The final report from the panel was released in April of 1999 and recommended that the project be allowed to go forward provided that a set of 107 recommendations contained in the report could be met, including an agreement on impact and benefits with the indigenous groups involved. This was clearly a tall order for Inco Corporation.

Inco Corporation

Inco, created in a merger between Canadian Copper Company and the Orford Copper Company, was incorporated in 1902. At the time, the potential for nickel was realized by very few, and Inco quickly became the world's largest nickel mining and processing company. This was largely the result of both the size of the high quality deposits it controls (particularly in Sudbury, Ontario) and its advanced patented techniques of reducing nickel by pyrolysis and electrolysis. Fundamental to Inco's early growth was its close ties with the consumers of metal, notably the steel and arms industry.

During the past thirty years, Inco has gone through a series of very serious slumps due to the caprice of nickel prices and labor issues at its huge complex of mines and smelters in Sudbury, Ontario. The Sudbury smelters were a recurring cause for protest by environmentalists all across Canada and some of the local communities also joined forces to voice their misgivings in this regard.[26]

In 1999, Inco had annual revenues of $2 billion, with sales of nickel as follows: 24 percent to the United States, 15 percent to Europe, 21 percent to Japan, and 35 percent to other Asian countries. Eight percent is sold in other world markets.

Despite its history, Inco has made a definite effort to improve its environmental performance. Most notably, in 1993 Inco completed the largest environmental project ever undertaken in North America: the rebuilding of their Sudbury, Ontario, smelting complex at a cost of $530 million to reduce emissions of sulfur dioxide. This change has even received kudos from environmental researchers in Europe such as Alyson Warhurst (1999).

Inco also owns several smaller businesses, including the International Metals Reclamation Company, Inc. (or Inmetco, as this company is known), and operates the only facility in North America that recovers saleable metals from steel-making wastes and from nickel-cadmium batteries. Since 1978, Inmetco has recycled more than one million tons of materials that might otherwise have ended up in landfills.

Development Plans and the Prevalence of Resistance

Inco currently estimates that up to 150 million tons of mineral resources will be developed as part of the Voisey's Bay project. Based on current knowledge of the mineral resources at Voisey's Bay, three primary mineralized areas will be developed: the Ovoid, Eastern Deeps, and Western Extension, including the Reid Brook zone. These zones have different characteristics and require different mining methods. The Ovoid deposit is located near the surface, which allows it to be mined from the surface as an open pit. Eastern Deeps and the Western Extension, however, lie well below the surface, thus requiring the use of underground mining methods.

The ore to be extracted from the open pit and underground mines will be processed into concentrates at the mill. The main components of the project are forty-seven kilometers of gravel roads, a port facility, an airstrip, an accommodation complex, a sewage treatment facility, a diesel generating plant, a mill, warehouses, and office facilities. Mining facilities will include mine rock and overburden storage areas, as well as a tailings disposal area. The mill is designed to operate at a rate of 20,000 tons of ore per day. The open pit will be approximately 500 meters wide, 1 kilometer long, and 125 meters deep.

Construction and other preproduction activities will generate 7,400 jobs. The open pit phase will generate about $1.1 billion in earned incomes and approximately 19,000 person-years of employment. During the underground mining phase, the company estimates that 53,000 person-years of employment will be created and about $2.7 billion of income generated.

The Innu and Inuit sought to ensure through the MOU that the entire mine/mill operation would be subject to a single, comprehensive review through public hearings in each of the affected Innu and Inuit communities. However, in April of 1997, the Voisey's Bay Nickel Company registered with the government of Newfoundland its plans to construct a road and airstrip to support its ongoing exploration work at Voisey's Bay. It was the understanding on behalf of Innu Nation and the Labrador Inuit Association that this type of activity was contrary to the MOU, which was already in place to assess these activities. On the other hand, it was the contention of the company that their activities were outside of the scope of the MOU because they were for exploration purposes and did not affect the plans for operation of the mine.

The Innu and Inuit decided that these advanced exploration efforts should not happen without their consent. This is especially understandable in light of the fact that Voisey's Bay area has never been ceded by treaty or other agreement. The Innu Nation and the Labrador Inuit Association sought an order from the Newfoundland Supreme Court preventing the Newfoundland minister of environment from approving the company's plans on the ground that the project was already undergoing an assessment under the MOU. However, the Court ruled in favor of the government and the company and work on the road and airstrip started in August. The Environmental Assessment Panel established under the MOU expressed strong concern over the government's decision to split the assessment of the project.

The indigenous groups jointly filed for appeal and engaged in protest action at the exploration site. Finally, in late August, the appeal court decided in favor of the indigenous groups. In a decision praised nationally, Judge Marshall wrote that although the purpose of the road was not for operations, the impact of the road, for whatever reason, would be the same, and the company should not be allowed to construct any further infrastructure until the entire project had undergone environmental assessment.

This judgment was a major victory for the Innu and the Inuit. It reinforced the importance of comprehensive environmental assessment and slowed down the pace of the development to give the communities more time to digest and understand the changes happening as a result of the mining development.

Resistance to the project continued. Following the Canadian Environ-

Table 5.1
Framework for Analysis and Synthesis

Subquestions	Issues and Implicit Hypothesis	Related Theories Tested	Relevant Sections
When does resistance arise?	Scientific, economic, and cultural determinism (shadow hypotheses); negotiation process (central hypothesis)	Various reductionist theories of scientific primacy; powerlessness theory (Gaventa); theories of negotiation	Chapter 6, 9
When does the resistance prevail?	Issue linkage and strategic alliances	Linkage politics (Aggarwal); civil society theories	Chapters 7, 8, 9
Is the resistance environmentally motivated?	Native/nature relations; greening of sovereignty	The "ecological" Indian (Krech); new pluralism in environmental justice (Schlosberg)	Chapter 7
What advice can we give to stakeholders in both countries?	Planning for sustainable indigenous development; role of government and corporate responsibility	Lesson-drawing in public policy (Rose)	Chapter 10

mental Assessment Agency's conditional approval for the project, the Innu Nation filed a case in federal court in September 1999 for judicial review of this contingent approval, which is still pending. Meanwhile, the province of Newfoundland is trying to get assurance from Inco for a smelter to be built in Argentia on the island of Newfoundland. During a special broadcast on 29 February 2000, CBC radio reporter Michael Enright described the mood over Voisey's Bay as follows: "The chances of nickel being mined in Voisey's Bay look about as remote as the location of the nickel mine itself" (Enright 2000).

However, largely through focused mediation efforts and a constructive nonintrusive engagement from NGOs, a workable impact-benefit agreement was accepted by both the Innu and the Inuit in June of 2002. The agreement was ratified through a referendum in which 82 percent of the

Inuit and 68 percent of the Innu voting population supported the deal, which will bring an estimated $300 million to both communities over the next thirty years.[27]

Toward Analysis

Table 5.1 gives a schematic of the main themes that will be developed in addressing the central question of "Why does environmental resistance to mining development arise in certain cases of mining development and not in others?" The related prescriptive question the cross-country comparison will address is "What lessons, if any, can be drawn from the Canadian and U.S. governments' experiences in dealing with such conflicts?"

Chapter 6

Science and Elements of Social Construction

Some Shadow Hypotheses

Environmental discourse has historically been predicated on certain absolute scientific foundations about ecology—in terms of scarcity, distribution, and quality of resources. The debates in environmental studies for much of this century, such as the classic bet between the late Julian Simon and Paul Ehrlich, were premised on predictions that were at least ostensibly scientific.[1] As Connie Ozawa states in her analysis of how science is commonly perceived in environmental conflicts, "In the economic and cultural context of the late twentieth century science is looked upon as a source of authority. This authority derives from a popular notion of the scientific endeavor. Science is conceived as a process that yields an objective, rational, politically neutral body of knowledge. Decisions consistent with scientific knowledge therefore command acceptance" (Ozawa 1996, 221).

However, much of the primacy of science as a touchstone for objectivity for substantiation of resistance or adjudication of conflict has been challenged by a host of social theorists, most notably Bruno Latour (1999). This group of theorists posits that science is socially constructed and hence trepidation is warranted when evaluating ostensibly objective science. This debate has roots in the philosophical distinction between epistemology (our representation of the world) and ontology (what the world really is). By intellectual standards, this is a fairly acrimonious and somewhat circular debate, as reflected in the title of Ian Hacking's most recent book, *Social Construction of What?* (1999). While in certain areas of scientific endeavor there are indeed levels of uncertainty, which can potentially give rise to multiple constructions, there are clearly other scientific metrics that can be stated quite objectively and evaluated as such. The real test of science lies in how such data is interpreted by society and what measure of importance is given to its findings. Scientific determinists would argue that the actual environmental impact of a mining venture as manifest in various contextually sensitive criteria—such as water quantity in a desert, crop quality in an agricultural area, or economic and demographic characteristics—more generally determine the emergence of resistance.

A Comparison of "Technical" Environmental Impact between Cases

While the word *technical* may seem somewhat reductionist in its usage, it is important to tease out the environmental impact of each project with regard to conventionally accepted criteria of ecosystem viability. In other words, the aim in this section is to understand and compare the asocial impact of the projects on the natural environment in order to test the proposition that resistance may arise based on the severity of environmental impact in a scientific framework. In the following individual case analyses, data is presented for various levels of environmental impact of each project with particular reference to impacts that have been most notably highlighted by resistance movements and the media.

Case U1: The Black Mesa/Kayenta Mine

Coal mining presents a rather interesting management situation for environmental health and safety professionals. From a purely environmental point of view, it can often be deemed relatively innocuous since it usually does not involve chemical extraction procedures. However, from a health and safety point of view, coal mining can be very dangerous. Apart from the respiratory ailments caused by coal dust, there is also a danger of coal combustion during operations in hot climates, particularly the combustion of "gob piles" of ore that are often left in the open.[2]

Two principal systems of coal mining are used: surface, or strip, mining and underground, or deep, mining. Strip mining, such as the Black Mesa/Kayenta operation, is a form of quarrying and is possible only when the coal seam is near the surface of the ground. At Black Mesa/Kayenta, huge power shovels and draglines are used to remove the earth and rock (overburden) from above the seam. The chief advantage of strip mining over underground mining is the enormous saving of time and labor. The daily output per person in strip mines or open cast mines is many times that of underground mines.

As a supplement to strip mining, or when other mining techniques are not adequate, augers are used to bore horizontally into exposed coal seams. The loosened coal then flows into a conveyor for loading into trucks. A newer development is a boring machine, called a push-button miner, that can tunnel as deep as three hundred meters (1,000 feet) into the coal seam, dumping the coal into mobile conveyors pulled by the machine.

In this regard, the Black Mesa/Kayenta is probably less deleterious than metal mining. Because of the Navajo/Hopi land dispute, the mines' environmental performance has come under particular scrutiny. In 1995 and 1996, the federal EPA conducted a compliance review that was prompted by a complaint filed by the Dine Alliance regarding environmental performance. A Comprehensive Environmental Responsibility, Compensation, and Liability Act site inspection was also carried out to focus on future liability issues. These reviews gave the mine a "good" rating.[3]

However, the most critical environmental impact of this operation does not ensue from the actual mining itself but rather the means by which the coal is subsequently delivered to the Mojave generating station some 280 miles to the west of the mine. The mine utilizes a highly unusual coal slurry pipeline to transport the coal—the only one of its kind in the United States. Most of the slurry water comes from confined aquifers (the N aquifer and parts of the D aquifer), which are also the primary source of water for municipal users within the 5,400-square-mile Black Mesa area (U.S. Geological Survey 1999). The aquifers also feed some of the terrestrial springs *(paahu)*, which have been historically sacred to the Hopi, and the water has also been used for terraced agriculture (see Whiteley and Masayesva 1998).

Figure 6.1 shows the extent of water usage by the mining operation over the past few years according to the Office of Surface Mining Control and Reclamation. For a water-scarce area, this water usage constitutes an enormous environmental challenge, which the tribes have decided to absorb, though concerns are frequently raised about the long-term viability of this water extraction. Interestingly enough, the revised EIS for the mine was completed in June 1990 and the following year witnessed an enormous increase in water usage, though this was apparently due to a water-intensive development project in Tuba city, Arizona.[4] While the EPA in its 1996 re-

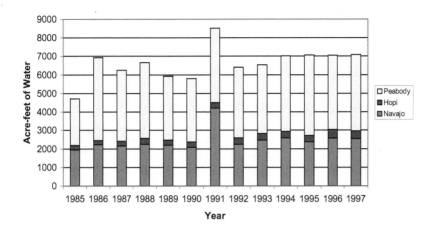

Figure 6.1
Water consumption from the N aquifer, Black Mesa.
(Data from Office of Surface Mining, Western Data Center, Denver)

view concluded that the mine was in good working order, initially when the EIS was presented to the EPA for review, it had classified the project as "EO-2: Environmental Objections — Insufficient Information." The impact of mining on the piñon and juniper was also a contributing factor in this evaluation.

Even though OSM now maintains that the recharge rate for the aquifers is enough to sustainably harness the water from the N aquifer, the government is already beginning to plan for alternate sources of water to meet growing demands in the region. Preliminary plans for a pipeline from Lake Powell and ongoing litigation over water rights to the Little Colorado River, which now has more than eleven thousand claimants, reflects the seriousness of the water scarcity situation.

Thus, water quantity concerns constitute an extremely important environmental impact, which could have been a major stumbling block in the renegotiations of the lease for the mine in 1990. However, despite these concerns, the project has gone ahead. While resistance has been voiced to water extraction by such notable tribal leaders as Vernon Masayesva (Hopi), no one in the tribal establishment has gone so far as to say that the mining should immediately be stopped. In 1979, the Hopi passed a tribal resolution (H-83-79) that established a moratorium on all *additional* energy resource exploration and development. However, this resolution recognized the existing activity at Black Mesa, and, to do away with any further ambiguity regarding the mining, on 26 May 1998, the Hopi Tribal Council, by majority vote, approved mining on the reservation limited to the current leasehold area and the J7 pit. The Navajo have similarly favored mining development despite their collective misgivings about the earlier lease arrangements with Peabody.

The protests that have been voiced in this case pertaining to the Big Mountain land relocation dispute, which we will see in the next chapter, is yet another story.

Case U2: The Crandon Project

The technical environmental impact of the Crandon project has gone through numerous phases as the company has tried to assuage regulatory and community concerns. While the location of the mine is in a particularly problematic area because of the high water table, the mitigation measures that are being proposed currently are also quite extraordinary by mining industry standards.

The most important environmental concern from this project is groundwater and surface water contamination caused by acid leaching from the tailings piles and also the depletion of groundwater that would take place as a result of the mine's usage of water in the milling process.

Since Rio Algom had full ownership of the project, its subsidiary, NMC, agreed to much greater environmental mitigation than the earlier owner, Exxon, had proposed. NMC has agreed to separate potentially acid-generating pyrite from the rest of the mine tailings. The pyrite would be mixed with cement and placed underground in a paste backfill. Ultimately, it would be submerged in the reflooded mine. The balance of the tailings would be placed in a landfill-like tailings management area. Due to the pyrite separation, the area is being reduced in size to about 75 percent of the originally proposed 345 acres. Currently, 282 acres are proposed to be used for tailings management development. Average tailings depth is expected to be about ninety feet.

Groundwater flow into the mine would be reduced by underground injection of cement grout in order to minimize the volume of water that would need to be pumped and treated. NMC would dispose of treated mine waste water via a system of groundwater seepage cells, at a location about two miles north of the plant site. NMC is reviewing data for site alternatives. Exxon's earlier proposal to pipe this water 38.3 miles from the site, for discharge to the Wisconsin River, south of Rhinelander, has been withdrawn on environmental grounds by NMC and will be discussed in the Department's Draft Environmental Impact Statement as part of the alternatives analysis required by the Wisconsin Environmental Policy Act.

NMC has also been obligated to provide examples of three mines with similar characteristics that have performed without incidence of pollution for at least ten years. The mines that have been chosen and the criteria that they meet are shown in table 6.1. Critics of the mine are quick to point out that the Crandon project would be bigger and in a more sensitive area. However, the company has gone forward with commensurately more stringent mitigation regimes as well. The McLaughlin mine is considered across the industry as a benchmark for responsible mining and was given the nod even by the California Sierra Club. While these submissions are being reviewed by the Army Corps of Engineers and the Wisconsin Department of Natural Resources, the resistance continues to gain pace.

The company's mitigation measures have been acknowledged by a former tribal leader of the Hochunk Nation, Joanne Jones, of Wisconsin, who has agreed to act as an adviser on Native American negotiations for the company.[5] However, even this effort has not caused any reduction in the resistance of the Mole Lake Chippewa, the Menominee, and, indeed, the greater activist community to the mine site. Here, too, it appears that scientific and technical criteria are not able to explain the emergence of resistance.

Case C1: The Saskatchewan Uranium Mines

In terms of both short-term and long-term environmental impact, uranium mining is by far the most environmentally problematic of any mining activity — owing to the simple fact that radioactivity of the ore presents an intangible that cannot be chemically mitigated. Moreover, the potential use of uranium for nuclear weapons adds to the arsenal which resistance movements already have toward nonrenewable resource extraction. Perhaps a silver lining to this cloud is offered by the absence of greenhouse gas emissions from nuclear power plants. But this comparative advantage is easily eclipsed by the imponderable task of managing nuclear waste from such facilities. Furthermore, the history of uranium mining near indigenous communities in both the United States and Canada has given rise to the term *radioactive colonialism*, which is often used by activists.[6] Given this backdrop, it is truly remarkable that uranium projects have continued to proliferate in Saskatchewan with relatively little resistance from indigenous communities.

Table 6.1

Summary of Mines Presented by NMC as Candidates for Exemplary Compliance

Mine	Sulfide Ore Body with NAGP (secs. 293.50 [1][b], [2][a] and [b])	Statutory Criteria under Wisconsin Mining Moratorium Law				
		More than Ten Years Operating/Closed (sec. 293.50 [2][a]/[b])	No Pollution of Groundwater or Surface Water from Acid Drainage or Release of Heavy Metals (secs. 293.50 [2][a] and [b])	Not listed on NPL (sec. 293.50 [2m][a])	Operator Still in Business/Responsible successor (sec. 293.50 [2m][a])	No Significant Environmental Pollution from Acid Drainage or Release of Heavy Metals (sec. 293.50 [2m][b])
McLaughlin mine, California	X	15 yrs. / —	X	X	X	X
Cullaton Lake mine, Northwest Territories, Canada	X	— / 13 yrs.	X	X	X	X
Sacaton mine, Arizona	X	12 yrs. / 14.5 yrs.	X	X	X	X

While the McArthur River mine, which is the principal focus of my study, is a state-of-the art operation, the environmental hazards of the project, particularly in comparison to other mines where much greater resistance has occurred, cannot be overstated.

Owing to the extremely high grade of the ore (and its commensurate radioactivity), planning for the mine was an enormous challenge. All mining methods requiring workers to enter the mining area had to be eliminated. Non-entry mining methods were required due to the high radiation fields from the ore. Other methods were eliminated if not compatible with grouting or freezing techniques for groundwater control. Strict adherence to the principles of limiting the time of exposure, maximizing the distance between the workers and the ore, and the placing of shielding between the workers and the ore were necessary in order to limit worker gamma radiation exposures. Radon gas released from the ore and groundwater adjacent to the ore meant excellent ventilation practices were required. The need to capture radon gas at its source has also affected mining method selection. Seven potential mining methods were proposed in the EIS submitted for McArthur River, with final selection dependent upon ore grades and ground conditions. These methods are the following:

—Raise boring
—Box-hole boring
—Remote box-hole stopping
—Blast-hole stopping, including vertical crater retreat
—Remote raise-bore stopping
—Jet boring
—Remote box-hole stopping with Viscaria raise mining

The preferred options for the mining of the high-grade ore are raise boring, box-hole boring, and remote box-hole stopping, which the mine has been using since production began in 1998.

Waste rock is generated both by mine development and by ore production. The production of waste rock is relatively small due to the low tonnage of ore required to be mined each day. However, the potency of the waste rock in terms of environmental impact is much higher, even in comparison to other uranium mines. Potentially problematic material (waste rock containing >0.03 percent U_3O_8 or with a net neutralizing potential of >3, i.e., neutralizing potential to acid-generating potential of <3:1, despite the low pyrite content) is hoisted conventionally via the main service shaft and stored on lined pads at McArthur River. This material is either used for backfill underground at the mine site or is transported to Key Lake for final placement in existing approved storage areas. During the development phase, 140,000 tons of potentially mineralized non-ore material and 75,000 tons of potentially mineralized sandstone were generated. Cement grout is being used extensively to mediate any residual pyrite content of the rock. Some of the concerns that ensue from tailings storage (in this case at Key Lake) include leaching of hazardous material to the groundwater supply; aerial release of radiation and radioactive dust; and the danger of dam failure due to erosion, heavy rain, or earthquakes.

The control of radiation has been the primary factor in determining the designs for the mine and plant layout, equipment selection, and the processing of the ore at McArthur River. In order to minimize exposures, the following criteria were applied:

— Radon gas is controlled by a dual ventilation system; a primary fresh air flow is always maintained in all active work areas, with a secondary exhaust system to remove contaminated air from particular sources.
— Radon is also controlled by the freezing and grouting techniques used to control ground water.
— During all mining and processing stages the ore is fully contained.
— Gamma radiation is controlled by utilizing the principles of shielding, distance, and time. The use of heavy-wall steel pipes, thick vessel walls, concrete, and sometimes lead sheeting is standard practice.
— Mining and ore handling and processing are accomplished remotely with computer control.
— Due to the low tonnage required to be mined, there is a long period between scheduled maintenance work.

A total of three shafts are utilized to provide 455 cubic meters per second of air at full production. Two shafts will supply fresh air (the main service shaft #1 and shaft #2), while a third shaft will exhaust the mine workings. According to Cameco, "every operation has been analyzed for exposure time, and distance and shielding calculations have been done to ensure that radiation doses are acceptable. Design calculations have been confirmed by doing physical measurements of radiation fields around pipes filled with high-grade ore from the test mining at Cigar Lake, and at the existing Key Lake and Rabbit Lake mills. As a result of these design criteria, the predicted annual doses for the workers are well under the regulatory dose limit" (Jamieson and Frost 1997).

Nevertheless, the long-term impact of the mine and the risk factor whenever dealing with radioactive material of this nature is highly capricious as indicated by the following calculations estimates performed by an independent consulting firm, Radioactive Waste Management Associates:

According to the McArthur River EIS, 3.3×10^6 Bq/sec of radon will be emitted from McArthur River operations, and annual radon concentrations will increase by over 50 Bq/m^3 at Key Lake. An area forty km long will have increased radon concentrations as a result of Key Lake operations. A 1979 Key Lake EIS estimated that the total radon release rate from the Key Lake mill, open pits, ore storage, and tailings would be 3.6×10^7 Bq/sec. More recent calculations use a source term of 3.8×10^8 Bq/sec. Radon levels observed at Key Lake from 1986 to 1993 were highest in summer (0.289 Bq/L) and were 0.4 Bq/L right over the tailings.

If we divide Cameco's estimated 3.8×10^8 Bq/sec of radon by the area of Deilmann Pond (580,000 m^2), one gets an estimate of 655 Bq/m^2/sec. Dividing this by a factor of twenty-five, to account for reduced radon emissions through the pondwater cover, one gets 26.2 Bq/m^2/sec emanating from Deilmann pit. This is less than the value RWMA [Radioactive Waste Management Associates] calculated for radon emission from the JEB pit at McClean Lake, which will use a similar subaqueous method. The smaller emission rate is due to the effect of "blending" the very hot McArthur River ores with Key Lake materials, bringing the Ra-226 concentrations of the tailings down to 325 Bq/g. Without blending, Ra-226 can be up to 1350 Bq/g. If in the future blending does not occur, or if the tailings do not remain underwater, radon emissions could increase dramatically. (Resnikoff, Knowlton, and Island 1996, 16)

This is just an example of the problems of risk management at a uranium mining facility. Thus the technical impact of the mine and the environmental hazards associated with the mined product in this case are once again an insufficient explanation for the relatively low level of indigenous resistance.[7]

Case C2: The Voisey's Bay Project

Like the Saskatchewan uranium mines, the Voisey's Bay project has also been the subject of numerous environmental reviews by various tiers of government and by independent consultants.

An environmental review was begun by the Canadian Environmental Assessment Agency in January 1997, with Inco, the provincial and federal governments, and the indigenous organizations participating, and was completed in November 1999. The Environmental Assessment Panel Report included a community benefits analysis.

The panel conducted hearings in Labrador and Newfoundland and consulted with the indigenous organizations and with the company. It sought and obtained detailed information concerning VBNC's mining plan, its proposed methods for managing the anticipated environmental problems, and the social and economic benefits for the local communities. It examined issues of air quality, shipping and its impacts on aquatic life, tailings management, freshwater fish and habitat, seals, whales, polar bears, birds, caribou, black bears, and general contaminants. It explored the impacts of the mine operation on the traditional economy of the Innu and Inuit, including the disturbance of wildlife, loss of habitat for animals traditionally hunted, contamination of country foods, disruption of travel across traditional territory, and reduced access to traditionally utilized resources. The panel also focused on economic concerns such as employment, the effects on local business, training, families, and communities. A number of additional issues were also addressed, namely the size and viability of the relevant ore bodies, the expected mine life, and the rate of ore extraction, these being the key determinants of the sustainability of the benefits that would flow from the mine. Its report was made public on 1 April 1999.

The most significant environmental impact of the mine according to the panel would be from the finely ground solid tailings remaining after the concentration process, as well as some waste rock. They are to be "stored under water in two tailings basins made from existing lakes . . . to prevent . . . them from being in contact with both air and water simultaneously which would cause them to release acid" (Canadian Environmental Assessment Agency 1999, 8). The panel concluded that VBNC's proposed methods of dealing with the tailings were appropriate and that the "best locations" to reduce environmental impact had been identified (starting with Headwater pond and then constructing the North Tailings Basin when the underground phase began).

The panel recommended that the project proceed. However, this was subject to the terms and conditions spelled out in a large number of specific recommendations. The panel concluded that "the Project could contribute significantly to sustainable social and economic development on the North Coast and in the rest of Labrador, without harming vital ecosystem functions and habitats or the ability of Inuit and Innu to keep using the lands in traditional ways" (Ritter 1999, 9). The rest of the document delineated the conditions that would have to be fulfilled by the company if it were to proceed with the project.

Perhaps the most detailed technical analysis for the project from a fairly conservationist perspective was carried out by Dr. David Chambers of the Center for Science and the Public Interest, an independent nonprofit organization that provides technical services to environmental groups. Dr. Chambers made numerous recommendations in a fifty-page report that critically evaluated the EIS for the project, the most significant items of which are summarized in appendix 2.

VBNC has tentatively agreed to address these concerns, in addition to several other concerns about the shipping of material from the site and its impact on the migration patterns of traditional gaming animals for the Innu and Inuit.[8] However, these technical mitigation measures are still not striking a favorable chord with the Innu and the Inuit. There tends to be a degree of cynicism about the measures being proposed. For example, the Labrador Inuit Association (LIA) mineral adviser, Chesley Anderson, commented in an interview that the company's proposed concession not to ship during April and May was motivated not by the indigenous concern, as it was advertised to be, but rather because the melting ice would prevent shipping in any case (Rio Algom 2000).

On the Innu side, resistance toward the project had been even greater. The Innu articulated their resistance most potently through protests at the mine site and in Labrador, through a Web site (www.innu.ca), and through articulation of the impact of mining on lifestyles of the people, thereby shifting the discussion from the technical environment impact. This is exemplified by the formation of an ad hoc committee on indigenous women and mining in Labrador, which has voiced vociferous opposition to the project, arguing that the mining may exacerbate social problems. This organization is particularly interesting since it includes both Innu and Inuit representatives (Tongamiut Inuit Annait). Historically the two communities have tended to work independently, owing to different cultures and territorial disputes.

Similar to the Crandon Case (U2), the technical criteria and mitigation allowances on the part of the mining company do not translate into a concomitant reduction in resistance to the project. However, here the communities are at least willing to talk and ostensibly negotiate with the company, which is not the case with the Mole Lake community in Wisconsin. This difference will be highlighted in part 3, which will focus on prescriptive measures for various stakeholders in the negotiation process, which in the case of Voisey's Bay can ultimately lead to an agreement.

Demography, Geography, and Economic Clout

Demographic characteristics of a region are often used as a measure of political clout and hence may be linked to the emergence of resistance. Table 6.2 summarizes some of the demographic characteristics of the communities in question. This table shows us that the cases that have large population (and hence larger physical presence and voting presence in a democratic system) do not necessarily have the most pronounced resistance (the Navajo tribe, for example). It may be argued that lower population allows for resistance to be more easily consolidated in communities. However, in that case, the Hopis could arguably have resistance formation more quickly, or, for that matter, the communities in Saskatchewan could also have formed resistance movements more easily. Cross comparison of the cases reveals that neither theory of resistance based on demographic criteria alone can explain the emergence of resistance.

Similarly, if we look at the proximity of the mine sites to actual communities, one could hypothesize that the communities that are further removed from the actual mine site would have lesser resistance to the mining. While this may hold for the Saskatchewan case and the Crandon case, it does not hold for either the Voisey's Bay case or the Black Mesa cases. Part of this may be explained by the fact that indigenous communities have historically led itinerant lifestyles, and while they are now living in permanent communities, they still consider the greater land base as their territory. The point again is to highlight that geographic location alone cannot account for the emergence of resistance either.

Economic considerations are often used as the bottom-line explanation for much of social science research. While monetary concerns clearly have an important role to play and may be the way in which concerns are articulated, the comparison across these cases reveals that finances offer only a partial explanation for the emergence of resistance. In the context of indigenous communities, particularly in the United States, the phenomenon

Table 6.2

Demographic and Geographic Comparison between Cases

Case	Indigenous Population (within 100-mile radius of mine)	Proximity of Nearest Community to Mine Site (miles)	Other Sources of Private Employment (presently)
U1: Black Mesa	20,000	5	Tourism, manufacturing
U2: Crandon	1,000	5	Casino, forestry, tourism
C1: Saskatchewan	5,000	60	Forestry
C2: Voisey's Bay	2,000	50	Forestry, local airline

of native gaming, after the Indian Gaming Act of 1982, has certainly created economic alternatives for tribes. The Crandon case may be used by economic determinists to show that when a tribe has an alternative source of income (namely, casinos, in this case), they can afford to resist mining. However, a closer analysis of the Crandon case reveals that the Mole Lake gaming operation is not particularly successful. While the tribe is reluctant to release exact numbers or information about the percentage of its revenues that comes from gaming (and the Freedom of Information Act does not apply to tribal accounting), the fact that one of its two casinos recently had to be shut down reveals that gaming at this reservation is not a very lucrative proposition. Nevertheless, that does not prevent them from resisting the mine, which could conceivably bring in average salary ranges of $55,000 per annum, in addition to compensatory payments for environmental and social impact.

Similarly in Canada, the Voisey's Bay project is located in an exceedingly remote area where the communities have numerous social problems and are facing severe economic hardships. However, they too were willing to resist the project despite the enormous economic benefits it could bring to them. Even the LIA, which was more amenable to negotiations with Inco, expressed the nonmaterial aspirations of the community as follows: "Today, as in the past, we live in a world where resource industries, governments and other interest groups work to have their beliefs become our rules, their values our way of life and our resources their wealth. But unlike the past, we may not be able to adopt what we find good and reject what is a threat because now it is our land that is being devoured."[9]

Conversely, the Navajo and the Hopi are currently engaged in mining activities that do indeed provide substantial royalties and constitute a major part of their budgets. The same is true of the Saskatchewan tribes. It is difficult to refute causality when the nested dependent variable (economic benefit) is in fact present in the case. However, the argument can be made that these communities also have other alternatives for developing other industries apart from mining. The most comprehensive study of Navajo attitudes toward mining and prospects for alternative development was carried out in the early eighties by Schoepfle et al. (1984). It reveals that mining has been accepted or chosen by various chapters (a Navajo local government unit) and individuals in spite of other economically viable alternatives.[10] It is also interesting to note that these tribes have decided not to engage in casino gambling, despite the possibilities for additional revenues from tribal gaming. Another point to keep in mind regarding the Hopi in particular, which defies the economic determinists, is that since 1979 the tribe has maintained a policy of no additional mining exploration on its reservation despite its enormous dependence on mining revenues. While this has not translated into direct environmental resistance against the existing facilities, it does show that the tribe has certain nonmonetary considerations in its decision-making process.

Economic factors no doubt play some role in the decision-making process for tribal leadership, but they are again not a sufficient determinant of resistance.

Culture and Conflict in the Black Mesa and Labrador Cases

Now that we have dealt with the hypothesis from the natural and quantitative social sciences, let us turn our attention to the qualitative social sciences. All too often, we are tempted to use culture as a sort of residual category for explaining away phenomena that cannot otherwise be explained. However, in this section I will test the cultural hypothesis and argue that, in fact, the forces that guide environmental resistance can transcend cultural differences.

The Black Mesa (U1) and Labrador (C2) cases provide us with an opportune set of circumstances to test this hypothesis. In both cases, there are two culturally distinct groups that have historically been quite antagonistic toward each other and also have very different approaches to negotiation and conflict resolution.

In many ways, the Innu are analogous to the Hopi, and the Navajo are analogous to the Inuit, given their history and lifestyles—despite the divergent climatic zones in which each pair of communities is situated. The Inuit are the descendants of the Thule people who migrated to Labrador from the Canadian arctic seven hundred to eight hundred years ago. The Innu, formerly known as the Naskapi-Montagnais, are descended from Algonkian-speaking hunter-gatherers who were one of two indigenous peoples inhabiting Labrador at the time of European arrival. The Inuit also have separate government designation than the Innu and have their own intertribal assembly called the Inuit Tapirsat Council, which is distinct from the Assembly of First Nations. The Inuit are thus newcomers to the ancestral lands of the Innu, and their situation is similar to the Navajo, who, by most archaeological accounts, arrived in the four corners region around five hundred years ago—around the same time as the Inuit arrived in Labrador.

There has been some historic hostility between the two groups in both cases. The Navajo/Hopi land dispute has been exacerbated (though not necessarily initiated) by this historic rivalry. In the case of the Innu and the Inuit, there are also contested claims to territory and a general feeling among the Innu, similar to the Hopi, that they are the "original" occupants. There is even a location in northern Labrador called Massacre Island, which is supposed to have been the sight of a battle between the two groups. However, as executive director of the Okalakatiget Communications Society, Fran Williams, puts it: "just who massacred whom, I'm really not sure" (Lowe 1998, 45).[11]

The differences between the Navajo and Hopi should also not be understated.[12] Nevertheless, despite differences in culture and historical antagonism, the two groups have had a remarkably similar stance on mineral development. In the case of Black Mesa, both tribal governments have generally accepted Peabody's operation, and when misgivings have arisen, such as the recent legal challenge over royalties, they have also worked collectively. The same is true of the LIA and the Innu. Granted that their approaches are somewhat different and Inco has had an easier time talking to LIA than the Innu, they have still managed to work together in organizing protests and sharing a collective vision. An example of collaboration despite difference was highlighted in the 1997 protests against Inco, as recounted by former Innu President Katie Rich. "I got a call from the LIA mineral person, Chesley Anderson, asking 'Who's your protest coordinator?' A typical LIA question. I laughed and said we don't have one! We are just going to go out there and protest!" (paraphrased from a quote in Lowe 1998).

At another level, the cultural hypothesis would also suggest that the tribes that are more traditional would likely show the greatest resistance to mining (that could change their lifestyle). While this may partially explain the Innu resistance, it does not explain the vehement resistance at the Mole Lake reservation in Wisconsin, which is probably the most assimilated of the tribes among the four case studies.[13]

Cultural differences among native communities must certainly be recognized, and it would be naive to suggest homogeneity of native traditions from lands as far apart as Labrador and Arizona. Nevertheless, there are some underlying similarities and common threads of association between all Native Americans and, for that matter, all indigenous people.[14] Thus culture may be a contributing factor in determining how resistance is articulated, but it is not a sufficient means of understanding the dynamics by which resistance may arise.

Placing the Shadow Hypotheses in Context

The case analyses in this chapter reveal that scientifically determined criteria are by no means a sufficient or even necessary condition for the emergence of resistance. This does not mean, however, that they are of no consequence. Rather, their contribution to resistance formation is indirect and is much more amorphous than is often presupposed by determinists. Scientific facts and objective statistics can be rendered subjective by how they are selectively used by parties in a conflict. Jasanoff (1990) has also argued that science in this vein has an important role to play in current regulatory regimes that would otherwise be deadlocked: "Scientific advice may not be a panacea for regulatory conflict or a failsafe procedure for generating what technocrats would view as good science. It is, however, part of a necessary process of political accommodation among science, society, and the state, and it serves an invaluable function in a regulatory system that is otherwise singularly deficient in procedures for informal bargaining." She also goes on to state that just as science has an important role to play in the policy making process, so too does the policy process have an important effect on science: "Negotiation commits scientists, no less than other actors, to moderating their views toward a societal mean."

Social construction hypotheses are, however, not just limited to the discrete world of science but have also been applied to the conception of human rights issues per se. Neil Stammers (1999) has argued that by using "the triadic relationship between human rights, social movements and power as an organizing focus for analysis, we get a very different picture from those offered by the dominant discourses, not only in respect of the origins and development of human rights, but also their potentials and limits." Thus it is established that while scientific indicators of impact may not adequately explain the emergence of resistance to mining, they can be an important means by which other latent factors are articulated in a negotiation. The same may be said of culturally specific factors as well, which on their own cannot account for the emergence of resistance. The aim, in subsequent chapters, is to gain a better understanding of these latent factors that give rise to the emergence of environmental resistance and also the relative prevalence of the movement.

Chapter 7

Indigenous-Environmentalist Relations

External Influence and Resistance Outcomes

This chapter examines a significant determinant of the prevalence of the resistance movement: nongovernmental organizations (or "civil society"), which are becoming an increasingly important area of social science inquiry. I will focus on nonnative ENGOs as agents of change; indigenous rights NGOs such as Cultural Survival or Survival International do not fall into this category, though I will look at some NGOs in the Black Mesa and Crandon cases that have attempted to blend native and environmental causes. The task at hand is to try and understand the native/environmental relationship and how that can effect the emergence and prevalence of resistance.

There are certain peculiarities about ENGOs that must be considered. In their award-winning study of advocacy networks around the world (movements inter alia to combat slavery, violence against women, and environmental protection), Margaret Keck and Kathryn Sikkink describe these peculiarities as follows:

> Environmentalism is less a set of universally agreed upon principles than it is a frame within which the relations among a variety of claims about resource use, property, rights, and power may be reconfigured.... Since environmentalists are often talking about public goods such as clean water or air rather than recognized "rights," they have a harder time giving their campaigns a human face—and must choose whether to do so. Environmental issues are treated in a wide range of institutional arenas. How activists frame an environmental conflict may determine its institutional location as well as the receptivity of target audiences. (Keck and Sikkink 1998, 121)

The most salient aspect of Keck and Sikkink's observation is that many environmental groups are all too often challenged by policy makers for not having a "human face" to their activism, and for this reason they may reconfigure their debate around health impacts and, in these cases, toward indigenous rights. They may indeed be genuinely concerned about indigenous rights as well, but whether that cause is the primary or secondary motivation for activism can be critically important in how conflicts emerge and how they may be resolved.

At another level, ENGOs that can provide technical knowledge to communities have received accolades from some scholars as a means of catalyzing consensus rather than promoting resistance. Haas posits that since environmental issues are often predicated on scientific knowledge, they can lead to the emergence of "epistemic communities," who are able to dissociate themselves from political bickering and catalyze cooperation. He argues that it was the emergence of such communities of knowledge that led to the Mediterranean Action Plan and also to other agreements such as the Montreal Protocol on Ozone Depletion.

Haas has been criticized for inferring too much from his observations about the plan. Zartman (1992) suggests that "the much-vaunted epistemic community is a result rather than a motor of environmental negotiations." Susskind (1994) has argued that Haas's model breaks down when actual policy responses to environmental harms are in fact being negotiated. He goes on to state that this hypothesis has the potential to relegate scientists to the role of another interest group, and that any potential for cooperation through the supremacy of science is likely to alienate developing countries, who are all too often complaining about disparities in scientific and technological expertise.

While Haas makes an important point about the role of knowledge as a source of objective "empowerment," his "epistemic communities" are by no means well represented in most conflicts involving minerals. As I have argued elsewhere (Ali 2000), the evidence regarding ENGOs as a source of knowledge-based empowerment is relatively scant with regard to indigenous community conflicts against mining.

These cases also challenge the common perception that international recognition for a cause is important for exerting environmental influence —a view voiced by, among others, Elise Boulding (1997) in her analysis of ENGOs and conflict resolution: "Precisely because ENGOs are transnational, they provide important inputs to national decision-makers in each country where a given ENGO has a national branch." Indeed, such larger transnational groups as Greenpeace tried to get involved in the resistance efforts in Saskatchewan and at Black Mesa but were marginalized and did not further pursue these causes.

Nevertheless, NGOs come in all shapes and sizes. In order to further our understanding of this phenomenon the efficacy of civil society must be tested at a case level. Only then can we gain an appreciation for the processes by which their involvement in indigenous causes can be constructive or destructive for both stakeholders. In the words of Tom Goldtooth (2000), of the Indigenous Environmental Network, "We have come a long way in bridging ties with green groups but we still have a long way to go."

Black Mesa Resistance

For the small group of families living on Hopi partitioned land (HPL) near the Black Mesa/Kayenta coal mine complex, 3 February 1998 was a momentous day. The area, which is known as Big Mountain, received a visit from the UN special rapporteur on religious intolerance, Abdelfattah Amor. This visit was the culmination of efforts by numerous activists—native and nonnative. However, the role of the nonnative activists in this regard was soon revealed to the visiting Tunisian diplomat when he was informed upon arrival that he was technically trespassing by visiting the HPL without asking for permission and was infringing on a Hopi religious ceremonial month. As a Hopi writer later observed, a nonnative activist named Marsha Monestersky had, by cochairing the UN NGO Human Rights Caucus while in New York, "seemingly managed to convince the U.N., with endless testimony from Navajo resisters and a wealth of other 'green' testimonials, that the poor Navajo of Big Mountain were being denied their very right to practice their religion by jack-booted Hopi Rangers in thrall to the U.S. Government and the 'nefarious' Peabody Coal Company."[1]

It is thus not surprising that when Mr. Amor eventually wrote his report and presented it to the UN Commission on Human Rights regarding his visit to Black Mesa, there was hardly a mention of the Navajo or Hopi tribes, but rather a vague reference that reads as follows: "On the subject of Black Mesa, the Special Rapporteur calls for the observance of international law on freedom of religion and its manifestations." The involvement of external representatives in articulating the conflict at Black Mesa ranged from Greenpeace to the Methodist Church to a professor at Caltech.[2] Even two European parliamentary officials visited the location and wrote letters of support for the small group of Navajo families that were ostensibly fighting against relocation on grounds of coal mining.

Nevertheless, the external support being accorded to these individuals led to serious divisions within the community. The situation was particularly sensitive because the conflict involved two tribes, and even within the tribes there was potential for tremendous polarization between the traditionalists and the modernists. It appears that the external nonnative activists in this case portrayed the Hopi authorities and the government as villains who were out to get the Navajo settlers. They even tried to attack the archaeologically established evidence regarding the Hopi historical association with the land.[3] Activist literature emanating from the region used the inflammatory rhetoric of division by comparing the Hopi tribe's activities to the Japanese internment camp program. In another instance, in May 1999, an e-mail was sent to an Arizona judge, accusing Hopi authorities and the BIA of shooting the horse of a Dineh elder. Two days later the accuser admitted that a Navajo neighbor had accidentally shot the horse — but that the behavior of the Hopi and the BIA was still "genocidal."[4]

While the international attention galvanized by such activists may have given some degree of satisfaction and financial support to the community organizations, the overall effort has not prevailed as a resistance movement because the community does not follow the kind of linear decision-making model that is offered by many environmental and labor activists. Thus, even the organization for which Monestersky has worked as a consultant, the Sovereign Dineh Alliance, asked her to disassociate herself from the Big Mountain cause in 1996:

> Go now, beyond the Four Sacred Mountains of our traditional indigenous homeland as none of the true resisters on Hopi Partitioned Land will hear from you any longer. The bad feelings, division, and confusion you bring is unacceptable and is not our way. I will continue to pray for you.
>
> Thank you once again for your assistance that benefited The People. . . . I will also continue to carry on with my labors as I always have, with trusted others who share my vision for the Dine' of Big Mountain and Black Mesa. In prayer, song, and ceremony, we remain strong as traditional Diné, unified in heart and spirit.[5]

At the same time, the Hopi government has issued exclusion orders for certain activists. These orders are an unusual step taken by the Hopi authorities to bar certain individuals from entering Hopi land. Perhaps the most disturbing aspect of the activists' stance has been the splintering that has occurred within Hopi society as a result of the way in which some of the activists have approached this issue. There are a few Hopi individuals who have allied with the environmental activists, and they are portrayed as spokespeople for the entire tribe by much of the ENGO community, which has exacerbated the situation. Local community organizations at the village level, such as the Hotevilla Wiwimkyam Assembly, have issued press releases to this effect.[6] Such splintering tactics and demonizing of the tribal government by nonnatives has in fact brought some of the Hopi who previously had second thoughts about mining to the defense of their government.

During the exclusion hearing for Marsha Monestersky, some Navajo families who are being relocated also testified against her. Betty Tso, a Navajo Nation employee who works with families in negotiating their homesite leases and grazing rites on the HPL said some Navajo families requested she urge the Hopi tribe to oust Monestersky from the Hopi reservation. At the hearing, Tso represented the families of Diné Dayikah Ada Yalti, an organization of three hundred Navajo families, who have signed accommodation agreements that allow them to remain on the HPL. She told the hearing that "the families had real concerns and recommended the exclusion of Marsha Monestersky and Arlene Hamilton. Non-Indian people are coming in, trying to provide assistance. With all good intentions, they are trying to help the families. This is not always helpful. . . . If something happens, the supporters go away, creating hardship for the families. . . . The negotiations are complicated, and it is frustrating when some outsider comes along, stirs the pot and disrupts the negotiations. Something is lost."[7]

At this juncture, it is important to note that the activists (or "human rights defenders," as they prefer to be called) have indeed played a constructive role to a limited degree and are certainly well intentioned. For example, Arlene Hamilton has facilitated a local weaving enterprise for Navajo women and has helped in securing grants to promote small business enterprises for the Navajo elders. Although some of the families, including prominent Dineh elder Roberta Blackgoat, have supported the activists, particularly Arlene Hamilton, their popularity has waned. Part of the problem is that the activists are not cognizant of the complex pattern of decision making that is involved in alliance formation among the

Navajo communities in this area. The activists adopt a rather simplistic approach to environmental and social resistance.

The ethnographic decision models for Navajos in the HPL area developed by Schoepfle and colleagues for the EPA in 1984 are instructive in better understanding the decision-making process for the Dineh resistance movement around Big Mountain (fig. 7.1). The researchers used extensive interviews and survey data and methods from cognitive anthropology to develop this model, which was also profiled by William Millsap in *Applied Social Science for Environmental Planning* (see Millsap 1984). The model shows the nonlinearity of the decision-making process that is involved in terms of the community's interaction with the mining company. It is not just a matter of environmental impact or land relocation issues that factor into resistance in such a circumstance.

Thus the Black Mesa case, which at the surface may appear to be a hallmark of environmental resistance at the international level, is actually a story of divisive resistance brokerage within indigenous communities that has not had any particular bearing on the mining or on the land dispute. The linkage between mining and land rights has in effect been quite contentious.

Canadian NGOs and the Saskatchewan Mines

Institutionalized environmental activism on nuclear issues on a global level can be traced back to Canada with the inception of Greenpeace in 1971. Greenpeace was started by a group of Canadian activists in Vancouver who were opposed to nuclear proliferation. As Canada became an ever-increasing contributor to the nuclear industry, the pitch of their opposition increased, but the voice was also diluted by numerous other environmental problems, such as population control, water quality, ozone depletion, and global warming. However, as Nova Scotia–based environmentalist David Orton reminds us, the native/environmental debate is still somewhat tabooed in Canada: "The relationship with indigenous peoples is an extremely sensitive topic within the environmental movement (more sensitive even than discussions of ecofeminism/gender relations or the relations between workers/the working class and environmentalists); among greens; and in the Canadian Left. . . . Realistic public discussion is usually avoided by environmentalists and greens. Avoidance of contentious native issues is considered good manners."[8]

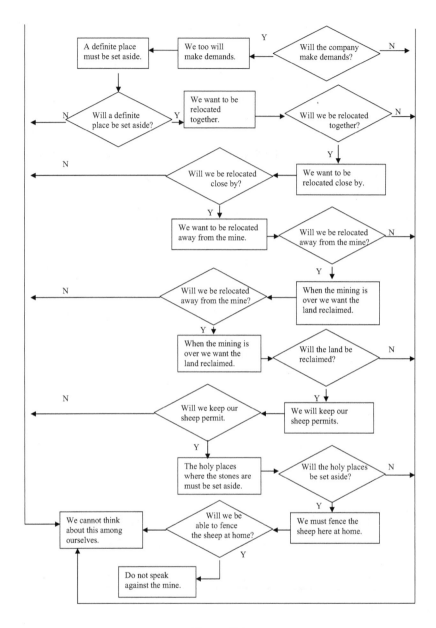

Figure 7.1
An ethnographic decision model for Navajos and energy development.
(Adapted from Schoepfle et al. 1984)

In Saskatchewan, the most vocal opposition to uranium mining came from church groups and a few regional environmental organizations. The Inter-Church Uranium Committee and the Saskatchewan Environment Society most actively participated in protest rallies and tried to galvanize support from northern communities. Greenpeace and other large multinational organizations were more preoccupied with environmental problems such as logging and biodiversity conservation. There were also several individual activists from abroad who had visited the region and developed particular associations with certain groups.

In the early eighties Eldorado Nuclear (now part of Cameco Corporation) entered into an agreement with the provincial government of Saskatchewan to begin mining activities in the vicinity of Wollaston Lake. The native communities of the region felt that their subsistence lifestyles of hunting and fishing would be threatened by water pollution from the mining development. Their opposition was partly due to the past experience of affected communities in Uranium City. They were also galvanized to action by an activist named Miles Goldstick, who had several connections with environmental groups in Scandinavia. The result was a considerable opposition movement that was even supported by some notable chiefs, such as Chief Hector Kkhailther: "I tried my best to get the government and the mining companies to discuss how it will affect our people for years to come. I tried my best to have a meeting with the people involved in uranium mining, and the people looking after it, running it, the ministers. It seems like those people are only looking out for the money. . . . We have to keep on bugging them until they close the mine. That's what we're after."[9]

A formal protest and blockade was organized in June 1985 involving 150 community members. The protesters blocked the road and received national press coverage including a brief parliamentary debate spurred by a member of Parliament from Manitoba: "Members will be aware, I hope, that at this very moment, and since Friday, there has been a blockade going on at Wollaston Lake, in northern Saskatchewan having to do with the concern of people there about the extent of uranium mining going on there and its potential expansion. I think it is high time that Canada got out of the uranium mining business."[10]

Within four days of the blockade, Eldorado met with a number of Déné chiefs and were successful in garnering their support. The chiefs were quick to point out that the alliance between the environmentalists and the indigenous communities had been opportunistic because of the opposition of the Green groups to traditional hunting and trapping: "These same protesters up there right now are the same ones involved as well in trying to stop the leg hold trapping . . . trying to stop the traditional livelihood of the people that the Chiefs represent. So we cannot sit by and let people run over us like that, whether they are pro-developers or antidevelopers. We are going to make a choice about how things are going to move ahead."[11]

Despite all the preparatory work and the media coverage, the blockade was generally unsuccessful in changing policy. Even some of the environmentalists disapproved of the way in which this movement had been organized. Soon thereafter, Miles Goldstick published a rather dramatic account of the blockade in *Wollaston: People Resisting Genocide* and subsequently moved to Sweden. According to Jamie Kneen, an activist based in Ottawa who worked with the Hatchett Lake band in Saskatchewan and the Inuit Taparisat Coalition, the blockade was "premature and extremely damaging to the community."[12]

The environmental review process and the government review of uranium mining ventures in general picked up pace during the early nineties. The Hatchett Lake band, which had shown the most organized opposition to the mining, also hired professional economic consultants at the Economic Resources Group in Cambridge, Massachusetts, to help with a cost-benefit analysis of the proposed mining projects. They compiled a report and submitted certain objections to the analysis in the environmental impact statement for the McArthur River project. However, the company and the government largely dismissed these findings in a detailed report, and Cameco in particular felt that the consultants had little knowledge of the cultural dynamics and economic predicament of the region and had charged exorbitant fees to an impoverished Indian band for unnecessary services.[13] The company continued to directly communicate with the band and to work through some of their concerns.

Meanwhile, the environmentalists in southern Saskatchewan, who had been the most vociferous opponents to the mining, decided to withdraw from the formal environmental assessment process, citing the following reasons:

> In September 1996 we reluctantly ended our involvement in the environmental assessment review process for the McArthur River, Cigar Lake and Midwest uranium mine projects. . . . The good faith being expressed by the public was not being reciprocated by industry, government or its many-layered bureaucracy. The process had simply de-

generated into a tool of political legitimation. We had no choice but to uphold our own good faith and belief in public processes by withdrawing from further involvement in these particular reviews.[14]

At this point, there was a distinct lack of engagement between the environmental groups based in the southern reaches of Saskatchewan and the indigenous groups in the north.[15] Indeed, very few of the environmental activists had actually visited the mine sites and were actively supported by only a few indigenous women living in urban areas, most notably Priscilla Settee at the University of Saskatchewan. As the director of the indigenous studies program at the university, she held certain academic legitimacy and had voiced her opposition to mining at conferences around Canada and Europe. However, because of her distance from the actual native settlements, she did not hold the same clout and authority among the decision makers in the native bands. Moreover, the alternatives to mining that were being suggested to the communities were not very lucrative. Ecotourism was the most promising. However, there were very few people who believed that there was a market for perennial tourist activities in the province. According to Cameco's Jamie McIntyre: "It's really unfortunate that the environmental groups were not involved in a positive way with the indigenous groups. They gave them alternatives but the indigenous people told them: If you want to go and pick berries, you go and pick berries, we will go and mine. The alternatives they have are to stay in the community on welfare or move. We have provided them a third alternative."[16]

The rift between the environmental movement and the indigenous rights movement and, indeed, the government was further widened by the debate on hunting and trapping, which continued to gain momentum: "I think it's time that we as indigenous people unite in a place like northern Saskatchewan, where we are really being exploited by these governments. You know we have to force these governments to come to the table to negotiate our land rights."[17]

Cameco and other mining companies kept a safe distance from such debates, which usually worked to their advantage.

Some Constructive Red/Green Alliances

While the previous two sections challenge the conventional confidence in ENGO-native alliances that tend to be depicted by the popular media, it is important to appreciate that there are indeed certain constructive alliances that have been forged by certain environmentalists and indigenous peoples. By *constructive* I mean their collective approach has been met with widespread support and has achieved most of the stated objectives for each "partner" thus far. This section explores how some of these alliances have been successful.

The Crandon case (U2) is particularly interesting since historically there has been considerable antagonism among the Indians, environmentalists, and sportfishermen of the region over the issue of spearfishing, which is a traditional Chippewa means of harvesting fish.

When Wisconsin reinstituted spearfishing in 1985, participation by tribal fishers was somewhat tentative. Public opinion opposing the spear-fishery appeared to vastly outweigh public support for treaty rights. Many fishermen preferred not to exercise their rights rather than suffer the verbal abuse and threats of physical violence that they encountered at boat landings. Slogans such as "save a fish / spear an Indian" were rife. However, during that first season, 2,761 walleye were taken in the spearfishery. The fishery grew steadily for the next three years with harvests of 6,940, 21,321, and 25,974 walleye. During 1989, a sudden recurrence of cold weather at the end of the spawning season curtailed fishing activity and only 16,053 walleye were taken. In contrast during 1988, all fisheries combined took 698,277 walleye from the waters of the ceded territories. Angling accounted for 672,303 of these fish, 96.3 percent of the catch (Spangler 1997).[18] Nevertheless, the conflict continued and became increasingly racist in its rhetoric. During this time a group of nonnative and native activists around Madison began a campaign to counter this tide by forming the Midwest Treaty Network (MTN) on 4 July 1989.

As defined by its cofounder, cartographer Zoltan Grossman, "The Midwest Treaty Network is an alliance of Indian and non-Indian community groups that support the sovereign rights of Native American nations. While founded in the context of the Chippewa (Ojibwa) treaty struggle, it is concerned generally with defending and strengthening native cultures and nationhood, protecting Mother Earth, and fighting racism and other forms of domination throughout our region. The Network has taken a stand against economic and political pressure on indigenous nations to give up their rights."[19]

In 1991, federal Judge Barbara Crabb issued a permanent injunction against protestors interfering "physically, whether on the lake or at boat landings," with the Chippewa spearfishing. Subsequently, thirteen members of Stop Treaty Abuse-Wisconsin, an antitreaty group, were forced to pay several thousand dollars in damages to the Lac du Flambeau Chippewa and the Wa-Swa-Gon Treaty Association in a case settlement arranged through the American Civil Liberties Union (Gedicks 1993, 185). The fisheries issue has also received some surprising support from the U.S. Supreme Court. In May 1999, by a five-to-four vote, the Court said that neither an 1850 presidential order nor Minnesota's statehood in 1858 stripped the Chippewa of the hunting and fishing privilege they received in an 1837 treaty.[20] Such judgments have generally silenced much of the spearfishing opponents in the Midwest and given the MTN an opportunity to focus on other issues — soon thereafter resistance to the Crandon project became a central campaign for the group. It is important to keep in mind, however, that the Mole Lake Chippewa community had already begun their resistance to the mining project in the late seventies, before the involvement of the ENGOs. This case is thus instructively different from some instances at Black Mesa where the activists came in after some families had signed for relocation and asked them to resist by giving them assurance of external support.

Even though some of the founders of the MTN have a very strong activist view on mining and are adamantly against any form of nonrenewable resource development, they have not articulated their vision for the group as an environmentalist organization. They have strongly adhered to the starting premise that sovereignty must come first. Indeed, the most strident environmental causes have also been lobbied for through a concerted campaign to promote tribal self-determination. This is highlighted by the MTN's logistical and political support for Mole Lake Chippewa's water quality standards and the Forest County Potawatomi's air quality standards.

The approach taken by the Wisconsin tribes in trying to formulate their own environmental regulations is the most institutionally astute means of resistance that could be offered. In 1974, when the EPA wrote the clean air regulations, the agency suddenly realized that its twenty-seven regulatory programs each had "three hundred holes" because they delegated authority to the states, which lacked jurisdiction on the reservations. "It was a nightmare," according to EPA's Indian coordinator at the time, Leigh Price. In 1986, Indian lobbyists succeeded in convincing Congress to add Indian amendments to three laws — the Clean Water Act, the Safe Drinking Water Act, and the Superfund law — that recognized tribal governmental authority as being identical to or very similar to that of states. Congressional action over the Clean Air act was delayed because of concerns about acid rain. Nevertheless, implementation of this phase is still largely delayed because most tribes do not have the resources or training to promulgate regulations. Moreover, tribes tend to view the environment holistically and resent the compartmentalization of air, water, and waste programs.

An even more remarkable aspect of this alliance network is that it includes erstwhile sportsfishers who are not the archetype of environmentalism by any means and have been adamantly antitreaty. Part of the reason for the success of the network is precisely that it is a network and is made up of dozens of smaller organizations that work on their own with regard to technical issues and meet together for lobbying purposes and information sharing. This structure allows for differences to exist without acrimony. It also makes the alliance much more difficult to demonize by opponents. As one of the cofounders of the network says: "We have so many heads, they don't know how to decapitate us."[21]

While the alliances formed between native and nonnative groups were helpful in pitching the issue to the government and the promulgation of the mining moratorium law, their importance should not be overstated. Indeed, as the activists themselves admit, the mining moratorium law was quite a "crow in peacock feathers." In reality, it only added an extra hurdle to the mining approval process and was not an unequivocal moratorium by any measure.

I would thus disagree with the scenario offered by Prof. Al Gedicks in his important book *The New Resource Wars*: "If Exxon could have limited the conflict over the mine to a contest between itself and the Sokaogon, there would not have been a decade-long protracted environmental conflict" (Gedicks 1993, 63). Professor Gedicks presumes that without the involvement of external ENGOs, the project would have gone ahead.

However, a closer analysis of the situation reveals that the actual factors that have led to the stalling of the project have much more to do with native regulatory primacy and the inclusion of native personnel at the local government's decision-making level. The alliance between the Chippewa and the nonnative locals was, however, facilitated by some of the work carried out by the ENGOs, particularly EARTH Wins, a one-person organization led by Alice McCombs, who sent out her weekly newsletter to interested Internet subscribers on a fairly regular basis from 1995 to 1997.

The election of Robert Van Zile on the Nashville town council board in 1999 has certainly been a welcome result of such efforts.

This observation is reminiscent of other studies of environmental advocacy networks observed by Keck and Sikkink in Malaysia and Brazil:

> Environmental advocacy networks have not so much gotten the tropical forest issue onto the agenda—it was already there—as they have changed the tone of the debate. To the frequent consternation of the epistemic community of scientists and policymakers who had succeeded in placing it on the agenda initially, the advocacy networks deliberately politicized the issues. While the epistemic community had sought to design policies and tried on the basis of their authoritative knowledge to persuade governments to adopt them, advocacy networks looked for leverage over actors and institutions capable of making the desired changes. (Keck and Sikkink 1998, 161)

There is also an emergent group of ENGOs starting from the premise of supporting indigenous movements that are already resisting certain forms of development rather than trying to "convert" pro-mining tribes per se. The alliance between Project Underground, a Berkeley-based antimining group, and the Indigenous Environmental Network is an important example of such an initiative. While Project Underground has a noncompromising stance on mining issues, their director, Danny Kennedy, states that "we are very conscious of social issues which can lead communities to support mining."[22] Project Underground has also worked with the Western Shoshone of Nevada in their resistance to gold mining around the Crescent valley region. This case is now being considered by the Inter-American Commission on Human Rights and is being argued for the plaintiffs by leading native lawyer James Anaya.

In Canada, there has been a congruent rise in antimining support groups as well as in nonnative groups that are prioritizing native sovereignty concerns. Mining Watch Canada is in some ways the Canadian equivalent of Project Underground, albeit milder in tone. Founded in April 1999, the organization describes itself as "a pan-Canadian initiative supported by environmental, social justice, indigenous and labor organizations from across the country. It addresses the urgent need for a coordinated public interest response to the threats to public health, water and air quality, fish and wildlife habitat and community interests posed by irresponsible mineral policies and practices in Canada and around the world."[23] This organization also shows much promise for constructive red/green alliances given its devolved structure and the deferential approach that was exhibited in its recent conference on "Indigenous Communities and Mining."[24] A notable feature of this conference was that it allowed pro-mining and antimining tribes and the representatives from the United Steelworkers of America to come together and discuss their mutual concerns in an amicable atmosphere. Seventy-three representatives from thirty-two indigenous communities attended the conference. The nonnative organizers at Mining Watch sought the direct cosponsorship of the Innu Nation for the event and let them set its tone. Interestingly enough, mining companies, government officials from DIAND or Environment Canada, and other ENGOs were not invited to the event. The purpose was to get the most closely affected stakeholders to the table to learn from each other—a model that has worked in other settings as well (see Susskind et al. 1999).

The Victoria-based group Settlers in Support of Indigenous Sovereignty (SISIS), which recently disbanded due to the death of key personnel in a car accident, was somewhat similar to the Midwest Treaty Network. However, it was distinct in being a purely nonnative collective with a decidedly nonenvironmental agenda, which was predicated entirely on indigenous rights. This group played an important part in defining the debate on tribal sovereignty versus environmental primacy—most clearly articulated in the controversy surrounding the Makah whale hunt.

There are thus clear examples of constructive alliances between ENGOs and native peoples. The key to their success has been in allowing the indigenous groups to make their own decisions and establish their own priorities. Zoltan Grossman, the cofounder of the MTN, has articulated four steps red/green alliances or native/nonnative alliances have taken: "The evolution (of the alliances) went through four general and often overlapping stages. First, Native American nations asserted their autonomy. Second a backlash emerged from some rural whites over proper resource use. Third, the two groups initiated dialogue over a perceived outside threat to the resources. Finally the groups began to cooperate" (Grossman 2000).

The rural backlash from nonnatives should by no means be considered a precondition for alliance formation. The Wisconsin case illustrates that alliances can form in spite of (not because of) such a backlash. Nevertheless, there is also tremendous potential for division and harm to both environmental and indigenous causes if the alliances are not carefully crafted and do not represent the underlying values of the people. This is where pluralist views of environmental movements can often be misleading, since they tend to assume that alliances and networks are inherently productive.

Critiquing the New Pluralists' Version of Environmental Justice

Environmental justice is clearly becoming an ever-expansive phenomenon (or perhaps cynics may say a buzzword). However, a major reason for this occurrence is the growing awareness in communities of the fact that environmental causes, apart from their substantive value, are also a means of legitimacy for anchoring discontent within a regulatory framework. By framing resistance within environmental boundaries, there is also greater leverage to use scientific information as a means of articulating one's argument (though this is all too often used selectively by communities).

As noted by Lois Gibbs of the Citizen's Clearinghouse for Hazardous Waste: "Environmental justice is broader than just preserving the environment. When we fight for environmental justice we fight for our homes and families and struggle to end economic, social and political domination by the strong and greedy" (Schlosberg 1999, 127). In a recent edited volume entitled *Liberation Ecologies*, Richard Peet and Michael Watts lay out a framework for how "the mediations between structured contradictions, deprivations, and various forms of sociopolitical actions are now seen as highly significant, rather than contradictions automatically producing organized opposition" (Peet and Watts 1997, 5). In this regard, there is a feeling that bridging of old social movements, such as unions and leftist parties, to new movements, such as organizations advocating environmental justice, is relatively easy—consequently, there is also a move toward bridging the environmental movement with the indigenous rights movement.

Network theorists have found many elegant ways of representing the strength of alliances between different kinds of organizations. There is a particular fascination with the new pluralism that alliances between groups as diverse as gay/lesbian activists, labor unions, environmentalists, and indigenous rights groups may embody. Most recently, Schlosberg, in his book *Environmental Justice and the New Pluralism*, has used the botanical metaphor of a rhizome to describe the organizing of groups such as those in the Wisconsin case study: "Rhizomes connect in a way that is not visible on the ground—they cross borders and reappear in distant places without necessarily showing themselves in between. . . . The rhizome metaphor may be helpful in discussing situations that may be localized but still be shared by people in different places."

Their "unity," it is argued, "does not emphasize uniformity." Interestingly enough, Schlosberg cites Brecher and Costello (1994) and their use of Jonathan Swift's metaphor of Gulliver (which was also used by a mining industry representative) being held down by the diminutive Lilliputians through a mesh (or network) of strings connecting them at different *positions*. The argument contends that the strength of the mesh comes from the different vantage points of each individual.

However, one must be cautious in presuming that such a network of alliances with different positions is necessarily beneficial. To carry the analogy further, the different positions of the Lilliputians may help in keeping Gulliver anchored in one place, but it is of little use in actually *moving* him anywhere. Therefore while such networks of resistance emanating from different vantage points may be effective in maintaining the status quo, they may not necessarily be useful in promoting lasting change. In order for change or *movement* to occur, all the individuals must concur on moving in the same direction. The new pluralists do not adequately address the efficacy of such movements in actually resolving disputes or administering change.

I concur with Schlosberg insofar that "a network, then, is not simply the connection between issues and groups, but is a particular method and practice of that connection as well. Function, in this case, follows form" (Schlosberg 1999, 120). However, after making this statement, he moves on like many other environmental justice analysts to applaud the extent of networking alliances without presenting data on efficacy in achieving lasting or "sustainable" reform. Part of the problem lies in the propensity for political theorists to summarily cite negotiation literature without fully appreciating the core of the latter's argument. At the heart of negotiation discourse is the notion of differentiating positional from principled bargaining positions (see Susskind and Cruikshank 1987).

In any alliance formation, stakeholders must be fully appreciative of the kinds of issues that can in fact be conducive to linkage and those that can lead to deadlock, as explained in the previous chapter. Successful native-nonnative alliances on environmental concerns have also been those in which the environmental groups have played a supportive role decidedly ancillary to the actual decision-making structure. For contemporary native societies, sovereignty is the touchstone for judging any other endeavor, and sovereignty is most clearly manifest in exclusive control over decision making. In the words of Larry Innes, a nonnative environmental adviser to the Innu Nation, "we [nonnatives] have a role to play as translators, but the ultimate decisions are theirs."

Chapter 8

Ambiguous Property

The Linkage Politics of Land Claims

This chapter will continue to explore factors that can lead to the prevalence of environmental resistance and focus on the hypothesis that issue linkage, particularly the linkage between land claims and environmental conservation, can play an important role in resistance formation and prevalence.

Lessons can be gleaned about how to link issues from the field of linkage politics, which has its roots in international relations. The first organized effort to understand issue linkage in political science was initiated by James Rosenau (1969) and culminated in a volume entitled *Linkage Politics*. However, this book and subsequent work in the arena of linkage theory and field theory[1] were largely focused on understanding the linkage between domestic politics and international relations.

At the broadest level, issue linkage can be thought of as catalyzing consensus through Thomas Schelling's "focal points," which he defined as "intuitively perceived mutual expectations, shared appreciations, preoccupations, obsessions, and sensitivities to suggestion" (Schelling 1960). Environmental concerns could certainly be conceived as having the characteristics of focal points if appropriately articulated and understood by all players in a conflict.

Linkage can also be thought of in terms of as a substantive means of enlarging the zone of agreement between parties. This area of negotiation theory has been admirably studied by James Sebenius (1983, 1996), building on the analytically rigorous work of Howard Raiffa and colleagues at the Rand Corporation. Sebenius presented his insights about "negotiation arithmetic" in a paper by the same title in which he uses vector analysis to show how issue linkage can lead to constructive and destructive engagement in negotiations. This was a prelude to his later work on the sequencing of issues in negotiations (see Sebenius 1996). Clearly there are times when linking a certain intractable issue can lead to deadlock in negotiations. A sterling example of this phenomenon is the linkage of Jerusalem's independence in the Middle East peace process. The parties agreed earlier on to de-link this issue to avoid deadlock and stalemate. However, there are also numerous instances when issue linkage can clearly increase the zone of agreement and in fact allow for agreement between conflicting parties who would otherwise not achieve a resolution.

However, this approach basically reflects a bargaining outcome that does not necessarily mean that potentially adversarial parties will agree upon issue linkage per se, particularly if their BATNA is relatively high — in other words, the opportunity cost for no agreement is relatively low.

Moreover, it is still important to understand the factors that can lead to sustainable cooperation beyond such bargaining regimes. In order to do so, there must be a discussion of time horizons and discount rates. To test the sustainability of linkages, Susanne Lohmann conducted an elaborate study of issue and player linkage to provide a conceptual framework within which to think about sustainable cooperation. Lohmann predicates the sustainability of cooperation on a discount factor (δ), which essentially measures how much the future is valued by players relative to the present. A lower value of a discount factor indicates a higher discount rate (future is more heavily discounted relative to the present) and vice versa. The scale that she has formulated is quite instructive in understanding the dynamics of cooperation and could indeed be a starting point for further investigation of her theory within an environmental framework.

Figure 8.1 shows her scale for issue linkage reflecting the challenge for potential adversaries to cooperate relative to their perceived discount factors. More important, it shows us that there are times when issue linkage works and does not work, all within a spectrum of discount factors — simply how much we value the future. Issue de-linkage is likely to be more successful at lower discount factors, and issue linkage is sustainable on both issues with slightly higher discount factors.

The key is to find out where on the spectrum parties lie and how to move them in the direction of constructive engagement. The framework for issue linkage presented in table 8.1 shows how environmental cooperation may bring ostensible adversaries together. The structure is largely de-

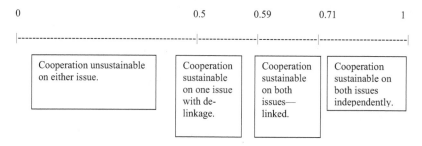

Discount Factor (δ) Scale

| 0 | | 0.5 | 0.59 | 0.71 | 1 |

| Cooperation unsustainable on either issue. | Cooperation sustainable on one issue with de-linkage. | Cooperation sustainable on both issues—linked. | Cooperation sustainable on both issues independently. |

Figure 8.1
Issue linkage and sustainable cooperation. (Adapted from Lohmann 1997)

rived from the work of Vinod Aggarwal, who is interested in studying ways in which institutions bargain with each other. Since many environmental issues are handled institutionally, this may be a particularly prescient framework to consider. The key problem in cases of environmental linkage arises when stakeholders do not perceive a substantive link (A) and instead think that environmental issues are tactical and opportunistic (B). In most cases, environmental issues are never in categories C or D, particularly if one is willing to take a long-term view of economic and social problems.

Land and Mining Disputes in Labrador and Arizona

The Black Mesa case presents a situation where the linkage between mining and the Navajo/Hopi land dispute has been made time and again by the activist community and, of course, the Dineh settlers on HPL. Even some respected journalists have tried to push a sort of conspiracy theory that there is a linkage between the displacement of the Navajo and mining activities, assuming in some way that the Hopi would encourage mining. This linkage has brought forth activists of all sorts to the site—many of whom would not have been attracted to the issue without the mention of a mining company in the midst. In a 30 January 2000 article in the *Boston Globe*, Gary Ghioto describes the scene: "Buddhist nuns and monks from Japan are joined by Native Americans, Europeans, and college students from across the United States chanting prayers and carrying traditional

Table 8.1
Dynamics of Issue Linkage

Linkage Type	Objective Reality	Target Decision Makers' Perception	Basis for Issue Connections	Outcome
A: Substantive link	Connected	Connected	Knowledge	Stable issue area
B: Failed substantive link (perceived as tactical)	Connected	Unconnected	Power	Temporary solution to externalities
C: Tactical link	Unconnected	Unconnected	Power	Unstable issue area
D: Failed tactical link (perceived as substantive)	Unconnected	Connected	Misunderstanding	Contingent (to unstable issue-area if consensual knowledge changes)

Source: Aggarwal 1998.

peace pipes." The linkage between mining and the land relocation has become accepted and embraced by the activist community and mentioned in forums across the globe. Peabody's record from thirty years ago and the nefarious dealings of the attorney John Boyden have been sloppily paraphrased into linkages with the current dispute with remarkable zeal, as shown in appendix 4.

This linkage, however, is by no means substantive and would fall into Category C of Aggarwal's typology. Despite the legacy of unfair lease arrangement, there is no evidence to support that the land dispute has been motivated by the mining itself. Indeed, the Hopi have already passed a resolution that prevents new mining projects from taking root.

Marjane Ambler, who has been a vociferous critic of the mining industry and the U.S. government's policy toward Native Americans, commented on this linkage: "Those who prefer simple black-and-white explanations argue that Navajos and Hopis could have continued to live peacefully in the Joint Use Area if the mineral companies had not insisted upon clearing title to the minerals" (Ambler 1990, 145).

Ambler goes on to quote Navajo history scholar Peter Iverson, who argues persuasively that the Hopis would have demanded relocating the Navajos to make room for the Hopis even if minerals had not been involved: "Even though energy companies complicated the issue and had a stake in the outcomes they should not be used as a convenient explanation for the policy that was implemented." The division was inevitably controversial because, as the activists pointed out, it resulted in the biggest relocation of people since the internment of Japanese Americans during World War II.

However, both tribes have been immersed in mining activities, and there is no firm indication that even under Navajo control mining would in any way be discouraged. In the aftermath of repeated activist allegations concerning Peabody's involvement in the land dispute, the presidents of both the Hopi and Navajo nation have written to the company, categorically denying that there is any such linkage, despite their misgivings regarding the leases with the company (which are now being argued in court).

The linkage of the mining to the land dispute has been an attempt on the part of environmentalists to give a human face to their crusade against mining, while for the Big Mountain settlers it has been a means of injecting an internationally recognized norm, such as environmental protection, into the debate. This is not to say that the attachment elders such as Roberta Blackgoat have to the land is strategic. Their feelings on this issue deserve respect. However, the linkage between their proposed relocation and the assumed de facto land use to be mining is not substantive. It is thus not surprising that even the Indigenous Environmental Network (initially founded at the Navajo reservation) and Honor the Earth (founded by Winona La Duke), the two largest indigenous environmental organizations in North America, which generally oppose mining, have distanced themselves from the Big Mountain activists.[2]

Such linkage politics are clearly destructive because they reduce the credibility of both the environmental movement and the indigenous rights movement, which could, on their own merits, argue quite convincingly for their own motives. Moreover, false linkages can also lead to divisions within the community that are widened with each aspersion that is predicated on misinformation. In this case, the linkage has also widened the rift between the tribal governments and the mining companies and has gone to reinforce negative stereotypes about environmentalists and native groups among representatives of the mining companies. Clearly the past conduct of Peabody vis-à-vis the lease arrangements has been quite reprehensible, but so too has been the past performance of almost every development enterprise dealing with native issues during the past century. The linkages that have been established in this case may have helped to galvanize resistance initially, but they have not succeeded in allowing for resistance to prevail because of the shaky ground of the linkage being posited in the case of the land dispute. Interestingly enough, there is an important linkage between the mining activity and the water depletion of the aquifer, a technical linkage, but then that should be tackled on its own merits rather than being linked to an intertribal land dispute.

If the Big Mountain settlers and the environmentalists felt that the key reason for their reluctance to relocate were in fact the fear that the Hopi would allow Peabody to mine on their ancestral graves, then they should have articulated it as such. Through a process of engagement they could have directly asked the Hopi, the government, and the company about this particular issue and use that as the principle for the negotiation process. If the process were articulated in such a fashion, then the linkage would still hold some ground and could be expressed constructively. Instead, there has been a presumption of a preexisting linkage that has no substantive merits, and conspiracy theories have been built around it.

The Voisey's Bay case presents yet another example of issue linkage that has played an interesting, and markedly more constructive, role in resistance emergence and prevalence. The key issue here for the indigenous groups has been a linkage between land claim settlements and environmental impact assessment for the mining itself. Like the Navajo and the Hopi, here, too, there are overlapping claims to the land between the LIA and the Innu, and there is a history of antagonism between the two groups.

However, the linkage between land claims and the assessment process was institutionally anchored through a negotiation process that was overseen by the government. The special panel on the Voisey's Bay project recognized this linkage in its recommendation:

That Canada and the Province conclude and ratify land claims agreements in principle with the Inuit of Labrador, represented by the LIA, and the Innu of Labrador, represented by the Innu Nation, before issuing any project authorizations, or, failing that, negotiate equivalent alternative measures before issuing any project authorizations, which must provide for Innu and Inuit consultation and compensation in respect of the project in keeping with the fiduciary obligations of Canada and the province. (Canadian Environmental Assessment Agency 1999)

The Innu and the Inuit have remained resolute and united in their assertion that the land claims should be settled before the project goes forward and have even gone to court in this regard. Another important feature of this process that has led to a constructive linkage of issues has been the memorandum of understanding, which was signed by the government of Newfoundland, the federal Canadian government, the LIA, and the Innu Nation in 1997, which led to the panel process and has been an anchor for much of the ensuing negotiations (Canadian Environmental Assessment Agency 1997).

The Innu are very conscious of the fact that their connection with the land has been highly romanticized and that their conservation ethic is different from that which most nonnative environmentalists may espouse: "We walk on the land. The Akeneshau (white man) is different. His feet never touch the ground. He walks on the pavement, and his feet are off the ground all the time. Then he comes to Labrador and says what a beautiful country" (Akat Piwas, Innu elder, quoted in Lowe 1998, 35).

In 1995, the Innu Nation decided to set up a task force to provide information on mining issues to the two Innu communities at Sheshatshiu and Davis Inlet. The result was a report entitled *Ntesinan, Ntshiniminan, Nteniunan: Between a Rock and a Hard Place*. The document reflected strong misgivings about the Voisey's Bay project but concluded with twenty-four recommendations for the Innu Nation, the mining industry, and government. The most pervasive theme throughout this report was a feeling that the Innu had not been accorded due respect by the other stakeholders. There was a major cultural divide that the Innu felt was not being understood. In the words of Katie Rich, the former president of the Innu Nation: "First declare a six month shutdown at Voisey's Bay. Then come and stay in our community for six months and ask the people's permission for what it is you want to do. You'll be surprised how many people will react if you ask permission" (Katie Rich, quoted in Lowe 1998, 91).

In their own way, the Innu tried to reach out to the mining industry as well. A professional guidance brochure produced by the Innu Nation was entitled *Mineral Exploration in Nitassinan: A Matter of Respect: Innu Nation Guidelines for the Mining Industry*. The document clearly reflected the strong apprehensions of the Innu about the project. However, it ended on a conciliatory note: "The Innu Nation is committed to working with mining companies who are prepared to respect our rights, our land and our way of life." While both groups initially resisted the mining, they brought forth constructive linkages that are credible and improve their negotiating stance. The strategy has clearly worked in reaching a workable agreement and in recognition of the outstanding land claims.

Delinking Royalties and the Panel Process

On account of strong pressure from lobbying groups in Canada and abroad, the government of Canada and the provincial government of Saskatchewan decided to form a panel to review the various uranium mining projects in August 1991. The panel was entrusted with the duty of looking objectively at the environmental and social impact of the mining projects that were being proposed and presenting its recommendations to the government. The panel comprised five members who were chosen on account of their scientific expertise and their experience in working with northern communities.

The chairperson of the panel was Prof. Donald Lee of the chemistry department at the University of Regina. Other panel members were Dr. Richard Neal, of the biology department at the University of Saskatchewan; Dr. James Archibald, of the mining engineering department at Queens University; Dr. Annalee Yassi, of the School of Public Health at the University of Manitoba; and Vice Chief John Dantouze, of the Prince Albert Grand Council of Saskatchewan.

The mining companies were not directly involved with the deliberations of the panel. However, the panel did confer with the companies to procure technical information and also to ascertain the terms of employment assurance and other social impact indicators. The panel also held sessions to get input from the public.

In early 1996, the panel began to plan a series of hearings across Saskatchewan in order to have an organized means of public involvement in the process and to expedite the reports the panel was obliged to issue after almost five years of deliberations. Despite its small size, there was considerable dissent within the panel as to the nature and timing of these hearings. Dr. Annalee Yassi was particularly opposed to having the hearings held at a time when the public was not completely informed of the various impact measures. "I want to reiterate that I think it is cynical to be proceeding to 'Public Hearings' when the public will not have the information they need to properly evaluate the EIS. It was clear to me at our meeting that there is a political and industrial agenda that we must follow." [3]

The majority opinion of the panel was that the environmental impact statements for the various projects had been available for several months at all public libraries, and public notices had been sent informing people of their availability (this had been preceded by a formal EIS review public notice as well). The hearings for Cameco's projects (McArthur River and Cigar Lake) were held in 1996, from 4 September to 11 October, at eleven different locations across Saskatchewan. However, certain misgivings between the panel members and some of the northern leaders caused the hearing meetings at Wollaston Lake were canceled because of the community's disapproval.

The Resignations

Dr. Annalee Yassi, the epidemiologist on the panel, had for some time felt isolated in the deliberations of the panel. She was insistent that more emphasis be given to occupational health exposure on a long-term basis. Her reluctance to hold the hearings on account of insufficient public awareness further estranged her from the panel chairperson and various government regulators. According to the panel report, she officially resigned on 15 August 1996. However, in her correspondence with another panel member, she claimed that "as there was no resolution, I was effectively pushed off the Panel."[4] In fact, she had written in an earlier communication: "As much as I am tempted to quit on principle, I realize that this would be exactly what some 'stakeholders' would want, and having spent almost five years in this process, having had to fight attempts to get me to quit all along, I am not about to do so now."[5]

Perhaps emboldened by Dr. Yassi's resignation, Chief John Dantouze, who had also expressed misgivings about the panel regarding revenue sharing, announced that he would also resign from the panel on 1 October 1996. Chief Dantouze's resignation had the potential of severely damaging the negotiation process in northern Saskatchewan. The panel was scheduled to hold hearings soon thereafter and with the announcement of his resignation, a few northern leaders announced that they would not like to host the public hearings in their communities, most notably the hamlet of Wollaston Lake. While Cameco was not directly involved with the activities of the panel, the resignations were undoubtedly a matter of concern to the company. In Cameco's assessment, however, Chief Dantouze did not have the constituency to make a difference in the cause, and, in fact, his departure would probably make the process more objective and less politically charged.[6] This was a delicate time for Cameco since the direct contact with the community members had to be maintained and strengthened to dispel the negative publicity that statements such as the following from Chief Dantouze would generate.

> Their allegation demonstrates that the fundamental problem in the panel process is not any conflict between my political obligations to the Athabasca First Nations and my mandate on the Panel, but the pressures from the federal and provincial governments and the mining industry to proceed prematurely with decisions in their favor. The Premier and the Panel Chairperson have stated that our request for direct negotiations is inappropriate at this time. . . . This delay tactic is transparent. . . . To employ the Premier's hockey analogy: I and other northerners have never been in the game, we have either been in the stands or the penalty box. We have a team and we want ice time.[7]

The panel was now down to three members and there was a serious credibility problem. Nevertheless, the chairperson of the panel continued with the panel's activities and the government continued to support them. A statement on the resignation was quickly issued by the panel and faxed to various stakeholders, including Cameco:

> We are sincerely sorry that the northern leaders have decided to withdraw invitations to hold public hearings in their communities. Despite the departure of Vice Chief Dantouze, I have absolute confidence in the ability of the remaining panel members to finish this review in a completely reputable fashion. . . . The Chiefs inferred that their withdrawal will discredit the review process. We are, however, of the opinion that allowing the panel to be deterred from its duty by political maneuvering on the parts of the chiefs would cause greater discredit to the review process. . . . As indicated in our previous report, we share many of the same general objectives expressed by the Northern Leaders and we have no objections regarding to discussions concerning the principle of revenue sharing; however, the specifics regarding the projects and their impacts should not be negotiated at this time.[8]

Jamie McIntyre, the manager for northern relations, had his work cut out for him in trying to avert a serious lack of trust and a breakdown in communication. He had lived in northern Saskatchewan for many years and was generally well liked by most of the communities there. However, he knew that the problems in the panel's ranks were the government's business, and by staying away from the conflict between the government and the panel members, the company could maintain a certain degree of objectivity that would be available in the future. The most critical issue in this regard was revenue sharing.

Revenue Sharing

The panel's recommendations for the McArthur River project (in which Cameco had the greatest interest) were published in February 1997. The government issued a response to the panel's recommendations soon thereafter in which most of the thirty-one recommendations were endorsed. On the most critical issues of employment and revenue sharing, the government stated that it "supports the objective of increasing the employment of northerners by 1 percent annually until a level of 67 percent is reached."[9]

However, this was not enough to assuage the long-term concerns of the community members. They felt that a certain percentage of the revenues that the government was getting from the mining should be directly funneled back to the communities. The issue of revenue sharing first came up when the panel began its scoping meetings in late 1991. In its report on the McArthur River exploration project, the panel stated in 1993: "Although formally on Crown Land, several of the indigenous peoples who appeared before the panel referred to it as 'our land' and indicated they had assumed a traditional right to use it for gathering purposes. As a consequence, it seems to be a matter of natural justice that the indigenous people should share in any revenue provided by development and that they should logically benefit from mining operations in larger proportion than do the people living in the southern part of the province" (Canada 1993, 4).

The issue was, however, being negotiated primarily between the government and the community. Cameco made it clear that they were paying all the legally requisite royalties and taxes to the government and they had no control over how the money was subsequently distributed. The northern communities did not press the company to give additional or separate revenues to them since the technical owner of the land was actually the government. Cameco distanced itself once again from any lobbying efforts and continued to work on other proactive initiatives with the communities. According to Jamie McIntyre:

> Several meetings with the government, however, dissuaded us from tabling any of our ideas or actively supporting, in any obvious way, the

concept of revenue sharing. The issue of revenue sharing involved much more than the uranium industry and they [the government] saw any attempt to facilitate it in this circumstance as the thin edge of the wedge, and they would be faced with pressure from other constituents to share revenue from other resources. So essentially Cameco backed off and let the debate continue with no real comment.[10]

The Athabasca Working Group

Bernard Michel, CEO of Cameco, and top executives from the McArthur River and Cigar Lake operations met with twenty-three community leaders and representatives, including those of Wollaston Lake, in March 1993. The aim of this meeting was to improve communications between the company and the community. According to the review panel, the discussion identified three major issues:

— a desire for more opportunities for jobs, training, and business, but not at the expense of the environment (see fig. 8.2)
— a need for a written guarantee stating that companies would protect the environment and compensate for any damage that might result from mining activity
— a desire to receive benefits and revenues beyond those jobs, training, and business opportunities (Canada 1997b, 43)

To address these issues, it was decided at this meeting that the Athabasca Working Group would be created to ultimately draft an agreement of understanding between the communities and the companies. Cogema joined the process in 1994.

The group consisted of two members from each of the six Athabasca communities and at least one representative each from Cameco, Cogema, and Cigar Lake. The members of the working group were the elected leaders of each Athabasca community and a designated community representative chosen by the elected leader. To remain free of any political involvement, it was decided that government agencies or officers of the Federation of Saskatchewan Indian Nations, the Prince Albert Grand Council, or the Métis Society would not be included, except by invitation.

The meetings of the Athabasca Working Group, particularly meetings in crisis situations, such as the resignation of Vice Chief Dantouze, were often animated. Cameco perception and behavior at these meetings were described by Jamie McIntyre:

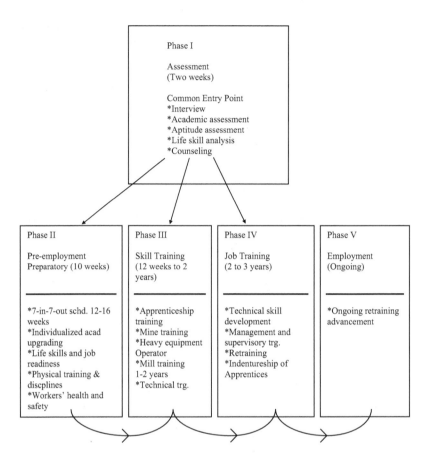

Figure 8.2
A multiparty training program in northern Saskatchewan.

The discussion and debate would get emotional and heated very quickly and escalate into these long 30–35 minute books, particularly by elders. They are particularly eloquent in their own language. After what could be a 7–8 hour meeting the meeting would break, sometimes in the wee hours of the morning. Everyone then gathered around and just shoots the gab, we used to talk about all sorts of things, often not at all related to the discussion that took place. It would literally switch into this very friendly conversation with some of the most genuinely nice people you would ever want to meet. And you always had to keep that in mind and not take things too personally or seem too defensive. They just wanted us to listen and once we got good at that, the meetings were generally very productive and rewarding experiences.[11]

In 1993, the Joint Panel on Uranium Development recommended that a consultation mechanism be set up by the government "for the people of Saskatchewan to be reassured that the mines are operating in compliance with all regulations and that northern economic benefits are being maximized." The provincial cabinet subsequently authorized the establishment of a Northern Mining Monitoring Secretariat (NMMS) and three regional Environmental Quality Committees. The committees' aim was to garner community opinions on mining developments and provide information on the projects on a regular basis. They were profiled in the Eighth Annual Report on Indigenous Participation in Mining as follows: "The EQCs [Environmental Quality Committees] are a bridge between northerners, government and the uranium mining industry—a bridge based on trust, respect, consultation and involvement. The NMMS is an administrative support structure for the 'bridge', offering co-ordination, information and communications services" (Canada 1997c).

In 1995 the work of the environmental quality committees was supplemented by the formation of an Office of Northern Affairs by the Saskatchewan government. A native Cree lawyer, Keith Goulet, was chosen as its director. At the Uranium Institute's symposium in 1997, Keith Goulet was an invited speaker, and while referring to the various initiatives of the Environmental Quality Committees, he commented that "cooperation and collaboration between the north Saskatchewan mining industry, governments, and local communities is now working well, deserves recognition, and must continue to develop."

Gleaning Lessons from Red Dog and Raglan

The particular sensitivity of indigenous groups to mining operations has led the mining industry to focus on certain case studies of success—where mining has proceeded without much resistance. The Uranium mining in Saskatchewan, which has been one of the core cases in this book, is one of the cases often heralded as a success story by the industry. However, the two cases that most often make their way into conferences and industry association pamphlets are the Red Dog mine in Alaska and the Raglan mine in Quebec.

There are two reasons why I did not focus on these cases in this work. First, both mines, which are zinc and nickel deposits, are located in areas where there is no indigenous habitation within a sixty-mile radius. Thus, even though the region does fall within traditional hunting grounds for the indigenous communities, the impact is much more indirect. Second, both mines are situated in areas with unique jurisdictions, which would thus prevent broader applicability of the lessons drawn to other indigenous areas. However, in this regard, both projects, even though they are located in two different countries, share an important common feature—they both involve agreements with "native corporations" rather than with tribal governments.

Alaska is of course the only state in the union that has a series of native corporations that were set up under the Alaska Native Claims Settlement Act. Similarly, the Ungava peninsula (Nunavik territory) of Quebec falls under the special regulatory regime of the James Bay and Northern Quebec Agreement, which created the Makivik Corporation of Inuits with whom the Raglan mine's agreement was signed.

Despite their unique characteristics, we can still glean some important lessons from these agreements. Incidentally, Raglan is owned and operated by Falconbridge, a close competitor of Inco (Voisey's Bay project), and Red Dog is operated by Cominco, a competitor of Rio Algom (owner of the Crandon project and now a part of BHP Billiton).

An important difference between the two agreements concerns employment guarantees. While the Red Dog agreement stipulated a target for employment of 70 percent by 1999, the Raglan agreement did not stipulate any particular percentage of employment, given the skill level of the workforce. The Raglan case reveals that while employment opportunities and training are an important linkage in such agreements, they should not become an essential prerequisite to consensus. Instead, the agreement has focused on profit sharing and contributions to an Inuit trust fund that over eighteen years (projected life of the first phase of the project) could total $70 million.

For the Red Dog operation, NANA receives 4.5 percent net smelter return as a royalty. After Cominco recovers its capital investment in the mine, NANA will receive 25 percent of the net proceeds, increasing 5 percent every five years until NANA and Cominco share equally in the profits. NANA-qualified shareholders in the NANA region (Alaska natives) receive first preference on all Red Dog jobs. Approximately four hundred people are employed at the mine and port facility, with slightly more than two hundred of these employees being NANA shareholders.

Raglan has a less acrimonious history than Red Dog, which may provide some lesson-drawing regarding the United States versus Canadian experience in such matters. In the early history of the Red Dog project, Cominco filed a lawsuit against the Secretary of the Interior, the Bureau of Land Management, the state of Alaska, and the NANA Regional Corporation to gain full tenure of the Red Dog site. However, in 1980 President Carter signed the Alaska National Interest Land Conservation Act, which securely established NANA's right to select land in the region for claims. This decision led Cominco to move toward direct agreement with the NANA Corporation (Koehler and Tikkanen 1991, 270).

As early as 1976, NANA's erstwhile president John Shaeffer told an interviewer that the mission of the corporation was "to provide people with an opportunity to participate in Western culture at whatever pace and degree they feel is possible for them" (Colt 1999, 35). In his detailed analysis of the comparative economic success of Alaska's twelve regional native corporations, Stephen Colt comments on this distinctive feature of NANA, perhaps a hallmark of its relative success as compared to the other corporations, many of which have languished close to bankruptcy:

> NANA saw itself as a bridge to Western society which no one had to cross if they did not wish to. From this basic self-conception followed a number of operating practices that appear to be unique among all regional corporations. These include the early and consistent separation of ceremonial leadership from day to day operations, a continuing emphasis on pride in culture, and an almost fanatical pursuit of employment on terms compatible with traditional Eskimo (Inupiat) subsistence. (Colt 1999, 112)

NANA was the first regional corporation to merge with its villages, and when the question arose in 1991 of whether to issue new stock to younger natives not originally included in the Alaskan Native Claims Settlement Act, the shareholders changed the bylaws to grant new shares to all subsequent descendents of current shareholders. The major concern thus far has been the tendency of NANA shareholders to move from the north down to Anchorage (and commute to the mine) because of the free transportation currently provided to shareholders on a fortnightly basis between the mine and Anchorage. This is contrary to the effect that is often hoped for in mining ventures marketed as a means of preventing community flight to urban centers by providing employment in remote areas.

The Raglan project, however, has not focused as much as NANA has on employment as a means of leverage; rather, they provide direct payments and royalties as well as environmental mitigation arrangements. For example, as part of the agreement negotiations, Falconbridge agreed to clean up a neighboring abandoned asbestos mine (which had no corporate connection to Falconbridge). Given the location of the project within the James Bay region, the approval process had to go through the Kativik Environmental Quality Commission. As in the Voisey's Bay case, there was a memorandum of understanding signed *before* the negotiation process commenced.

A key aspect of the Raglan case is that the negotiations with the Makivik Corporation spanned a period of five years, from the late 1980s to 1993, when the memorandum of understanding was signed. Meanwhile, the reduction of nickel prices allowed the project to lay fallow for some time, permitting the negotiations to be carried out without any external pressure for hurried results. The company made some substantial compromises on the work shifts, shipping schedules (to prevent disturbance of wildlife migration patterns), as well as regulations on firearm usage, exclusively for the Inuit workers at the mine site. Falconbridge does not have a special indigenous policy, as do several other mining companies, but it does have a sustainable development policy, which has been closely followed. In June 1998, the president of the Makivik Corporation, Pita Aatami, described the relationship between the Inuit and the company: "This project represents a vivid illustration of how development between a major mining corporation and indigenous communities can take place. Makivik is proud to have signed the Raglan Agreement with Falconbridge" (quoted in ICME 1999, 12).

Both of these cases illustrate the possibilities for cooperation that may arise under certain circumstances while also revealing some of the constraints of cultural difference that remain despite the ostensible capitalization of the two native communities at Raglan and Red Dog. Even here it can be seen that the key linkage that resulted in a clear agreement was the linkage of the issue of land rights and property. Various other factors such as the cultural match of negotiations between a native corporation and a mining corporation also played a part in facilitating dialogue. Subsequently, similar agreements have also been negotiated with diamond mining projects in the Northwest Territories and the Musselwhite project in Ontario. Environmental concerns that the communities raised and addressed were a manifestation of this lasting commitment to property but not vice versa. At the end of the day, these projects gave the communities a pivotal role in decision making and hence reaffirmed their sense of sovereignty — which is ever so important to native peoples.

Part III

The Prescriptive Synthesis

Chapter 9

Resistance and Cooperation

Understanding Indigenous Proclivities

The analysis thus far reveals the primary issue at stake for contemporary indigenous communities in the planning process is a reassertion of their sovereignty. Environmental conservation is subservient to this larger objective; hence, resistance based on environmental grounds can take root only if it is articulated within a framework of tribal self-determination. Ultimately, tribes decide whether to go ahead with a mining project or to resist it on environmental grounds based on which of the two options is a greater threat to their sense of sovereignty.

The preceding statement sums up the argument that I have tried to make throughout this book. Given the discursive nature of the topic, the key claims and the evidence on which they are premised are widely dispersed throughout the work. This chapter aims to present the key attributes of this argument and how they are supported by the cases in a concise and coherent form, thereby providing the basis for theory building and policy advice in the subsequent chapter.

Before discussing the key arguments, I would like to revisit the initial puzzle that led me to focus on this research. My starting point for this project was the observation that scientific criteria alone could not explain the emergence or prevalence of resistance. If scientific measures of impact were the primary motivation, one would have found greater resistance to mining in the uranium mining case in Saskatchewan and the mines in the Four Corners region. If economic concerns were an issue, then the Innu and Inuit would be expected to show least resistance to the mining given their remote location and lack of alternative options for economic development. Similarly, the Mole Lake tribe in Wisconsin would have much to gain economically from the mining given their relatively impoverished condition at present. Comparative review of impact criteria in chapter 6 aimed to provide evidence in this regard, thereby opening the way for a test of alternative hypotheses. Given these observations, the alternative hypotheses focus less on the product (environmental impact and amelioration) and more on the process by which stakeholders are collectively engaged.

Framing the Argument

The process by which stakeholders in a mining development project are engaged, particularly with reference to environmental impact, can largely be understood within the framework of institutional negotiation analysis.[1] I have tried to articulate my argument about the causes of resistance prevalence among native communities by focusing on two particular elements of a negotiation: *issue linkage* and *player linkage*.

With regard to issue linkage, the focus of my research has been on the linkage between land disputes and environmental impact negotiations. At the same time, my analysis of player linkage has focused on the interactions between environmental NGOs and native people, given that these two groups have most frequently been perceived to be strategic allies.

My analysis has sought to understand whether these linkages are *synergistic*—meaning that combining the issues or having certain coalitions of players increases the opportunities to create value and promote agreement, thereby reducing the level of resistance—or *antagonistic*—meaning that combining the issues or having certain coalitions of players decreases the chance of an agreement and thus promotes resistance.

Antagonistic linkages deserve further analysis, which is often missing in much of the commercial negotiation and planning discourse that tends to start with the premise that "any agreement is good." Instead, I focus on how to arrive at an agreement that is sustainable, if at all possible, by seeking ways in which the negotiation process can better incorporate causes of resistance.[2] In this regard, my approach may be categorized as "conflict resolution," whereas the former approach may be categorized as "conflict management." Jay Folberg and Alison Taylor differentiate between these two approaches as follows: "Conflict resolution creates a state of uniformity or convergence of purpose or means; conflict management only realigns the divergence enough to render the opposing forces less diametrically opposite or damaging to each other" (Folberg and Taylor 1984, 25).

There might be certain kinds of proposed agreements that may well be worth resisting. In such cases, antagonistic linkages might be the optimal route to take until, and unless, the agreement can be better crafted to meet the desires of all the stakeholders. Nevertheless, there are clearly some parties in a negotiation for whom there is no zone of possible agreement. When establishing player linkage, an appreciation of this dynamic is essential. The following sections present the key claims of my argument and synthesize the evidence from the case studies presented in part 2.

Player Linkage

The term *player linkage* can be used in various connotations depending on the scale of the analysis. Here I have tried to focus on the player linkage at the level of institutional alliances. In particular, I have explored alliances between ENGOs and native communities, given the usual articulation of resistance movements to mining in environmental terms. This focus also questions the common assumption that native peoples have some inherent environmental proclivities.

There are two separate but related claims that I am making in this regard. The first claim questions the role of NGOs as a source of empowerment, and hence resistance formation, among native communities. The second pertains to the essential ingredients for any constructive alliance between native peoples and environmentalists. To better understand these claims, it may be instructive to look at various perceptions of linkages and which are, in fact, supported by the evidence. Figure 9.1 shows a model of player linkage that reflects the common perception that indigenous people are empowered by civil society through knowledge transfer while providing environmentalists with traditional knowledge about ecosystems. I am referring to this as the "resource wars" model that is espoused by most activists. However, the evidence from my case analysis challenges many of the key attributes of this model.

The resource wars model is largely predicated on notions of resource dependency and presumes that indigenous communities are deficient in certain essential resources needed to form resistance. Knowledge about environmental harm is often presented as the key missing link for resistance formation by many of the key proponents of this model, who argue that NGOs and indigenous people have an epistemic relationship. At the same time, this model, which often ensues from the activist world, also

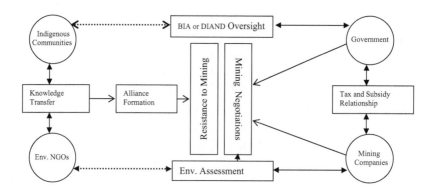

Figure 9.1

The "resource wars" model of player linkage for mining development.
Filled arrows indicate transfer material; lined arrows indicate progression
to a new step in the process; dotted lines represent an interaction that
may have repercussions on the negotiations in certain cases,
depending on how the negotiations unfold.

configures mining companies and governments as allies who have a mutually advantageous relationship based on tax revenues. The government can collect such tax revenues from the government, as well as certain subsidies that the government often gives to primary industries to promote economic development.

Compelling as this model may seem to many activists and social critics, the empirical evidence from my cases does not support many of its features. First, in all four cases, I found little evidence to support any substantive knowledge transfer taking place from the NGOs to the indigenous communities. Much of the information concerning environmental impact was directly collected by the tribes through either governmental channels or through their own initiatives to hire particular consultants and environmental specialists. Second, the texture of the alliances, if any, that formed in the cases was not one of unified resistance against a common foe but rather independent action taken by indigenous groups and environmentalists on their own. The only case of more institutionally organized alliance formation was observed in the Crandon case (U2), and here too the indigenous communities most effectively resisted through individual regulatory initiatives. Finally, the evidence in my cases *does* support a strong relationship between mining companies and various tiers of government.

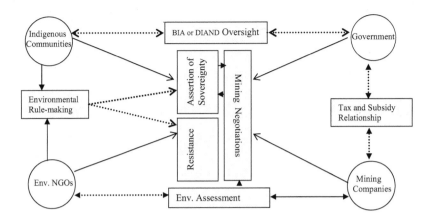

Figure 9.2
The "sovereignty is first" model of player linkage in mining development.

However, this too is not bilateral by any means, as activist groups often propose in their campaign literature. Any collaborative efforts are presented through the mining development negotiation process. With the exception of the Black Mesa case (UI), this process was fairly transparent in both the United States and Canada.[3] Even at Black Mesa, the historically surreptitious behavior of the government and Peabody Coal is now widely acknowledged by the government, and the renewal of the permit in 1990 was fairly transparent.

The case analysis reveals that the presumed natural alliances between NGOs and indigenous communities are more illusory than initially thought. While there is potential for alliance formation, the basis for such alliances is usually not knowledge transfer. Moreover, alliance formation is not an essential prerequisite for resistance formation, nor is resistance channeled through NGOs per se. Tribal decision making regarding environmental issues in North America is in fact much more sophisticated than the resource war model. Figure 9.2 shows my model of player linkage as supported by the evidence in the cases.

In this model the key difference is that resistance is not a monolithic outcome on the part of the indigenous communities. The primary stake for indigenous communities is an assertion of their sovereignty, which can sometimes manifest itself as resistance movements to development ventures, such as mining. This was observed in both the Wisconsin and Newfoundland cases (u2 and c2). Environmental issues are a means by which tribes may want to assert their sovereignty but that should not necessarily mean that the underlying values are in synch with the NGOs. Indeed, the only form of environmental alliance building between NGOs and indigenous communities has been predicated on this acknowledgment of native self-determination. In practical terms, the relevant field of engagement that has worked well for these two groups is environmental rule making. NGOs have channeled their alliance-building efforts through the support for tribal environmental laws (tribal primacy or treatment-as-a-state rule making).

Another notable feature of figure 9.2 is the arrows leading from the "assertion of sovereignty" field to the mining negotiations. This connection illustrates the empirical observation that mining negotiations within federalist states can also reconcile concerns of native sovereignty if they are appropriately undertaken by the government and the companies. The Saskatchewan case (c1) illustrates such an interaction, which has resulted in a relatively successful mining venture. In the Saskatchewan case the sense of sovereignty of the bands was reinforced by the mining company through various forums such as the Athabasca Working Group—a means of direct involvement of top management with the tribal negotiators (including the appointment of a tribal leader to the board of the company). The failure of environmentalists to garner native support in Saskatchewan, despite a history of deleterious mining activity, showed how native communities were able to discern the lack of legitimacy urban environmentalists often have when advocating preservation in remote areas.

In the Wisconsin case (u1), where constructive alliances were observed, the axis of alliance formation was not environmentalism but treaty rights. It is also important to note that in this case the natives initiated the protests without necessarily being galvanized by the NGOs. Alliances did form later on, but they were brought about through the Midwest Treaty Network rather than by a particular environmentalist agenda.

Apart from appreciating the limitations of native-NGO alliances and the ingredients for making such alliances productive, I have also tried to recognize the negative effects of certain misconceived alliances. This aspect of my player-linkage claim is exemplified by the Black Mesa case, where environmentalists allied themselves with certain elderly Navajo residents in a disputed land area and diluted the efficacy of their claims while also antagonizing the neighboring Hopi tribe. The environmental activists, despite their good intentions, tried to form alliances with Navajo resistors by presenting the mining company as a common foe. However, in this regard they circumvented layers of tribal authority and due process and approached the issue with a presumption that the tribal authorities and the government authorities were beholden to mining interests. Thus, their rhetoric was targeted at discrediting tribal leadership and pitching one tribe against the other. The lesson in alliance formation or player linkage is to appreciate the difference in BATNAs between parties before forming alliances.[4] In other words, the opportunity costs for various stakeholders are quite different, and the way in which they present issues in the negotiation process or as a resistance movement are consequentially different and have a strong bearing on the outcome.

Issue Linkage

While alliance formation can have a significant impact on the way parties organize themselves and the degree of power that they can leverage, the linkage of issues plays a pivotal role in determining the zone of possible agreement. My analysis, once again, does not seek to assume that a larger zone of agreement is necessarily good; rather, it seeks to understand how the linkage of issues can help or hinder the attainment of the ultimate objectives for each stakeholder.

The three key issues that were conceivably at stake for the indigenous communities (though not to the same degree in each case) were land rights, financial benefits (employment and royalties), and environmental protection. The way in which each of these issues was linked to the mining development negotiations, and to each other, determined the degree of resistance from the community as well as the prevalence of any resistance movement. While negotiation processes ostensibly present issues collectively, that does not necessarily mean that the issues are linked. Formal issue linkage requires parties to consciously use issues for bargaining, contingency, and commitment.

Earlier in this chapter, I briefly discussed how linkages could be synergistic or antagonistic, depending on whether they increased or decreased the zone of agreement. With regard to issue linkage, it is also important in this context to consider *competitive* versus *reciprocal* linkages (Watkins and Passow 1996).

Competitive linkage occurs when agreement in one negotiation precludes agreement in other linked negotiations. While competitive linkage is often operationalized in the context of bidding contracts for small businesses, it can be a useful frame of reference within the context of development ventures. Mining companies have very little leverage about where they establish a mine, since many of their decisions are based on geology. They do not have many options for site location, as do manufacturing businesses. Hence, they are not really in a position to establish competitive linkages among communities. However, communities may, in certain cases, have the option to choose between different development options. For example, a competitive linkage may be made between mining and tourism within the context of a development plan.

Nevertheless, the more prevalent form of linkage within the context of indigenous communities in remote areas, where mining concerns are most prevalent, is reciprocal linkage. Often, competitive linkages are not even an issue because there may not even be a competing development alternative. The alternative is often a status quo (which in certain cases may also be more desirable). Reciprocal linkage implies that agreement must be reached in all issue areas in order to gain an overall agreement.

How issues are linked, and by whom, are both key determinants of resistance formation and prevalence. For example, issue linkage was a salient factor in the failure of environmentalists to galvanize support across both Hopi and Navajo tribes (which are in fact mutual adversaries on most issues but relatively united when it comes to positions on mining). The environmental groups often caused serious divisions within the community, and by posturing nonsubstantive linkages between mining, the ecology, and territorial disputes, they reduced the credibility and legitimacy of their own cause, as well as those of the land disputants. However, cross-case comparison revealed that the linkage of land claims to the mining negotiations in the case of the Innu and the Inuit made sense since there was no treaty settlement in the area. This was also supported by the peripheral Raglan and Red Dog cases, which are heralded by the mining industry because there are existing land agreements in place (the Alaskan Native Claims Settlement Act and the James Bay and Northern Quebec Agreement, respectively). However, in the case of the Navajo and the Hopi land dispute the linkage was not substantive since the decision regarding the allocation of Hopi territory was made by the federal government and conspiracy theories linking Peabody to the Hopi did not hold ground, particularly when articulated in an environmental framework.

The linkage of financial concerns to project development may seem fairly obvious to some economic observers. However, there were clearly different approaches to internalize financial considerations within the negotiation process and their relative impact on the tribe's decisions. In the Saskatchewan case, revenue sharing was a key issue that sparked resistance from Chief Dantouze and led to his resignation from the federal/provincial uranium review panel. Environmental groups attempted to link the resignation to environmental concerns but were not able to garner support on this basis. The mining company distanced itself from the revenue sharing negotiations and let the government deal with the political concerns of certain tribal leaders while focusing on the community consultation process through the Athabasca Working Group. In the Wisconsin case, financial remuneration was dismissed by the tribe, which had an uncompromising resistance to mining. While a tribal leader briefly accepted some monetary compensation for exploration rights, the check was torn up at a tribal council meeting, and no further financial offers were entertained. In this case, the money was perceived by the tribal members as a sort of bribe because Exxon, the original owner of the project, had not interacted positively with the community and had not conducted prior consultations. This had poisoned the views of the tribe toward mining prospects, so such a sudden financial overture thus appeared contrived and insincere.

Within financial linkages, employment guarantees are often used as a development incentive by mining ventures. In the Saskatchewan case, the mining company offered employment targets and a plan to achieve them to the tribal leadership. This worked well but is not a necessary prerequisite to a workable agreement. At the Raglan mine, employment was de-linked from the negotiation process and still a workable agreement was achieved.

The Canadian experience of direct bilateral negotiations between the tribe and the company for impact-benefit agreements in the Labrador case alongside a supervisory panel process was able to deescalate the conflict. Therefore, even though the resistance to mining in the Labrador case was just as pronounced, the government was able to prevent the communities from walking away from the negotiating table. The three-track process, which may initially seem somewhat inefficient, actually worked well in allowing for negotiations to continue—linkage between land claims, mining, and environmental harm was made, but the issues were not confounded.

From another perspective, the constructive ENGO-native alliance in

Wisconsin was exemplified by the fact that the ENGOs articulated their struggle purely in terms of treaty rights and acknowledged that if the tribes decided to go ahead with mining they would respect their decision. Moreover, they articulated their opposition by lobbying for tribes to get treatment-as-state environmental regulations, thereby reinforcing a sense of sovereignty for the tribes.

The competitive linkages were not developed by any of the stakeholders in each of the cases. This is an area of further inquiry in other case studies where clear development options are presented before tribal communities. Indeed, for ENGOs seeking a constructive role in indigenous development planning and lasting alliances, this may be an area to explore further. It is not enough to suggest competitive alternatives to mining but to be able to present them with analyses that can be useful in decision making.

Toward a Typography of Environmental Resistance among Indigenous Communities

"We must move away from the sterile question of whether efforts to cope with ecological problems erode or bolster some reified conception of sovereignty to the more interesting question of how such efforts lead to a reconfiguration of political space" (Litfin 1998, 2).

Following this advice from Karen Litfin in her volume *The Greening of Sovereignty in World Politics*, I focus on the reconfiguration of political space. The phenomenon of environmental resistance on the part of indigenous communities exists because of a fundamental disconnect between the perception of goals between stakeholders as played out in their respective interactions, rather than differences in perceptions of the technical environmental impact of mining. This is manifest in strategic alliances, which, due to misplaced issue linkage, often exacerbate divisions rather than generate consensus among the communities. Figure 9.3 shows a typography of the three key stakeholders with reference to their goals—a static corollary for what is at stake for each stakeholder. The layout should be considered a conceptual map rather than a Cartesian plane. This diagram is only meant to present a two-dimensional view of outcomes, and the underlying power dynamics discussed in the earlier part of this chapter lead to this ultimate outcome. From a prescriptive standpoint, a more reciprocal view of power as developed by Emerson (1962), and exemplified in much of the contemporary dispute resolution literature, is needed. It is possible to

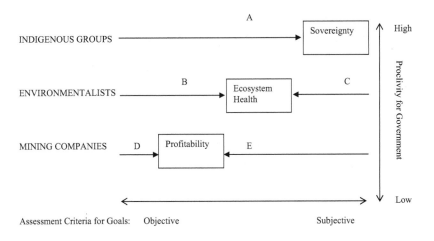

Figure 9.3
The general typography of resistance formation.

move beyond zero-sum views of power and to focus on ways in which specific needs and resources of each stakeholder can be negotiated. This process requires an appreciation for how interdependence can allow parties to mutually gain power.

The rectangular boxes positioned horizontally along a continuum of assessment criteria, ranging from objective to subjective, represent the goals for each stakeholder. I am using these terms (objective and subjective) in the classical sense, where the former implies a relative unity of measurement parameters, whereas the latter implies multiple measurement parameters. This range is meant to indicate the degree to which the assessment criteria can have multiple interpretations and also takes into account the perennial tension between the constructivist notions (the subjective end of the spectrum) and realist notions of discrete data and empirical observation (the objective end of the spectrum).

The primary goal of mining companies—profitability—is assessed in high realist currency and thus is near the objective end of the spectrum. However, it is important to note that here too there are some important subjective issues at play regarding how to account for one's profits—therefore, the companies' goal rectangle is not at the extreme end of the range (hence arrow D). Environmental goals rely on objective criteria such as scientific studies but also have an important normative dimension based on judgments about consumerism and social justice, hence they are somewhere in the middle. The primary goal of indigenous groups—sovereignty—is operationalized through highly subjective assessment criteria and hence it is on the other end of the spectrum.

The more interesting attribute of this diagram's features is the arrows that depict predominant strategies for reaching the desired goals. The length of the arrow indicates the general prevalence of the strategy and the direction indicates the part of the spectrum toward which that particular strategy is inclined. However, in this analysis it is important to keep in mind that attaining the full measure of the goal in question requires an application of both arrows. In comparing the situation of the goals across stakeholders, these arrows can be considered vectors, and thus a difference in direction indicates a subtraction *across* stakeholders of total efficacy where a similar direction indicates a reinforcement of strategy.

Arrow A indicates the overwhelming desire for indigenous groups to attain sovereignty. This is the frame of reference for this analysis (hence the single arrow leading to it) since there is so much unanimity among indigenous communities about achieving this goal. There is only one arrow here also because achieving sovereignty is not predicated on a balance between different approaches, as is the case with the other two goals.

Arrow B has the same direction as A and refers to those issue areas whose strategic use can indeed lead to sovereignty as well as ecosystem health. This refers to initiatives such as the Midwest Treaty Network in the Crandon case or the role of environmental activists such as Larry Innes in the Voisey's Bay case. This arrow also embodies the normative attributes of environmentalism that advocate small-scale economies (Schumacher 1973) that are often congruent with native aspirations for sovereignty.

However, the goal of ecosystem health is situated in a place on the typography that also requires certain actions that undermine native sovereignty (Arrow C). These are the issue areas that can lead to tensions between natives and nonnatives, such as the Makah whaling controversy, or issues that were raised in the Saskatchewan uranium mining case.

Arrow D reflects those practices in the mining industry that support indigenous sovereignty through employment and self-sufficiency and that can be effectively harnessed, as reflected in the Saskatchewan case and, to some degree, in the Black Mesa case. However, the profitability goal of mining companies is often directly incongruent to the sovereignty vector A. This is related most acutely to the issue of royalties and land claims. As we saw in our discussion of even the most widely acclaimed indigenous mining agreements such as the Red Dog case, there was a history of litigation and an initial attempt to get title to the property.

In the vertical dimension, I have aligned the cases along a continuum of a "proclivity for government involvement." The government is a stakeholder with multiple goals that are truly embedded across both dimensions. The vertical scale is meant to indicate what degree of government involvement each of the three stakeholders prefers.

Indigenous groups are at the top here because they are in fact aspiring for their own government and hence have a very strong proclivity at that level. There is also the love-hate relationship that they have with the federal government and the difference between self-determination and termination that we have already discussed. Environmental groups certainly want government involvement at some level to regulate pollution, but they are also skeptical about centralized authority and are therefore in the middle again. Mining companies have the least proclivity for government involvement, as is to be expected of a private corporation; hence, they are at the bottom of the spectrum. However, in terms of power dynamics, they are clearly not at the bottom of the spectrum, and power is a central locus of theory development in this context.

Configuring Capacity: Beyond the Development Planning Paradigm

To understand why resistance arises, or, conversely, why it may not arise despite provocative circumstances, I am arguing for an approach that transcends scientific or economic determinism about environmental factors in understanding tribal resistance. Rather, my argument focuses on the effectuation of sovereignty as the prime frame of reference for understanding contemporary resistance movements among native communities in North America. However, sovereignty is a somewhat amorphous term that needs further grounding:

> Sovereignty is an especially odd phenomenon. Everyone seems to want it. Those who claim to know it all tell us that sovereignty is just what we have, although some may have more of it than others. It seems to have been around for as long as anyone can remember. Even so, for such an established fact of life, and for such a cherished ambition, there is a disconcerting uncertainty as to what it is exactly, or where it is to be

found, or who has it and who does not, or where it came from in the first place, let alone what is happening to it now. (Walker 1996, 16)

Despite its elusive nature, sovereignty is still a very real concept for indigenous people and hence must be understood. Native groups in the United States and Canada (at least), are at a critical juncture in history that is often not fully appreciated by planners and corporate negotiators involved in development ventures. Nonnative stakeholders tend to focus on microlevel impact concerns or simplistic economic arrangements in order to placate many tribal communities. However, I argue that, at present, tribal communities are evaluating development projects and processes with the purpose of nation-building in mind. They are focusing on long-term viability of their communities with the power to decide upon, or plan, projects on their own. Native people are acutely aware of their status of anachronistic dependency in a postcolonial world and are determined to change their fortunes by invoking the most cherished democratic ideal of self-determination. However, self-determination is perhaps just as ambiguous a concept as "sovereignty" or "inherent right" (as the Canadians like to state it), and such grand declarations have essential prerequisites for realization. Native communities are most concerned at present with developing a capacity to build institutions and power structures that further their goals of governance.

The use of the word *capacity* in this context is perhaps somewhat reminiscent of development discourse and the frequent exhortation from the World Bank and other agencies to build capacity. However, my argument is not so much about building capacity as it is about configuring capacity. The difference is critically important, since my cases are based in countries that are considered developed by all socioeconomic indicators. Building infrastructure and providing for basic needs of native communities has been the preoccupation of government institutions in the United States and Canada for much of the twentieth century. There are clearly abundant resources within both these countries to achieve these aims and to even delegate these resources to local tribal governments. However, the problem remains that in the long term such communities are often not able to sustain the outcomes of well-intentioned development planning.

Capacity building is a neutral term that implies some sort of resource transfer of either physical or social capital. However, this still begs the question of "What are we trying to build toward?" It may be instructive to

Table 9.1

Configuring Capacity: Explaining Resistance

	Capacity Building as Means	Capacity Building as Process	Capacity Building as Ends
Capacity building in indigenous civil society	Strengthen capacity of primary stakeholders to implement defined *activities*	Fostering *communication*: processes of debate, relationship building, conflict resolution, and improved ability of society to deal with its differences	*Strengthen capacity of primary stakeholders to participate in political and socioeconomic arena according to long-term objectives defined by them*
Capacity building in NGO	Strengthen organization to perform specified *activities* (one of which may be to build capacity among primary stakeholders)	Process of reflection, leadership, inspiration, adaptation and search for greater *coherence* between NGO mission, structure, and activities	Strengthen NGO to survive and fulfill its *mission* as defined by the organization

Source: Adapted from Eade 1997.
Note: Italicized text indicates the focus of my argument.

try to understand how capacity can be *configured* instead. Table 9.1 shows the various dimensions of capacity-building approaches that Oxfam has identified in its activities around the world. In this chart, my argument about resistance is articulated in the italicized text.

In essence, the explanation of why resistance may arise in certain cases and not in others is predicated on whether the issues and the stakeholders who articulate them are able to strengthen the capacity of tribes to realize long-term objectives as defined by them. Currently, tribes are trying to configure attempts to build their capacity toward governance, and this aim is an end in itself, rather than a means to an end, as much of the environment and development literature may presume. In fact, environmental criteria are means to an end in this context, which is why there is often a disconnect between NGOs and indigenous communities during attempts at alliance formation. Furthermore, from an operational perspective, NGOs are often constrained by their agenda or mission, which is why Oxfam has delineated separate categories for NGOs and civil society. Often these two terms (NGOs and civil society) are used interchangeably, but it is important to keep in mind that civil society refers to one of three spheres that constitute a democratic society, alongside the state and the market. Civil society is the sphere in which social movements become organized. NGOs may emanate from activities within civil society, but their focus tends to be much more narrow — hence the term *special interests* may often be applied to them.

Within the literature on capacity building there is a tendency to focus on meso-level strategies such as strengthening of individual organizations and sectors, or microlevel functions such as human resource development. However, native people in North America are more interested in macrolevel capacity configuration toward nation building and governance.[5] For this purpose, the locus of reform needs to be the negotiating process through which development contracts are undertaken. Such changes in processes beyond the material attributes of capacity building have interesting parallels in the political economy literature as well. For example, Arturo Escobar (1995), in his seminal work *Encountering Development*, presents a compelling argument for how technical training and classic capacity-building efforts failed to improve conditions for the trainees or capacitados in Colombia. Escobar argues that the exiting power structures, in effect, prevented a realization of appropriate development trajectories.

Native people appreciate that the power to decide their own development trajectories is more important than any particular short-term agenda. Their resistance to particular projects is thus inextricably connected to the perception of power that a certain process may engender.

Perceptions of Power and Resistance among Native People

"Indigenous people shall be people living in countries which have populations composed of different ethnic or racial groups who are descendents of the earliest populations which survive in the area, and *who do not, as a group, control the national government of the countries within which they live*" (Anaya 1996, 47). This definition of indigenous peoples, which was arrived at by a consensus process involving hundreds of indigenous representatives from around the world, reveals a seminal feature of indigenous politics and its relation to the kinds of resistance movements described in this book. Contemporary indigenous societies define themselves in terms of their lack of control and, consequentially, in terms of a struggle for certain basic rights that may often take the form of environmental resistance movements. The formulation of any meaningful theory that would explain the dynamics of environmental resistance in indigenous communities must first come to grips with the self-actualization of power.

At a general level, this approach was initially discussed by Emerson (1962) and further developed by Lukes (1975) and Gaventa (1980). In the context of Native American development, this theory is particularly compelling given the historical dependency of tribes on natural resources, which were then appropriated by the government. Stated quite simply, Emerson's theory presumes that "the power of A over B is equal to, and based upon, the dependence of B upon A." Furthermore, B's dependence on A is (1) directly proportional to the importance B places on the goals (mediated) by A and (2) is inversely proportional to the availability of these goals to B outside the A-B relationship.[6] While this may appear to be a rather self-evident and commonsense theory, it has some profound implications.

As W. Richard Scott (1998) has pointed out, Emerson's work leads us to think of power not as some "generalized capacity but as a function of specific needs and resources that can vary from one exchange partner to another" (110). Thus, it is possible for a government organization to have relatively little power with respect to one company and much greater power over a tribe. This approach also avoids a zero-sum view of power where it is assumed that one actor gains power at the expense of another. Instead, it is possible for actors to mutually gain power by increasing interdependence (see Pfeffer 1992; Pfeffer and Salanick 1978). Differences in perceived bargaining power can often lead to disillusionment with the process of negotiation. Indeed, there is sometimes a perception that the mere process of negotiation is perhaps a concession to the other side. This has been the case in many ecological disputes where value systems may be at stake (Crowfoot and Wondolleck 1990). Developing and refining a non-zero-sum view of power is thus critically important to dispute resolution, particularly concerning environmental matters.

As we have seen throughout the case analysis thus far, the key demand that surfaced, amidst the environmental tenor of the debate, in all the negotiations and protests from the indigenous groups was predicated on a strong sense of self-determination — which would necessitate the power to make decisions without external involvement. Negotiating within the confines of the Westphalian nation-state model, the tribes have also repeatedly used terms such as *sovereignty, control*, and *self-determination*. At the same time, they do not want to be divorced from the superstate structure — hence the dilemma and the resulting paradox of their movement. Even the Innu, who had at one point advocated non-Canadian citizenship, have reconciled to and embraced Canadian citizenship. In the United States, there is a common aphorism among native people that the distance between self-determination and termination is only a few letters (Ambler 1990).

A reconciliation of these seemingly paradoxical stances on power is offered by the psychologist Edward Deci (1980) in his work, *The Psychology of Self-Determination*. Deci advises readers to keep in mind the difference between control and self-determination. Control is outcome-oriented and is often operationalized as being the boss, whereas self-determination means the freedom to decide for oneself. The distinction between the two terms may help us understand the demands of indigenous people vis-à-vis resource development ventures: "Being a boss or succeeding at a task (which is called being in control) will often leave people feeling self-determining, yet one need not be the boss, or succeed, in order to feel self-determining. Further, being in control does not guarantee self-determination, for people often feel trapped in positions of control. . . . One may at times prefer to be a passenger than to be the driver, even though the driver has more control" (Deci 1980, 112).

Another way to think about this imponderable is to consider the two different kinds of freedom that political philosophers often allude to and anthropologists have also used in approaching the study of culture and power. Westcott (1988) believes that there is a dialectical process occurring in all cultures between negative freedom (freedom from) and positive freedom (freedom to), which is spurred by five factors: (1) some external as well as internal strife, contention, or dissatisfaction; (2) a perception of incompleteness and some effort to cope with it; (3) opportunities for risk taking; (4) anticipation of change; (5) aloneness within a matrix of relationships. All these factors are clearly present in resource development decisions confronting native peoples.

In exploring theories of power to explain resistance, it is important to differentiate between subjectivist notions of power, which imply the question of who governs, and economic notions of power, which ask the question of how much a party is able to accomplish.[7] Goran Therborn differentiates the two as "power over" versus "power to." He goes on to differentiate further between utilitarian[8] and sociological approaches[9] to power within an economic framework. "Although they can be said to share a common approach to power, inspired by liberal economics, concentrating as they do on nonconflictual 'power to,' the two main variants of the economic approach also show differences that are by no means insignificant. In the sociological variant, power is generated and operates in social relationships, whereas in the utilitarian conception it is basically a nonrelational asset."[10]

Kenneth Boulding (1989) also offers a useful framework to understand perceptions of power when he describes the linkage between power and the economic concept of possibility boundaries, which divide the total set of future possibilities (or plans) into those that can be implemented and those that cannot. More important, Boulding develops the notion of "integrative power," which he defines as "an aspect of productive power that involves capacity to build organizations . . . to bind people together and to develop legitimacy." At one level, native decisions to resist mining and other development projects appear to be about this aspect of power. The argument can be made that in order to reify sovereignty native people are striving for integrative power in order to build their institutions. However, my case analyses reveal that in fact this manifestation of power is embedded in a more basic proclivity for subjectivist power—where who governs is often more important than what is achieved. Environmental issues are usually invoked if they are a means for developing a sense of legitimacy for achieving subjectivist power within the larger federalist state.

These contending views of power are also reflected in the international legal status of indigenous peoples. Describing this ambivalence toward indigenous peoples, as well as the environment, Nico Schrijver (1997), writes in *Sovereignty over Natural Resources*: "States are increasingly accountable, also at an international level, for the way they manage their natural wealth and resources, but for the time being indigenous peoples, humankind and the environment as such are *objects* rather than *subjects* of international law" (Schrijver 1997, 390). Therefore, indigenous people feel that they are often used as a means to an end, which again reinforces the need for self-determination.

There is thus a perception of power differentials at work, which in turn leads to resistance. The preceding discussion of power was about what is desired. The next step is to understand what forms of power are available to native people, and how the disconnect between desired power and avail-

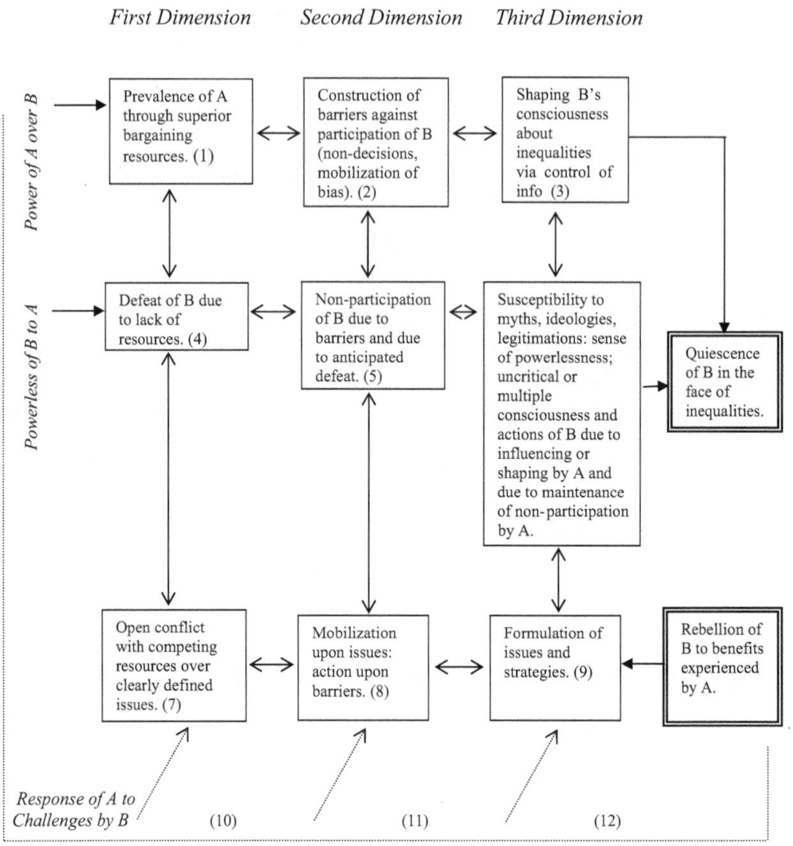

Figure 9.4

Various dimensions of power. (Adapted from Gaventa 1980)

able power can lead to resistance. Gaventa (1980), in his detailed study of social movements in the Appalachian coal mining region, has developed a compelling framework for looking at power and resistance that may be instructive in the next phase of this analysis. Unlike many other social scientists who have studied power and social resistance, Gaventa began with the premise of not why resistance occurs but rather why and when resistance may not occur in the face of gross inequalities and perceived injustices. The typology of power that he has developed building on Lukes (1975) is presented in figure 9.4.

However, I do not fully concur with Gaventa's argument that the ab-

Table 9.2

Scott's Typology of Domination and Resistance

	Material Domination	Status Domination	Ideological Domination
Practices of domination	Appropriation of grain, taxes, labor, etc.	Humiliation, disprivilege, insults, assaults on dignity	Justification by ruling groups for subjugation
Forms of public declared resistance	Petitions, demonstrations, boycotts, strikes, land invasions, and open revolts	Public assertion of worth by gesture, dress, speech, and/or open desecration of status symbols of the dominant	Public counter-ideologies propagating equality, revolution, or negating the ruling ideology
Forms of disguised, low-profile, undisclosed resistance, infrapolitics	Everyday forms of resistance — e.g., poaching, squatting, desertion, evasion, foot-dragging	Hidden transcripts of anger, aggression, and disguised discourses of dignity — e.g., rituals of aggression, tales of revenge, use of carnival symbolism, gossip, rumor, creation of autonomous social space for assertion of dignity	Development of dissident sub-cultures — e.g., prevalence of millennial religions

sence of resistance is caused by a third dimension of power that "shapes their consciousness" and leads to quiescence (box 3 in fig. 9.4). My case analysis reveals a remarkable ability of communities to be guided by their own imperatives. Indigenous communities have repeatedly shown their resilience against assimilation. I am inclined to believe that the third dimension of power, and hence quiescence, is more about strategy than powerlessness.

Let us now turn to how the misperception of powerlessness can translate into behavior at the negotiating table or the emergence of resistance. In his landmark treatise *Domination and the Arts of Resistance*, James Scott reminds us that the adage to "speak truth" to power does not hold true for much of what is observed in social movements. All too often there are hidden transcripts of resistance that can be neglected in cursory analysis. Scott urges us to look at the *infrapolitics* that may exist in a society (table 9.2). By this he means the "cultural and structural underpinning" of the more visible political action on which our attention has generally been focused:

> The bond between domination and appropriation means that it is impossible to separate the ideas and symbolism of subordination from a process of material exploitation. In exactly the same fashion, it is impossible to separate veiled symbolic resistance to the ideas of domination from the practical struggles to thwart or mitigate exploitation. The hidden transcript is not just behind-the-scenes griping and grumbling, it is enacted in a host of down-to-earth, low profile stratagems designed to minimize appropriation. (J. Scott 1990, 188)

Following Scott's theory, Ramachandra Guha, in his seminal study of the Chipko forest movement in India's Himalayan region,[11] urges us to distinguish "between the private face of Chipko, which is that of a quintessentially peasant movement, and its public profile as one of the most celebrated environmental movements in the world" (Guha 2000, 178). The revised edition of Guha's book (2000) also cites examples of various subsequent academic works published in the West that have romanticized the movement beyond its real intent and cautions intellectuals from selectively appropriating various dimensions of case studies such as the Chipko movement. Revisionist critics of the movement have argued that despite all its noble aspirations for ecological preservation alongside regional control, the movement in fact led to forest protection regulations that gave even less control over resource management to the local inhabitants (for example, see Mitra 1993). However, given the limited resource base of the movement, such policy ramifications are more illustrative of the failure of government to appreciate and understand the movement's demands than of a failure of the movement itself. Guha responds soulfully to such detractors: "The lack of sympathy is manifest, and unfortunate. This is a classic case of projection of the hopes of the middle class intellectual onto the people . . . the intellectual seeks total, systemic change, but the task of bringing this about is always left to others" (2000, 11).

Like the admirers and detractors of the Chipko movement, the various constituencies that follow native struggles against mining also have a propensity to swing either way, and the aim of this work is to provide an alternative means of evaluating options.

Chapter 10

Planning for Sustainable Development

Some Advice for Stakeholders

"It seems that resistance is a mirror image of planning. Every techno-environmental change project has both costs and benefits; in some cases, these are represented in the form of cost/benefit ratios. Resisters tend to focus upon the costs of a project, while planners tend to emphasize its benefits. Resistance begins with the identification of threats posed by a project and planning begins with the identification of needs."[1]

It is precisely the kinds of views about planning and resistance noted above by Schweri and van Willigen (in Millsap 1984, 134) that prompted me to pursue this book. Indeed, the internalization of resistance efforts within the planning process is essential in the new wave of planning toward sustainability (see Kenny and Meadowcroft 1999; Dobson 1999a). However, such a process is undoubtedly much more complex, and implementing it requires a fundamental shift in the way stakeholders interact with each other. In this final chapter, I will try to present some of the lessons learned from the cases in question, with particular reference to any policy differences between Canada and the United States which provide a mutual base for lesson drawing.[2]

Indigenous policy posits a challenge to policy makers because acceding to native demands for greater self-determination in the minds of many politicians has the propensity to generate anarchy, which is of course anathema to the modern nation-state. This challenge resurrects the concerns that were raised more than a century ago by the British philosopher Matthew Arnold in his seminal work, *Culture and Anarchy*.

Anarchy to Arnold was embodied in excessive materialism—what he contemptuously refers to in one of his chapters as "Doing As One Likes"

— and, most profoundly, in what he considered the "subversive pluralism" to which he felt his society had surrendered. This pluralism, for Arnold, meant the disintegration of a sense of shared, permanent values and a corresponding collapse of cultural standards.[3]

Around the same time thousands of miles and traditions away indigenous peoples in the Americas were thinking along similar lines.[4] Indians also shaped their politics and their statecraft around maintaining a community and a continuity of cultural values. It is important to keep in mind that they too were deeply suspicious of any convenient pluralism, and they believed, no less than Arnold did, that culture must maintain an orderly balance between convention and change, or else anarchy will take hold.

In trying to understand the indigenous notions of law and sovereignty and proposing resolutions to current conflicts, we can also glean some important insights from the writings of the nineteenth-century political philosopher Henry Maine, who argued that law and order, like art and culture, depend upon a sense of tradition. Maine drew his examples from across the world, most notably from the ancient tribal hamlets of India.

One aspect of Maine's argument is especially relevant to our discussion — the way in which he related tradition and authority. J. Edward Chamberlain has summarized Maine's argument as follows: "Traditions accommodate change — resistance and innovation, as well as appropriation, are their stock-in-trade. But they do not easily tolerate competition. Authority, on the other hand, thrives on competition and is often quite comfortable with contingent power relationships, provided only that boundaries are clearly established. Traditions, for their part, always want the field to themselves, though they accept — indeed sometimes even encourage — periodic changes in boundaries."[5]

That is why many post-Renaissance European societies could strictly separate the traditions of church and state at the same time as they continued to acknowledge contingencies of secular and sacred authority within each tradition. However, Chamberlain, along with numerous other scholars of indigenous history and politics, then makes a rather astounding and erroneous leap by asserting that for Indians "the contingencies of authority were always negotiable. Traditions, on the other hand, could never be contingent, and therefore could never be negotiated. Coherence and continuity were absolutes threatened more by pluralism than by power."[6]

While this perception concerning the negotiability of authority may well be true during the sixteenth and seventeenth century, that is certainly not the case at present. Indeed, authority as manifest in the tribal insistence on self-governance is the unequivocal demand in all our case analyses. The issue at hand is how do we reconcile these divergent perceptions about the environment and development amidst what is fundamentally a continuing clash of cultures.

The most violent conflicts in human history are ostensibly generated by a perception of difference that tends to be based on lines of ethnic differentiation. Before looking at specific lessons and recommendations for stakeholders, it may be useful to look at cases where ethnic differences have existed with the emergence of violent conflicts and compare those cases with other instances of ethnic difference in societies where conflict has not been manifest in any violence. Louis Kriesberg (1998) presents such a comparison of conflicts in the former Yugoslavia and compares it to the successful attempts of deescalating destructive conflict in Quebec. He presents a matrix of policies that can successively lead to de-escalation of conflict as shown in table 10.1.

A major problem with contemporary conflicts involving indigenous groups is that indigenous people feel that they are at stage E of the old conflict between the natives, whereas the government and industry, while acknowledging past issues, are framing their interactions with the indigenous groups vis-à-vis mining agreements more in terms of the present-day business contract, and working on stage A and B.

Norman Dale, in his insightful analysis of a resource planning conflict in the Queen Charlotte Islands of British Columbia (or Haida Gwaii, to the natives), also alludes to this fundamental issue of stages. Quoting from Edward Said's work *Beginnings*, Dale points out that "the point at which a storyteller chooses to begin is the first step in the intentional construction of meaning."[7] In his case, as with most cases involving native communities, the Haida begin their story much earlier than the nonnatives. Many of the preferred goals stipulated in this table are dependent on a degree of dispassionate involvement on the part of stakeholders, with an appreciation for all the processes at each stage that are needed to prevent escalation of conflict.

Contested Visions of Indigenous Development in the United States and Canada

Efforts at drawing lessons between the Canadian and U.S. experiences with indigenous policy have been few and far between. While both policies emanate from a common source, namely the Royal Proclamation of 1763,

Table 10.1

Policies to Prevent Destructive Conflicts

Phase	Preferred Goal				
	A: To Correct Underlying Conditions	B: To Prevent Destructive Acts	C: To Prevent Escalation	D: To End Fighting	E: To Move toward Resolution
1. Conflict emergence	Economic growth; dialogue; reduced inequality; integration, shared identity	Legitimate institutions; dialogue; conflict resolution training	Crosscutting ties; nonviolent training; unofficial exchange	—	—
2. Threat of isolated destructive acts	—	Deterrence; reassurance; external mediation or intervention; crisis management; precise policies	Noninflammatory information; limiting arms; tit-for-tat; humanitarian assistance; peacekeeping	Negotiation; reframing conflicts; confidence-building measures; mediation	Negotiation; mutual reassurance; unofficial exchanges; superordinate goals
3. Extensive destructive acts	—	—	Changing expectations of victory/defeat; intervention; constituency opposition; limiting arms	Mediation, external intervention; limiting arms; negotiation	Superordinate goals, interdependence; confidence-building measures; problem-solving workshops
4. Protracted and extensive destructive acts	—	—	—	GRIT;* problem-solving workshops; unofficial exchanges; step-by-step negotiations; constituency opposition	Acknowledging hurts; superordinate goals; no humiliation; external enemy; mutual recognition; shared identity

Source: After Kriesberg 1998.

*GRIT: Graduated Reciprocation in Tension reduction strategy (originally presented by Osgood 1962).

the policies diverged considerably because of a mutual repugnance between the governments in the nineteenth century. Legal scholar Michael
Asch reflects this divergence eloquently:

> Architects of Canadian confederation were determined to demonstrate
> their faith in the country's future by establishing a common culture that
> was based on something other than the revolutionary rhetoric of the
> American Declaration of Independence—whose phrases about "life,
> liberty and (especially) the pursuit of happiness" sounded almost as
> hokey to them as "the mother of all battles" (à la Saddam Hussein) does
> to some of us. The authority of the "monarch" along with the celebra-
> tion of the Victorian virtues of industry and thrift, seemed one good
> antidote to republican indulgence, extravagance, and anarchy; and a
> rhetoric of obedience and duty a wise part of the national discourse.
> (Asch 1997, 10)

It was thus not until the early part of the twentieth century that the
first concerted effort was made by academics on both sides of the border
to learn from each others' successes and mistakes in dealing with the common concern of indigenous policy. In 1939, the University of Toronto and
Yale University organized a seminar to discuss ways of learning from the
experiences of both countries. However, the tone of this seminar, given
the times, was decidedly assimilationist. Prof. Charles Loram, of Yale's
erstwhile Department of Race Relations, declared at the opening meeting
"that the Indian Problem was one of Acculturation" (Loram and McIlwraith 1943). The problem at present is still one of acculturation. However,
now it is becoming more a matter of how the federal government, environmentalists, and industry acculturate to indigenous concerns. Indigenous
society is clearly the most inertial of the other stakeholders (I mean that in
a neutral way) and is increasingly in a position to leverage power. Mining
negotiations are an example where this change is being played out, and
both countries are still trying to grapple with ways of most appropriately
planning for such projects in the most efficient and equitable way.

Lessons Canada Can Learn from the United States

Canadians have taken some truly monumental steps in furthering the
cause of indigenous people. The establishment of Nunavut in 1999 was

emblematic of their success. Nevertheless, there are still some areas where they may glean some lessons from their southern neighbor. In a speech before a Native American conference in Arizona, the erstwhile Canadian minister for indigenous affairs, Shirley Serafini, made a remark that sums up a key lesson for the Canadians: "sovereignty is a far more tabooed word in Canada than here in the United States. The most we like to say is 'inherent right.'"[8] She was alluding to the important historical path that U.S. indigenous policy has taken in recognizing the concept of self-government and not being embroiled in the somewhat archaic British legal regime of the sovereignty of the monarch and the primacy of Crown land. Kathy Brock describes this important distinction as follows: "American policy tended to regulate external aspects of tribal life while Canadian policy tended to extend into the internal life of tribes as well. Canadian policy was predicated on a disregard of First Nation and Métis governance while American policy was founded upon a begrudging acceptance of tribal governance."[9]

In the Crandon case (U2), this difference becomes starkly evident in the willingness of the Environmental Protection Agency against all the misgivings of the Wisconsin state legislature to encourage the Sokagoan Chippewa and the Forest County Potawatomi to form their own environmental regulations (which would of course be at least as stringent as the federal regulations). Particularly after the passage of the Indian Self-Determination and Education Assistance Act (1975) and the Indian Mineral Leasing Act (1982), the government made a conscious effort to reaffirm the nation-to-nation relationship between the U.S. government and tribes.

This brings up another important distinction between the United States and Canada that may be instructive to Canadians. The U.S. Congress has passed an enormous corpus of laws and legislation regarding Indians. While this may have in some ways made matters more cumbersome, the willingness to legislate changes and enact new statutes to deal with new concerns is something Canada has not exhibited. The Canadians tend to be more adept at megalevel changes such as the constitutional amendments in 1982 that incorporated indigenous issues within the constitution. However, in terms of economic development planning, it is often the more small-scale measures that can be most helpful. The U.S. Congress has approached the issue through a series of statutory revisions to facilitate self-government on reservations, most recently the Indian Tribal

Economic Development and Contract Encouragement Act of 1999. Under this new law, Section 81 of the U.S. Code will be amended to not require the BIA to sign off on industrial contracts. The oversight of various other government agencies vis-à-vis environmental protection will remain intact, but it will prevent any misuse of BIA authority. According to Ambler (1990), one of the most blatant examples of BIA's catering to industry rather than Indians occurred in 1980 during the uranium boom in the San Juan Basin. In this incident the BIA repeatedly tried to force Navajo families to accept a lease agreement with Mobil, despite several more lucrative bids from other companies. Subsequent legal action resulted in a federal ruling in which the judge concluded that the BIA had acted illegally and unconscionably, stating that "the BIA and Interior generally seem to have been more concerned throughout the leasing process with their relationship with Mobil than their relationship with Indian owners" (Ambler 1990, 234).

A similar concern exists in Canada with the DIAND's dual role as a department of Indian affairs and of northern development (which some would argue can be a conflict of interest). Furthermore, Canada has made important steps in Indian policy regarding *off-reserve* land claims but has been relatively inertial when it comes to *on-reserve* policy.

Thus, the U.S. government has tried to make the BIA increasingly an Indian organization over the past several decades. The budgets for both departments are comparable, though Canada, with its higher taxation rates, has a commensurately larger budget—around $2 billion for the BIA and around $3 billion for DIAND. The bureau currently has over 80 percent native employment, whereas the Canadian DIAND has less than 15 percent.[10] This difference in employment levels has an extremely important symbolic value for many tribes in the United States and is particularly important in cross-cultural negotiations such as those involved in mineral leases. The president of the National Congress of American Indians in a recent testimony before Congress quoted a frequent refrain in Indian country: "The BIA is a son-of-a-bitch, but it is OUR son-of-a-bitch!" Through Indian employment the BIA has carved a niche for itself, which may mean that it will not be an obsolescent organization, as many had perceived: "The BIA has functioned as the American embassy to Indian Country, and as a concrete symbol of the existence and continuation of a special relationship. It may be that some would like to see the end of the BIA. But if the non-Indian forces determine there is no longer a reason for the continued existence of the BIA, they may also conclude that there is no longer any reason for the continued recognition of Indian tribes."[11]

The emergence of this feeling of diplomatic association concerning the BIA is something that is missing in DIAND's experience and is an area where Canada may have some lessons to learn from the United States. In the long-run the role of the BIA and DIAND is likely to become one of an exclusive consulting agency for tribes to provide them with particular technical expertise, or perhaps in the even more remote future the organizations may take the form of a National Endowment for Native Americans.

At the level of environmental regulations and mining law, the United States and Canada are generally at par with each other. The one area where Canada can learn from U.S. experience is the enactment of a strong remediation law such as the Comprehensive Environmental Responsibility, Compensation, and Liability Act. Canadian environmentalists, particularly those working on mining issues, have frequently lamented the fact that there is no comprehensive clean-up law in Canada. Indeed, such a law is important given the huge number of mining clean-up sites in Canada. On 11 January 2000, Mining Watch Canada presented a plan for dealing with Canada's abandoned mines crisis to the eight members of cabinet most responsible for finding solutions to this issue. The plan calls for the following:

— a national inventory of sites for which the federal government carries responsibility, and incentives for the provinces to create compatible databases on sites under their jurisdiction
— physical and chemical assessments of all abandoned mines to verify hazards
— provision for resources to clean up the worst sites first with a plan to establish the priorities and more research dollars to figure out how to do this best
— and establishment of a funding mechanism to recover costs from industry to pay for cleaning up the sites. (Mining Watch Canada 1999, 2)

The clean-up issue all too often becomes a major stumbling block in contemporary mining contracts as well. Indeed, the successful Raglan agreement discussed in chapter 8 was partly a result of the mining company's offer to clean up an old asbestos mining site (this was entirely a good-will gesture, since the current company did not have any connection with the previous mining company).

Lessons the United States Can
Learn from Canada

Among modern nation-states the Canadians have shown a remarkable ability to balance cultural differences as exemplified by the "the Quebec phenomenon." On a smaller scale, the Canadian government has, of late, tried to embrace a similar stance on indigenous issues. Canada's handling of the land claims has been particularly instructive, especially given the added complexity of provincial involvement. In many ways, they have learned from their own mistakes with the reserve system and tried to follow a much more institutionally sound process of handling land claims as illustrated by the landmark Nunavut agreement of 1999. It is the success of the agreements in Saskatchewan and with Raglan (Quebec), and the agreement in principle in the Voisey's Bay case, that have allowed for conflicts to be contained. The Canadians have achieved this through an inclusive process of bringing together stakeholders and not taking sides with any particular party, unlike the unfortunate debacle in the Navajo/Hopi land dispute the U.S. government partly created by deciding on its own that certain territory was Hopi and certain territory was Navajo.

Mining agreements between indigenous groups and industry in Canada usually follow a two-track approach that has also been somewhat successful in terms of clarifying issues and avoiding destructive linkages. Such linkages were a major problem with the Black Mesa case. There is an environmental assessment process that is carried out under the Canadian Environmental Assessment Agency and a separate Impact Benefits Agreement process that is carried out between industry and the indigenous groups directly. The Impact Benefit Agreement (IBA) process arose as a voluntary effort facilitated by the federal government in the 1980s and has since then become a sort of best practice within industry. These agreements can be regional in scope or project specific depending on the context of the project. The IBA negotiations give indigenous people "the power of process," which they often feel is missing in the conventional environmental assessment process with their somewhat perfunctory hearings and town meetings. In his detailed analysis of IBAs across Canada for the National Round Table on the Environment and the Economy (another uniquely Canadian organization), Alex Kerr concludes that "the strength of IBAs appears to lie in their ability to deliver economic benefits locally, through jobs, commercial opportunities and fiscal benefits" (Kerr 2000, 12). Figure 10.1 shows the way in which the Canadian government

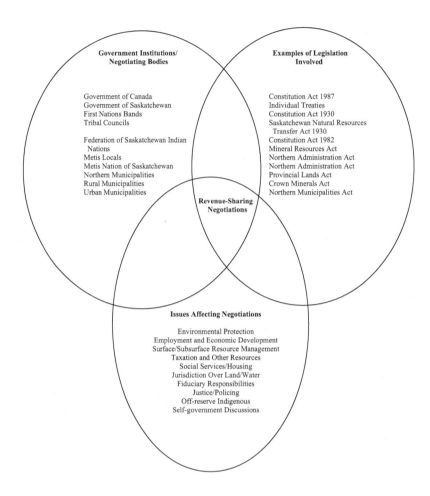

Figure 10.1
Some factors affecting revenue sharing in Canada.
(Adapted from Canadian Environmental Assessment Agency 1997)

handled the highly sensitive revenue-sharing negotiations in the Cameco case (CI).

Often there is a third parallel process of land claims agreements as well, which, as observed in the Voisey's Bay case, can be a major stumbling block for mineral negotiations. This is a much more delicate process than the IBA and the environmental assessment because in Canada it involves the federal and provincial governments and often involves overlapping claims. The most positive relationships among indigenous groups, mining companies, and First Nations have been those where the land claims were settled before going into the IBA negotiations (for example, the Saskatchewan case, the Raglan agreement, and the Musselwhite accord). The BHP Ekati Diamond mine is an example of a case where the land claim has still not been settled and the IBA has been signed and mining has commenced. However, in a review of the project, the Canadian Institute of Resource Law in Calgary concluded that "the lack of resolution of critical land and resource ownership and jurisdictional issues necessitated the creation of ad hoc mechanisms, some of which may ultimately be included in land claims agreements" (Canadian Institute of Resource Law 1997, 31).

Such ad hoc arrangements were facilitated by preexisting institutions in the Northwest Territories such as the Water Boards. These boards were created under the Northwest Territories Act as quasi-judicial tribunals "to provide for the conservation, development and utilization of waters in a manner that will provide the optimum benefit for all Canadians and for residents of the Northwest Territories in particular." Such boards are now being tested by DIAND across the northern region as a means of further devolving authority to the communities and may prove to be a useful model to emulate. Their performance thus far in the Ekati project has received positive acclaim from indigenous groups and environmentalists.

One of the reasons for the success of Canadians in land claim disputes, in particular, is the important constitutional changes of 1982. In U.S. political culture, the Constitution is a much more immutable and sacrosanct document, and the amendment process is too cumbersome for such changes to be initiated. However, such allowances in the Constitution would have been greatly beneficial to tribes that have not yet been recognized, or for large-scale land claim settlements such as the Alaska native claims settlement in the 1970s.

Despite the regalia of British and French traditions, Canada has also tried to circumvent a lot of extraneous governmental approval processes and paperwork. In 1985, Jed D. Christensen, director of the U.S. Office of Surface Mining, shocked states and tribes by trying to take $24 million from the tribes' Abandoned Mines Land accounts to reclaim high-priority, non-Indian sites in the East. Christensen did not notify the tribes of the plan or invite them to attend with the states the meeting where the reclamation was to be discussed. He claimed the money was going to waste because the tribes had failed to get congressional authorization. Christensen promised his agency would clean up the worst Indian sites anyway, using the federal funds. To the surprise of the Department of the Interior, states backed the tribes and unanimously opposed Christensen's idea, stating that they considered the proposal an "absolute travesty" and "almost criminal." The General Accounting Office (GAO) later found that the surface mining office had the legal authority to take the money without congressional action, but doing so would greatly limit the prospects for reclamation of Indian mines. Such debacles have not occurred in Canada because much of the funding is directly administered by tribes. The Native Development Corporations in the north have been generally quite successful in this regard. In the words of McGill management professor Leo Paul Dana, they have provided a "means for a socialist culture to participate in a capitalist economy" (Blunt and Warren 1996, 214–19). Unlike their Alaskan counterparts, the creation of these corporations does not preclude future land claims settlements.

The Canadians have also managed to focus specifically on mineral development and indigenous activities as a phenomenon that involves multiple stakeholders. They have done so at two levels. First, at the federal government level a special program was created in 1999 to focus on indigenous communities and nonrenewable resources development. This program compiled a detailed report presented to the National Roundtable on the Environment and the Economy, another uniquely Canadian institution, which is self-described as being "legislated by an Act of Parliament in 1994 to serve as a catalyst in identifying, explaining and promoting the principles and practices of sustainable development. Working with stakeholders across Canada, the NRTEE carries out its mandate by identifying key issues with both environmental and economic implications, fully exploring these implications, and suggesting action designed to balance economic prosperity with environmental preservation."[12]

Second, the Canadian government has established an Intergovernmental Working Group on Mining (among the federal and provincial governments), which has a special committee on indigenous participation in mining. This group publishes an annual report, which is sent to indigenous groups all across Canada. Such efforts, which may seem initially to be talk about talk, actually create important fields of engagement that are particularly important in cross-cultural dispute resolution (see Duryea et al. 1992).

As far as mining regulations are concerned, the Canadian government completed a major revision of its mining regulations in 2001. It used the

Whitehorse Mining Initiative as a touchstone in terms of multistakeholder involvement. Interestingly enough, this initiative was launched by the mining industry as a means for facilitating mining contracts with communities in northern Canada, particularly indigenous people. Since then the Canadian Department of Natural Resources and a few other departments have become "trustees of the process" (Natural Resources Canada 1998).

Conventional wisdom, or cynicism, about government may lead one to believe that such a proliferation of government departments and agencies with a panoply of ministers creates bureaucratic deadlock. However, if it is properly managed, the segmentation of authority in this form can actually prevent some of the interorganizational competition for funding that has plagued many U.S. departments. For example, within the Department of the Interior, there are agencies as diverse as the Bureau of Indian Affairs and the Bureau of Land Management. In his recent testimony before Congress, former Assistant Secretary for Indian Affairs Ross Swimmer alluded to this issue as follows: "We are constantly having to defend tribes and tribal reservations, tribal lands from the rest of the Interior."[13] Thus the Canadian model of departmental organization may also hold some lessons for the United States and elsewhere.

The expert panel process, discussed in the case of the Saskatchewan projects and the Voisey's Bay project, is also an interesting feature of the Canadian experience. This process allows for an overarching supervisory role to be delegated to an interdisciplinary group of leaders. The texture of the panels in Saskatchewan and Newfoundland was quite different—the former comprising mostly scientists, while the latter comprised decision makers from various constituencies. Part of the reason for this distinction was that the Saskatchewan panel was addressing the broader issue of uranium mining at a regional level, whereas the Voisey's Bay panel was focusing on local environmental impact. Despite their shortcomings, the panel process provides yet another measure of legitimacy to the process that can act as a buffer against cross-cultural tensions.

The Canadians have also been much more forthcoming in embracing culture as a policy imperative. The United States has no counterpart to the Canadian Heritage portfolio within the government, which is centered around the theme of culture. The introductory statement of the department (a cabinet-level department with its own minister) quite remarkably mentions the word *sovereignty* as follows: "The Canadian Heritage Portfolio was created to consolidate national policies and programs that maintain Canada's *cultural sovereignty* and promote Canadian identity. . . . In 1971, Canada became the first country in the world to adopt a Multiculturalism Policy. Canada's approach to diversity has evolved over the years and is embedded within a broad policy and legislative framework."[14]

In the United States, culture is still a tabooed term at the public policy level. Indeed, the closest the United States comes to such an organization is the National Park Service, but here the emphasis is much more on site-specific preservation and conservation rather than human-centered cultural exchange. The Smithsonian Institution, which is a quasi-governmental organization, is working toward a National Museum of the American Indian, but again the focus is project-specific curatorship rather than the broader vision concerning cultural education and promotion of cross-cultural dialogue, which the Canadians have achieved.

Continuing the Learning Process

To sum up the lessons learned, in many ways the United States was initially on a more progressive trajectory than Canada because of the American recognition of Indian self-government. However, the path soon became riddled with court cases and challenges and a poorly organized bureaucratic framework. Therefore, Canada despite its initial marginalization of Indian peoples, and the immense complexity of dealing with the highly devolved provincial government structure, was able to catch up with the Americans. This was largely because of a more efficient and malleable political framework, most notably through the 1982 revisions to the Canadian constitution and a willingness for the Canadian government agencies to make *sui generis* arrangements such as assessment panels and impact benefit agreements their U.S. counterparts have largely failed to achieve.

Nevertheless, both countries have a common problem of an increasing divide between perceptions of indigenous people among the larger settler populace. Publication of books such as Thomas Flanagan's *First Nations: Second Thoughts* (2000), in Canada, or Jeff Benedict's *Without Reservation* (2000), in the United States, both by mainstream publishers, reflect a persistent resentment among settler communities, largely because there are still so many misunderstandings about the plight of native people. A need for a comprehensive education program about the nature of indigenous sovereignty is absolutely critical in both countries so that the policy decisions are anchored in public understanding.

Another important lesson that can be gleaned collectively is that there are indeed certain cases that are nonnegotiable. One can try all of the most elegant and elaborate negotiation strategies, but in some cases the community simply does not want the mining, or other development ventures, to go ahead. The Crandon case (U2) illustrates this starkly. In this case Rio Algom tried to even involve another well-respected tribal chairperson from a neighboring tribe to act as a mediator to simply open communication channels (and remaining neutral on the mining per se). However, the tribe has refused to even talk to her. As Brock Evans of the National Audubon society stated in an address to the mining industry: "Just because an ore body is discovered does not mean that it has to be mined" (B. Evans 1994, 9). Mining companies and governments have to realize that just as a mining deposit under New York City would certainly not mean that mining will go forward, the same may be true for other places as well. This is where environmental justice arguments may start to creep in, despite the geological determinism of mining in general.

In the Crandon case, at an earlier stage, had Exxon been more adept at negotiating with the community, there may still have been a chance for the community approval for mining. But the key lesson to capture in the context of native negotiations is that beyond a certain point the articulation of sovereignty takes root in resistance—in this case, the wild rice fields of the Chippewa became a symbol of environmental sovereignty, in direct contrast to mining.

On a positive note, I think Canada and the United States provide an excellent example for much of the world, where indigenous people are in far worse circumstances. Even developed countries such as Australia and Japan (where the Ainu are largely assimilated) have much to learn from the North American experience in terms of a commitment to engage the past.[15] New Zealand's situation is somewhat more advanced than in any of the other three Anglo-majority nations because the Maori constitute a much larger percentage of the population.

With high population growth rates in many parts of the world, indigenous peoples are becoming an increasingly important presence that governments will no longer be able to ignore. However, in order for lasting reconciliation to occur there are also some areas where indigenous people need to show some signs of change as well. Some suggestions in this regard are given in the next section.

Tribal Sovereignty—But What's Next?

While governments have a major responsibility for facilitating efficient and equitable negotiations, some of the onus for allowing productive communication to occur also falls on the native communities themselves. There has been a tendency for tribes to posture and take ambivalent positions regarding mining negotiations. The Voisey's Bay case is an example of such a situation. As Ambler (1990) reminds us, tribes often seek "symbolic coups in contracts," even if it means giving up monetary returns. Companies consequently worry about the symbolic importance of contract terms, fearing their peers might think they are too generous. One tribe's bluff can become industry's stereotype of what the Indians really want. In one instance, for example, the Navajo director of economic development told a room full of energy attorneys that he advocated tearing up contracts, not because he really planned to do so but because he believed that overstatement was a valid tool in bargaining (Ambler 1990, 221). In the Makah whaling controversy, the captain of the Makah whaling vessel Wayne Johnson told a Sea Shepherd Conservation Society (SSCS) representative: "well if nothing else, we piss off the white man."[16]

Such positional attitudes on the part of native peoples are not helpful in achieving contracts or in moving toward sovereignty. They lead to a fundamental distrust on the other side and reinforce negative stereotypes. Native leaders are also beginning to appreciate that demands for sovereignty cannot exist in a vacuum and sovereignty must be followed by a strong sense of accountability within the nation's decision-making apparatus.

Indigenous people have shown much more proclivity for international forums than national ones—in such arenas their positions and roles become analogous to a lot of developing or southern countries (see Dallam 1991). For native people, there appears to be far greater trust in international regimes than in national ones. However, alongside other legal doctrines that reaffirm their rights to self-determination, they must also consider the time-tested maxim in international law: *sic utere tuo ut alienum non laedas* (use your own property so as not to injure the property of others). By this measure native people are increasingly realizing that there are certain pan-global issues that transcend, or perhaps transform, sovereignty—such as human rights, and in some cases even environmental concerns. The Native American lawyer James Anaya has suggested that Native

Americans should embrace "a modified integrationist" vision of sovereignty that acknowledges certain inherent connections between groups and hence acknowledges the imperative for collective decision making (Anaya 2000).

Native communities also need to reorganize among themselves to exchange best practices and to gather strength. The Council of Energy Resource Tribes (CERT) has been an attempt to achieve this aim in the United States, and the Canadian Aboriginal Mineral Association has attempted to do the same in Canada. CERT's highest budget thus far was in 1981 — $3.9 million, with the federal government providing 74 percent of the total and the tribes providing the rest. However, both these organizations have been beholden to the federal government or industry (respectively) and have not managed to develop as a strategic resource for native peoples. They have had their respective accomplishments, but given the tremendous resources of tribes at present, they have still not been able to reach their full potential. Their work has been particularly deficient in the area of environmental planning, which is all too often the way in which tribes articulate their decision-making authority. Donald Fixico (1998) in his detailed studies of CERT found that out of more than one hundred reports on various ideas and projects prepared by CERT, only five focused on environmental issues; the rest were about uranium potential, resource inventories, coal mining, power plants, synthetic fuels, and nuclear power plants. It is thus not surprising that many splinter groups within native populations end up resorting to environmentalist literature.

While this book may have reaffirmed that native views about environmental issues are clearly distinct from mainstream environmentalism, there is a spectrum of opinion even so within native communities. One can argue that the more environmentally inclined indigenous groups are, in fact, the modernists who are espousing contemporary environmental inclinations, even though they are often labeled as traditionalists. Native governments have to get over the fear of these groups as being indoctrinated by the environmental community. In fact, by embracing a divergence of opinion they can perhaps prevent destructive splintering that can occur when such individuals have to grasp whatever source of empowerment they can muster (as with the Big Mountain resistance).

Finally, I would like to add that regarding mineral contract negotiations, tribes should get involved at the exploration stage of a project and work through the details of each contract, preferably using the two-track impact benefit and environmental assessment models that have been relatively successful in Canada.

The Market and Its Meritocracy

Mining can be classified as a kind of windfall development similar to the establishment of a casino in an impoverished neighborhood, ushering in a sudden influx of wealth to a community. However, mining represents development that is very different from other projects, such as casinos, stadiums, or army bases because of its inherent obsolescence. Therefore, in order for such a development to be successful in the long run, it must be coupled with some other development strategy; otherwise, the result is a proverbial mining ghost town that is sadly the scourge of many pristine landscapes.

The mining sector can provide an opportunity for sustainable development only if it is viewed as a proximate solution to day-to-day technological necessities, not as an end in itself. Historically, primary resource extraction industries have been considered sacrosanct by many governments and have received numerous subsidies. Clearly this has not provided mining companies an incentive to diversify and think in the long run about alternative services they could provide in terms of recycling materials and investing in alternative material science research that employs renewable resources. This move would be congruent with the oil industry, which is now shifting gears to be considered an energy service industry, and investing in solar and other renewable forms of energy research.

Clearly these issues need to be addressed at all levels of governance. However, I think that the international level is most salient in this context to prevent the proverbial "pollution havens phenomenon." Given the multinational nature of most mining companies, there needs to be some way of standardizing best practices in the mining sector. There should be a series of International Standards Organization standards for nonrenewable resource extraction industries, considering their unique and obsolescent nature. Meanwhile, regional, national, and local oversight of mining operations is also essential. Just as human rights are nowadays trumping the past primacy of sovereignty, it is also likely that environmental issues will follow a similar path.

Mining is often a leading sector in the area where it exists and should therefore be used to encourage other businesses to invest in the region.

Since mines are usually located in remote parts of the world, it is difficult to get other manufacturing or service businesses in the area. A usual solution that is proposed is to develop a tourism industry (eco-tourism, in its most green incarnation). This is, of course, limited to the mine's terrain and is often not feasible.

Perhaps a preferable way of approaching this question is first to study and evaluate the lifestyle of the people before the mining activity, and then to see how that predevelopment lifestyle could be improved *without* the windfall development. Such an analysis would highlight some of the limiting factors that could be preventing a more sustainable yet inchoate sector from developing. For example, a poor agricultural economy may be deficient in appropriate farming technology. Now, once this evaluation has been conducted, the windfall developer can institute measures to specifically target that sector for improvement through direct financial means or through technology transfer. Education is a critical issue in many areas where windfall development is to occur, and the establishment of schools and other vocational training programs independent of their utility to the developers is critical. Hence a contingency development plan would be essential, particularly for projects of planned obsolescence, such as mining. However, plans for alternative development strategies should be strongly encouraged for any risky windfall development. Such a system will likely require regulatory enforcement, as it is a classic externality for the developer. However, the specifics should remain flexible given the highly diverse nature of alternatives that may exist for various communities.

Clearly some of the process issues, stakeholder involvement in decision making, organizational dynamics, and implementation would need to be ironed out in order for such a system to be effective. However, the take-home lesson in this study is likely to be that any windfall projects must not take place in a vacuum and should be catalysts rather than reactants in the synthesis of development.

Mining companies are beginning to consider the environment more as a cost of doing business and less as a regulatory hurdle. There is also a move toward having temporary infrastructure and not establishing permanent settlements, thereby making remediation and cleanup much easier and also preventing a ghost town scenario.

For example, Homestake's McLaughlin mine in Lower Lake, California, has received commendation from unlikely quarters such as the Sierra

Club. According to Raymond Krauss, the mine's environmental manager, "When we look at the total environmental cost, it is roughly 2 percent of our capital cost for the whole project. We want to protect our stockholders' investment. Creating an environmental liability doesn't serve their interests or ours" (quoted in Watkins 2000, 92).

In 1994, and again in 1996, KPMG Management Consultants conducted surveys of more than three hundred businesses and municipalities in Canada, questioning them about their environmental management programs. In both surveys, over 90 percent stated that their primary motivation for establishing environmental management systems was compliance with regulations. Approximately 70 percent cited potential directors liability, a factor also related to environmental laws. Only 25 percent claimed to be motivated by voluntary programs (KPMG Management Consultants 1996).

Another interesting dimension of this debate is the perception companies engender in culturally disparate stakeholders (who are often *not* stockholders). Resistance movements have a tendency to dehumanize corporations and make them a sort of apathetic entity without a human face. On the other hand, communities in rural areas can also humanize corporate motivation and react accordingly, as illustrated by the following observation from of a landmark study of coal mining in West Virginia: "They [the miners] have had little experience with relatively impersonal urban and bureaucratic relationships. Consequently, they tend to perceive coal company operations as if the company were a person. They tend to judge the company's motives by the characteristics of people whom they know to be associated with the company. As a result, opinions of the coal companies and their operations tend to be highly individualistic and strongly polarized, not necessarily related to socially objective criteria" (Weller 1965, 120). These cultural nuances are still seldom appreciated. The modus operandi tends to be that an anthropologist is hired to deal with cultural issues rather than to educate company officials about the delicacy of interactions in the negotiation process itself.

There also needs to be much more informed debate between the government and the mining sector, both of which often need to be galvanized to action by NGOs. The environmental movement's response to mining has been particularly uncompromising because of the nonrenewable nature of the resource extraction process. While some contention regarding mining ventures will always remain, there is some potential for consensus if the sector is manifestly identified as transitional—that mining companies are perceived as materials service providers searching for better ways to provide for the material needs of society and as being open to suggestions.

Civic Society and Strategic Alliances

Environmentalists, like native groups, must come to a more clear realization of their goals, and, as the case analysis has revealed, strategic alliance formation must be based on the set goals—otherwise, the results can be a mutual lack of legitimacy and efficacy.

A notable case in which many environmental groups had to adamantly distance themselves from tribal governments has been the Makah whaling controversy in the Pacific Northwest. Interestingly enough, here, too, there has been a clash of forces between environmental sovereignty versus tribal sovereignty, both within and outside the tribal community. However, the environmental groups have been quite clear in terms of their objectives in the campaign and have kept a somewhat tenuous balance between their support of self-determination of tribes and an overarching concern for the environment. The Sea Shepherd Conservation Society has come under attack from pro-treaty collectives, such as the Canadian-based SISIS. As the founder of the group, Paul Watson stated in reply:

> The Sea Shepherd Conservation Society categorically rejects any accusations of racism, and notes that our accusers are themselves demonstrating a basic tenet of racism by implying that the Makah, because they are Native American, cannot be criticized or opposed, even when engaging in an activity that is illegal under the definition of international law. Attacking conservation groups with accusations of racism serves only to benefit the powers that be, who oppose both conservation and indigenous rights. Should we let them drive a wedge between two movements that have so much in common?[17]

The approach taken by Watson has been strategically astute, since he has also stated that if the International Whaling Commission can officially recognize this hunt as being done for subsistence purposes (as allowed for by the international law on whaling), then he and his colleagues would not oppose the Makah hunt—thus, he has made his argument principled rather than positional. So far, the International Whaling Commission has refused to give the full go-ahead for the hunt in its official proceedings.

On the other hand, the U.S. courts, after remanding further environmental review, have given the go-ahead for whaling through the most recent decision on 8 August 2002, dismissing a lawsuit brought against the tribe by the Fund for Animals.

Another interesting dimension of this case is that some Makah elders contacted the Sea Shepherd Conservation Society on their own and expressed their opposition to the whale hunt. They contend that the hunt is being done primarily as a symbolic gesture to assert their treaty rights—again the primacy of sovereignty is eclipsing environmental issues and, for that matter, cultural necessity as well.[18] Unlike the Black Mesa case, where there was a direct linkage between the Big Mountain resistance groups to the land relocation, the tribal elders in this case do not have any larger agenda vis-à-vis the tribe itself.

In referring to a debate between the Jicarilla Apache and various stakeholders, Ambler (1990) observes that "although some environmental and industry interests tried during the debate to pigeonhole tribes as either anti- or pro-development, the tribes defied classification. Like the states, the tribes' primary interest was in protecting their options and their land base" (Ambler 1990, 230).

Opposition to mining and other development beyond Indian jurisdiction is far safer territory for alliance building. For example, in June 2000 the Sierra Club joined thirteen American Indian tribes fighting desecration of San Francisco Peaks, a mountain area sacred to them that is scarred by pumice mining. The struggle to preserve the sanctity of the mountain led Hopi runners to conduct a sacred run that year. Starting at the edge of the White Vulcan Mine, Hopi runners ran to a public hearing in Flagstaff. Urging protection of the Navajos' sacred mountain to the west, Navajo Nation Council Speaker Ed T. Begay gained council support to oppose mining on San Francisco Peaks as well. Begay, with support from Hatathlii (Navajo medicine people), said San Francisco Peaks are prominent in Dineh origin, clan and ceremonial stories (*Indian Country Today*, 15 June 2000).

New strides are certainly being made. Some constructive alliances such as the MTN in Wisconsin are paving the way for a better understanding of the issues at hand. The key lesson for environmental groups is to make sure that the goals are clear at the start of any strategic alliance formation and that there is a keen appreciation that there may be a profound difference of what is at stake for native communities.

Concluding Thoughts

When approaching any development project, "planning is always positive—for the fulfillment of some program—but democracy may negate its execution. This dilemma requires an understanding of the possible unanticipated consequences which may ensue when positive social policy is coupled with democratic procedure" (Selznick 1949,4). In the case of mining development on indigenous land, the dilemma Selznick speaks of is even more potent because of the enormous gulf in perception and cultural difference about what constitutes environmental impact. Through the case analysis, various theories were traversed to arrive at process-centered hypotheses for explaining resistance. Along the way, it was determined that resistance is a much more malleable form than may be initially evident—it has many hidden transcripts that may often elude planners. It also became clear that environmental concerns are perceived and articulated quite differently by indigenous people than they are by environmentalists, and alliance formation between these groups must be cognizant of their differences. Environmental resistance in the context of contemporary indigenous societies trying to define themselves in terms of territory and decision-making power has much to do with environmental sovereignty. Such dynamics of power are all too often misunderstood or ignored in the negotiation process.

In this book I have tried to explore ways of internalizing resistance within a planning framework in order to build consensus. At the same time, I have tried to embrace the realities of cultural difference. The key is to have a process that is judged to be appropriate by all stakeholders rather than to begin with a preconceived notion of what the substance of the negotiation will center on. Planning—and environmental planning in particular, because of its larger vision of ecosystem interactions—by this measure may be likened to Torgenson's view of *The Promise of Green Politics* (in his book of the same name). Environmental politics, he argues, is an art, but not just an artifact of "scientism"—rather it is a "performing art," where sheer performance (or process) possesses value (Torgenson 1999, 14).[19]

By examining the processes by which environmental conflicts in the highly polarized realm of mining on indigenous land are handled by two leading developed countries, I have tried to draw lessons that can hopefully ameliorate the planning process on, and around, indigenous land elsewhere. As a society with noble visions of sustainable development, we must try to contend with the complexity of environmental conflicts. This volume has been a modest step toward appreciating the vitality of different human perspectives on the environment, which may be reconciled through constructive engagement.

Appendix 1

Highlights of the Nunavut Land Claims Agreement

— $1.1 billion in financial compensation paid out between 1993 and 2007.
— 1.9 million square kilometers of land and water (Nunavut Settlement Area) — within that, title to 355,842 square kilometers of Inuit-owned land, including mineral rights to 35,257 square kilometers.
— Inuit employment in the government eventually proportional to the number of Inuit in Nunavut's population — 85 percent.
— A share of federal government royalties from oil, gas, and mineral development on Crown lands
— Equal representation of Inuit with government on lands and resources management decision-making boards.
— Policies ensuring that federal and territorial government contracts awarded for Nunavut-destined projects see increased participation of Inuit firms. Training and education provided where needed, and labor force hirings within contracted firms to reflect proportion of Inuit in Nunavut.

Note: Nunavut officially joined the Federation of Canada in April 1999.
Source: Nunavut Agreement, accessed at www.gov.nu.ca.

Appendix 2

Technical Concerns Regarding the Voisey's Bay Project

Application of the Precautionary Principle to Tailings and Waste Rock Issues

— Avoid using headwaters pond as a waste disposal site in order to minimize the potential for long-term impacts on the Reid Brook Watershed (an application of the Precautionary Principle).

— A commitment to backfill open pit to minimize the possibility of acid mine drainage. Pit backfilling would be environmentally beneficial in the following ways:

   1. It could reduce or avoid the need for additional waste disposal space.
   2. Combined with underground mine backfilling, it could significantly reduce the need for aboveground waste storage.
   3. Backfilling would ensure that the acid-generating waste materials would remain submerged in the long term.
   4. It could prevent the formation of a potentially toxic pit lake by covering the submerged acid generating waste with less reactive waste to a level above the water table.
   5. Pit backfilling would be better suited as a landform capable of sustainable use beneficial to both humans and wildlife.

Development of a Comprehensive Monitoring Plan Outline during the EIS Process

The plan should include the following:

— Suggested sample locations and sampling frequencies
— A list of contaminants to be tested for water-quality monitoring
— A wildlife-monitoring program outlined in some detail
— Duration, funding, and criteria for triggering other actions (e.g., more testing, less testing, or remedial actions) to be discussed

The monitoring plan that should be developed in conjunction with the EIS should discuss the following:

— Who will do the measurements, and the frequency (i.e., when), at which these measurements would be performed
— Where surface and groundwater quality and air quality will be measured
— What constituents will be measured for each category
— What biologic tests will be performed and the frequency of this testing

Development of a Preliminary Reclamation Plan, which Includes Obligations and Standards for Reclamation

A host of physical considerations are key to defining the reclamation plan and can be specified even before construction of the project has begun. Revegetation criteria should be developed in order to determine whether reclamation/revegetation has been successful. An example of revegetation criteria used for reclamation for the Zortman-Landusky Mine in Montana is 90 percent revegetation of native species compared to adjacent undisturbed areas of similar slope and aspect.

Commitment and a Financial Mechanism for a Reclamation Bond and a Financial Vehicle to Cover Long-Term Monitoring and Maintenance of the Facility Once Reclamation Is Complete

Bonding for reclamation should be required and discussed in the EIS. Although the bonding instrument is usually specified by government regulation, the amount of the bond is often an issue. In addition, a significant feature of this project is that the potentially acid-generating waste will have to remain under a water cover in perpetuity. Even though the dams and other facilities that must remain functional will be "constructed to provide long term and low maintenance containment," there will still be a need for long-term monitoring and maintenance (LTMM) after the mine is closed and fully reclaimed.

Source: Chambers 1998.

Appendix 3

Questionable Mining–Land Dispute Linkages
Used by Activists

"To aid Peabody Coal in their plans to strip mine, the U.S. government has been relocating the Dineh to less valuable land, downstream from the largest uranium contaminated site in the U.S." (Action Resource Center Web site, http://www.arcweb.org/campaigns/big_mountain/).

"Today, there are about 1,000 Dineh [Navajo] elders and their families resisting U.S. government efforts to forcibly remove them from their ancestral homeland in Big Mountain, Arizona. The reason behind the relocation: an estimated 22 billion tons of coal, which Peabody Coal is eagerly seeking to stripmine" (Greenlink Web site, http://www.greenlink.org/affinity/120196/bigmt.html).

"A struggle is occurring on Black Mesa between two divergent viewpoints on the relationship between humans and their environment. One group, led by male-dominated mining corporations and tribal council governments, view land as property, whose title-holders should exploit for the maximum profits regardless of the impact on the land, or on people who currently inhabit the land" (*The Case of the People of Sovereign Dineh Nation*, a report submitted to the Women's Environment Development Organization by the Sovereign Dineh Nation, 27 April 1998).

"The reason the U.S. government has given for the relocation is a so-called Hopi-Dine land dispute. However, the real dispute is between traditional Indians who wish to protect their land and the tribal councils and outside forces that support intense mineral extraction" (statement from Ableza, a Native American arts institute, at http://www.ableza.org/bigmtn.html).

"For a hundred years, Navajo and Hopi people have jointly lived on the land. However, energy companies discovered rich minerals under the soil. They inflamed a 'Hopi-Navajo land dispute' as an excuse to have traditional Navajo people expelled from this land" (*Revolutionary Worker*, 31 May 1998).

"Ever since it was discovered that Big Mountain sits over the largest coal deposit in the country, our government has done everything in its power to relocate the reservation's residents and open up land for mining by Peabody Coal Company. Congress passed a law authorizing relocation in 1974" (Steve Masek and Patrick Reinsborough, "Help Save the Dineh Nation at Big Mountain," *Minnesota Daily*, 20 May 1997).

"Elders of the Sovereign Dineh Nation have been resisting relocation at the hands of the United States government and major energy corporations including Peabody Western Coal Company" (Julia Butterfly Hill and Earth First! statement, http://csf.colorado.edu/bioregional/2000/msg00046.html).

Appendix 4

Charles Lipton's Eighteen Points on Indian Mineral Leasing

1. *Limited period.* An agreement should be for a fixed period, preferably twenty to twenty-five years, not for "so long as minerals can be profitably produced," as the 1938 Minerals Leasing Act provides.

2. *Exploration work program.* A work program should detail what work is to be done, including drilling, and when it will be done and should require spending a specified minimum amount.

3. *Data delivery.* A tribe should obtain all information resulting from exploration, including interpretation. A tribe should have the property rights to that information subject to confidentiality for a limited period and subject to the operator's right to use the information for carrying out the agreement.

4. *Prospect size and relinquishment.* If the agreement covers a large area, it should include a provision requiring the operator to relinquish percentages of the exploration area over a certain period. The area can also be divided into a number of blocks and specific blocks reserved for the tribe (traditionally in a checkerboard pattern) for future development should a discovery be made, which would increase the value of the reserved blocks.

5. *Sharing real profits.* The tribe should share in the true profits, including tax credits and allowances and other direct and indirect subsidies. The tribe's share preferably should increase on a sliding scale based upon revenues or profitability or after the operator has recovered its original costs. A tribe should be sure that an operator does not siphon off profits by overpricing or underpricing affiliated company transactions.

6. *Limitation of recovery rates.* Where a tribe shares in profits, the operator's recovery of its original costs should be computed within certain limits: Either the number of years should be specified or each year's costs should be limited by a specified percentage of the value of production.

7. *Royalty.* A tribe should be assured of a royalty equal to a percentage of the fair market value of production each year, regardless of profitability, preferably on a sliding scale that increases with price or revenue.

8. *Minimum cash payment.* A tribe should also be assured of a minimum annual revenue, as a rental or minimum royalty.

9. *Payments for surface and water rights.* The tribe should charge fair market prices for water and for the use of surface rights. Where a fixed annual charge is agreed upon, provision should be made for automatic adjustments according to a price index for changes in the cost of living.

10. *Bonuses.* Cash bonuses should be considered on signature, on discovery, and perhaps at different production levels, keyed to the value rather than the quantity of production. A tribe should focus on long-term benefits, however. It should not trade off a share of the profits or a higher royalty for front-end money if it is not to its long-term economic advantage.

11. *Employment preferences.* Tribal members should be assured of genuine employment and promotion preference in all employment categories, including supervisory, administrative, technical, and managerial. This preference should be combined with commitments to provide educational opportunities and on-the-job training.

12. *Preference for tribal enterprises.* Enterprises owned by a tribe and tribal members should be preferred for providing goods and services through mechanisms such as prequalification, advance notice, and a 15 percent edge in competitive bidding. (This 15 percent edge is required by the World Bank for local companies.)

13. *Tribal concurrence in basic decisions affecting the reservation and its resources.* These decisions should include location of drill holes or wells, plant, equipment, offices, and access routes; size, methods, and rate of operations; impact on air, surface, and subsurface water, and community facilities; conservation, reclamation, and restoration programs; marketing arrangements; and annual operating budgets if the tribe shares profits.

14. *Indemnification.* A tribe and its members, officers, employees, and agents should be fully indemnified against all liabilities arising out of operations.

15. *Record keeping and reporting.* All pertinent information on exploration, production, and sales should be recorded on a regular basis, with financial information recorded in accordance with agreed-upon accounting principles (not just those "generally accepted"), and reports should be rendered at least quarterly to tribal officials.

16. *Inspection and monitoring procedures.* Tribal officials and their advisers should be assured the right to inspect all operations and books and records at all times.

17. *Assignment.* Tribal consent should be necessary for any assignment of any interest in the agreement.

18. *Insurance, guarantees, and performance bonds.* Operators should be required to carry appropriate insurance in adequate amounts for all operations. Performance bonds should also be required unless the operator's performance is guaranteed by parent corporations with adequate assets, including cash reserves.

Source: Ambler 1990, appendix A.

Appendix 5

Marjane Ambler's Suggestions on Aboriginal Negotiations for the Minerals Industry

1. Do not generalize about tribes based upon your own—or worse, someone else's—bad experiences on one reservation. Before ever going to the reservation, recognize that the days are over when companies could deal with Indian lands as if they were federal lands and tribal governments as if they were rubber stamps for BIA contracts.

2. Be prepared to adjust your attitude; tribal sovereignty is a reality that has to be faced. Rather than launching litigation, companies should try to determine compatibility of interests between the tribe and the company. Do your homework before negotiations begin. Visit the reservation. Try to understand the problems there. Look at each tribe's treaties, constitution, tribal newspaper, and ordinances to see how it views its powers. Analyze tribal courts.

3. Contact the tribal energy department. On most reservations you do not need to "know somebody" to get in the door. Find out if the tribe still holds lease sales and, if not, the process for making a proposal, which usually entails getting on the agenda for a tribal council meeting. On other reservations, you must contact the tribal attorney.

4. Be prepared for delays. It may take time to build trust and understanding. Because many tribes try to reach a consensus among council members—and sometimes among all tribal members—their decisions may take longer. Consensus can protect enterprises from future delays, however.

5. Avoid unnecessary delays by involving BIA in negotiations from the beginning. Although BIA under law has six months to review proposed agreements, the contracts are often approved faster when BIA is already familiar with them.

6. Do not align with any factions or take advantage of factionalism.

7. Expect unusual requests for funding and accept reasonable requests regarding corporation's social responsibilities. Remember that Indian people often do not benefit from the more generalized giving of mineral corporation's foundations. Tribes will ask for assistance with education and job training and may also ask for help with supporting tribal infrastructures (such as tribal courts), paying for ceremonials, and clarifying lease records.

Source: Breaking the Iron Bonds: Indian Control of Energy Development, by Marjane Ambler, published by the University Press of Kansas © 1990. www.kansaspress.ku.edu. Used by permission of the publisher.

Notes

Introduction

1. Canadian Department of Indian Affairs and Northern Development Web site: http://www.inac.gc.ca.

2. The phenomenon of retributive politics has become particularly widespread since the end of apartheid in South Africa. For a detailed analysis of retributive politics, see Minow (1999).

3. There is also much debate in the literature about whether the environmental justice movement is serving the interests of Native Americans (Weaver 1996). Indeed, historical work on the native/environment relationship has been highly polarized, with detractors of native environmentalism arguing that the fur trade was a manifestation of native "plundering" of nature (see Martin 1978).

4. For a revisionist and co-optive view of corporate environmentalism, see Greer and Bruno (1996).

5. The term *planned obsolescence* is borrowed from the literature in science and technology studies where certain industries or organizations have to plan for the expected demise of a product such as the computer, which usually does not have a long market life.

There are, of course, parents who do not let go and children who never grow up, but Indian society has shown that it had immense potential for sovereignty and civilization, and the parental role of the U.S. BIA or the Canadian DIAND was questionable.

6. For a detailed review of development options for tribes, see Kalt and Cornell (1992).

7. Perhaps the first attempt to do this in an organized way is a recent volume edited by Litfin (1998).

8. Rosenau's classic edited volume *Linkage Politics* (1967).

Chapter 1. Mining on Indigenous Lands

1. A particularly engaging account of the mystery mines is given in Love (1974, chap. 1).

2. An authoritative history of Native American demography is Thornton (1990).

3. Churchill has also written on environmental concerns.

4. Some native leaders in western Canada also prepared a detailed declaration entitled "Ecocide as Genocide" in May 1992. See http: //www.vipirg.ca/.

5. *Booklist* review on the back of Fixico (1998).

6. Quoted in Sharon Venne, "Understanding Treaty Six: An Indigenous Perspective," in Asch (1997).

7. See Rabe (1994) for a detailed social science analysis of the nuclear siting dilemma in the United States and Canada. A more recent work that focuses on Native American issues in nuclear waste siting is Kuletz (1998).

8. Dobson borrows these terms from David Miller's work (1990). The "benefits and burdens" dichotomy is manifest in the Canadian process of "Impact Benefit Agreements," which will be discussed in the case analyses in part 2.

9. Based on data compiled by the U.S. EPA and the U.S. Bureau of Mines (no longer in existence).

10. The precursor of RCRA was the Solid Waste Disposal Act of 1965.

11. This question has recently been posed by the World Bank group but with characteristically inconclusive outcomes (see Ackermann 1999; McPhail and Davy 1998). The World Business Council on Sustainable Development has also commissioned a survey study on mining and sustainable development and the possibility of setting up a World Commission on Mining similar to the World Commission on Dams.

12. Personal communication, Robert Wilson, Department of Mineral Resources, BIA, Lakewood, Colo., 20 January 2000.

Chapter 2. The Resistance Brokers

1. Personal communication, Peter Penatshiu, president of the Innu Nation, Sheshashiu, Labrador, Canada, 25 March 2000.

2. A notable scholarly work that articulates the presence of a third nonprofit sector in the economy is Weisbrod (1975).

3. Berger and Neauhaus (1977) would define them as a "mediating structure" in public policy. They argue that such structures play an essential role in balancing the seemingly conflicting desires of the populace to have strong elements of a welfare state while maintaining an equally vehement hostility to big government.

4. The typology is outlined in a table where there are four categories of paragovernmental organization institutions: organization, authority, treasury, and nodality. Each one of these has a public and private division. These categories are correlated with three modes of emergence: top down, bottom up, and sideways across. Various combinations of these categories give twenty-four different kinds of institutional forms.

5. Interactional field theory provides a similar basis for thinking about the role of ENGOs in corporate/community interactions (Kaufman 1959). The ENGO, in the light of this theory, provides a *field of interaction* in which collective involvement and the social definition of principles can be manifest, based on the objectivity of technical expertise. Thus, the ENGO can be seen as the field of interaction between the "corporate community" and the "indigenous community."

6. A detailed exposition of social movement theory and its contemporary ramifications can be found in Morris and Mueller (1992).

7. A study of internal conflict within an environmental NGO is Predelli's study (Predelli 1995) of the radical group "Earth First!" However, the almost unique nature of this group renders it not very suitable for an inductive analysis for our purposes.

8. Charles Barbour, annual address to the American Mining Congress, 1981.

9. Personal communication, e-mail, Pratap Chatterjee, 12 February 1998.

10. Recent scholarship has also shown that, like George Washington and other American historical celebrities, Chief Seattle was a slave owner with a highly questionable moral outlook.

11. For a detailed and very convincing account of this debate, see Weaver (1996).

12. Personal communication, Prof. Sheppard Krech, Brown University, Providence, R.I., 18 February 2000.

13. For a comprehensive discussion of Maori self-determination, see Durie (1998).

14. Ibid., 12.

15. For an in-depth discussion of these issues see Fisher (2000).

16. The term "sovereignty of convenience" was used by Charles Johnson (1994).

Chapter 3. Mining Companies and Management Dilemmas

1. T. Dunbar Moodie's detailed sociological study of gold mining in South Africa (1995) is perhaps the most authoritative work that gives a balanced account of the lives of miners during Apartheid and beyond. For an account of the secretive diamond empire of De Beers and its related companies, see Kanfer (1993). For a somewhat older but highly comprehensive account of mining in Africa, see Lanning (1979).

2. "Tapping into Greece's Mineral Treasure Chest," http://www.ana.gr/hermes/1998/feb/mining.htm.

3. Despite all the negative publicity, Freeport continues to have a distinguished board, including the Nobel laureate and former Secretary of State Henry Kissinger, who has visited the Grasberg mine in Irian Jaya.

4. Danny Kennedy, director of Project Underground, Brownsville, Tex., 16 June 2000. "Project Underground" is a Berkeley-based NGO that aims to support communities resisting mining development.

5. Hoover's online profile of the mining industry at http://www.hoovers.com/industry/snapshot/0,2204,29,00.html.

6. An excellent study of smaller mining ventures and the adaptation of indigenous cultures to artisanal mining firms is Godoy's study of mining and agriculture in highland Bolivia (Godoy 1990).

7. Small-scale mining for gold in placer deposits was, of course, carried out by the ancient Mayas and Aztecs and is a tradition on its own in some parts of the world. However, my focus in this study is on industrial mining ventures, which have the most severe environmental impact.

8. Such arguments have frequently been made in the social sciences by such notable authors as Domhoff (1971), Mitchell (2001), and Useem (1986).

9. Cournot competition here refers to an oligopsony situation in which each firm believes that its rivals are committed to a certain level of production and that rivals will reduce

their prices as needed to sell that amount. Bertrand competition refers to an oligopsony situation in which each firm believes that its rivals are committed to keeping their prices fixed and that customers can be lured away by offering lower prices. The Lerner index is a measure of monopolistic and monopsonistic power given by $\lambda = (P - MC)/P = 1/\eta$ where η is the elasticity of demand / supply for the firm's output / labor; MC is marginal cost and P is price.

10. For an exchange of perspectives on the MMSD initiative from NGOs as well as industry, see Ali and Behrendt (2001).

Chapter 4. The Embedded Stakeholder

1. For an excellent overview of this literature, see Kenny and Meadowcroft (1999).

2. See, for example, the volumes by Lee (1993) and Glasbergen (1998).

3. Telephone conversation with Ward Churchill, Univ. of Colorado, Boulder, Dec. 1999.

4. Employees Mission Statement, Bureau of Indian Affairs, 1998.

5. Personal communication, Jean Louis Causee, Department of Indian Affairs and Northern Development, Ottawa, Canada, 10 January 2000.

6. The term *métis* historically refers to those people who settled in the Red River area of the Canadian West and were the progeny of Scottish or French settlers and native women. Under Riel and Dumont they formed a separate government, which was ousted by military action by the federal government in the late nineteenth century. However, their indigenous title is derivative, not original. Their land base, except for some settlements organized under provincial law, is nonexistent. All of these issues are obscured by the question of status. Are all people with some indigenous blood, but no other status or entitlement, Métis? Are Métis the descendants of the distinctive society in western Canada—led in the last century by Riel and Dumont—who did not take treaty? Much of this is still a gray area in Canadian law.

7. Http://www.inac.gc.ca.

8. Http://www.nrtee-trnee.ca.

9. See, for example, the excellent treatise on the history of the BIA by Taylor (1984).

10. The differences between Canadian provinces and territories are the following: (1) A province exists in its own right, a creation of the Constitution Acts, 1867–1982; a territory, however, is created through federal law. (2) Crown lands in the territories are retained by the federal government in the Crown in right of Canada; this differs from the provinces, which own provincial lands in the Crown in right of the province. (3) In territories, federal Parliament may enter into provincial-type affairs, such as school curriculum. (4) Territorial governments are not included in the constitutional-amending formula—which is how policies are changed in the Constitution of Canada; provinces get a vote when a change is proposed—territories do not.

11. See, for example, Benedict (2000).

12. For an excellent account of the history of anthropological research on native people in the Americas with particular reference to the discovery of Kennewick Man, see Thomas (2000). For a more in-depth appraisal of studies about the settlement of the Americas, see Dillehay (2000).

13. The U.S. Indian Gaming Act (1988) establishes a comprehensive system for regulating gambling activities on Indian lands and divides gaming into three categories or classes. Class I gaming consists of social gaming for minimal prizes and traditional gaming and is regulated exclusively by Indian tribes. Class II gaming consists of bingo, pull-tabs, bingo-like games, and nonbanking card games; for example, games such as poker that are played against other players rather than against the house. A tribe may conduct, license, and regulate Class II gaming if (1) the state in which the tribe is located permits such gaming for any purpose by a person or organization; and (2) the governing body of the tribe adopts a gaming ordinance that is approved by the National Indian Gaming Commission. All other forms of gaming that fall into Class III gaming may lawfully be conducted by an Indian tribe if (1) the state in which the tribe is located permits such gaming; (2) the tribe and the state have negotiated a tribal-state compact that has been approved by the secretary of interior; and (3) the tribe has adopted a gaming ordinance which has been approved by the NIGC (from NIGC, http://www.nigc.gov). Canadian information from Bill Henderson, "Virtual Law Office," http://www.bloorstreet.com/200block/brintro.htm.

14. A notable case recently filed involves a meteor sold by native tribes in Washington to the American Museum of Natural History in the early part of this century. It is now being demanded back by them on the basis that the rock is spiritually significant.

15. The three Marshall cases are *Johnson* v. *McIntosh* (1823), *Cherokee Nation* v. *Georgia* (1831), and *Worcester* v. *Georgia* (1832).

16. Bureau of Indian Affairs, http://www.doi.gov.

17. Personal communication, Robert Williams, Tucson, Ariz., 12 November 1999. A case in point concerning Indians and mining that was argued before the Supreme Court in 1998 is *Montana* v. *Crow Tribe of Indians*, in which the court denied the tribe's petition for restitution of tax revenues from Montana from mining operations.

18. See the Environmental Mining Council of British Columbia, http://www.miningwatch.org/emcbc/.

Chapter 5. From Nain to Navajo

1. There are a few revisionist archaeologists who claim that Navajo may have had a nomadic presence in the region alongside the ancestral Puebloans. However, there is scant evidence to support this view, even though the National Park Service has given credence to Navajo ancestral linkage to the Chaco Canyon ruins (Smith 1999).

2. In an alternative chain of causality, Emily Benedek (1999, 33–35) has suggested that the creation of the reservation was in fact spurred by a conflict between some white Indian agents over schooling decisions for Hopi children. The demarcation of the initial Hopi reservation was arguably quite arbitrary given the frenzy surrounding this internal squabble in the bureaucracy. However, it is difficult to establish with any measure of certainty the strength of this causality chain rather than the more common argument that Hopi were disturbed by Navajo grazing incursions and actually complained to the Indian agents.

3. Under The Dawes Allotment Act of the late nineteenth century, certain native

groups were allotted land in an effort to do away with the reservation system and to acculturate Indians in to the market economy.

4. Quoted in "The Church Rock Disaster," http://www.ratical.org/radiation/Killing OurOwn/KOO9.html.

5. Unless otherwise stated, the statistics quoted in this section are derived from the Web site of the Office of Surface Mining Control and Reclamation, http://www.wrcc.osmre.gov.

6. When Boyden wrote to the Peabody vice president as a Peabody attorney, he addressed him as "Dear Ed"; when he wrote to him as a Hopi attorney, he called him "Dear Mr. Phelps."

7. See *Denison* v. *Tuscan Gas and Electric Co.*, 1 Sup. Ct. 95 (1974).

8. See the article by Whiteley and Masayesva in Johnston and Donahue (1998).

9. Personal communication, Carl Johnston, Office of Surface Mining, Denver, 15 June 1999.

10. Telephone conversation with Tom Goldtooth, director of the Indigenous Environmental Network, May 2000.

11. Mining of lead by these communities for ornaments can be traced back to four thousand years. For an in-depth history of Native American involvement in lead mining, see Murphy (2000, chaps. 3 and 4).

12. Personal communication, Sylvester Poler, Mole Lake, Wis., 15 April 2000.

13. Personal communication, Zoltan Grossman, Madison, Wis., 14 April 2000.

14. Personal communication, Dale Alberts, Nicolet Mining Corp., Crandon, Wis., March 18 2000.

15. Personal communication, Maxine Wiber, vice president, Environment and Community Affairs, Rio Algom, Toronto, 15 January 2000.

16. Algom, Rio (2000), *Environmental Health, Safety and Community Report* (April).

17. Personal communication, anonymous Native individual, Saskatoon, 21 July 1998.

18. These surveys were conducted for Cameco by independent consultants Anderson/Fast Associates of Saskatoon. The respondents were chosen to proportionately represent six regions of the province's population of one million. The margin of error was plus or minus 3.4 points. Personal communication, Elaine Kergoat, 12 August 2000.

19. The way in which these resignations were handled by Cameco and the government will be discussed in detail in chapter 8.

20. The Wollaston Lake area was the subject of a notable activist book against uranium mining entitled *Wollaston: People Resisting Genocide* (Goldstick 1987).

21. Jamie McIntyre, presentation to the Saskatchewan Human Resource Association, 19 March 1998.

22. The term *Eskimo* is considered pejorative since it means "eaters of raw meat" in an Indian dialect. The epithet itself shows that considerable antagonism has existed between Indians and Inuit.

23. Personal communication, Chesley Anderson, Labrador Inuit Association mineral officer, St. John's, Newfoundland, 30 March 2000.

24. Personal communication, Larry Innes, Sheshatshiu, Labrador, March 2000.

25. Friedland's infamy largely rests upon his shady dealings in the Summitville mine in Colorado, which is now a major Superfund site. Friedland is under criminal investigation

concerning this project (though he lives in Singapore and it may be somewhat difficult to bring him to trial).

26. In one particularly embarrassing moment for the CEO of Inco, Mike Sopko, a community activist who was being awarded an honorary degree by Laurentian University alongside Sopko, got up and made a scathing speech about the company, commenting that Inco brings out "the truly nasty parts in people" (McNish 1999, 230).

27. Innu Nation Press Release via email, 25 June 2002.

Chapter 6. Science and Elements of Social Construction

1. For a sound resurrection of this Cassandran/Cornucopian debate, see the new edition of the late Julian Simon's notable work *The Ultimate Resource* (1999), which has an appreciation by Milton Friedman. In comparison to the Cornucopian view, the Ehrlichs' *Betrayal of Science and Reason* (1997) presents a coherent environmentalist response.

2. Personal communication, Prof. Erling Brostuen, Colorado School of Mines, Golden, 17 June 1999.

3. EPA Region IX, *Multimedia Review of the Black Mesa Mine Complex*, EPA Site ID NND 051452654, prepared by URS Consultants and reviewed by Des Garner, 18 October 1996.

4. Personal communication, Steve Parsons, Office of Surface Mining, Denver, Colo., 12 July 2000.

5. Telephone conversation, Joanne Jones, Esq., Madison, Wis., June 2000.

6. See the writings of Ward Churchill, Tom Goldtooth, and Winona LaDuke in the bibliography.

7. It is important to note that there has been resistance from nonindigenous environmental groups, but it has not been supported by indigenous people per se. The role of the Inter-Church Uranium Committee in this regard will be discussed in the next chapter.

8. Personal communication, Mark Sheppard, Inco environmental negotiator, St. John's, Newfoundland, 27 March 2000.

9. Personal communication, Chesley Anderson, Labrador Inuit Association Mineral Advisor, St. John's, Newfoundland, 27 March 2000.

10. The importance of the ethnographic research model and its particular application to environmental planning will be further discussed in part 3.

11. Formed in 1982, the Okalakatiget Society (pronounced O-HALA-HA-TEH-GEET) provides a local, native communications service for approximately 4,500 people of the north coast of Labrador.

12. For a systematic account of social organizational differences between the tribes, see http://www.mc.maricopa.edu/anthro/navajohopi/socialorganiz.html.

13. This can be measured by the fact that very few members of the tribal community speak their language. The proximity of the reservation to nonnative cities and the presence of casinos have also added to this situation.

14. It is important to keep in mind the somewhat amorphous definitions of *indigenous, Indigenous,* and *tribal* in international law. There has generally been a consensus that such groupings should be self-defined by the communities, who view themselves as distinctly different from the dominant culture.

Chapter 7. Indigenous-Environmentalist Relations

1. See "Who is Marsha Monestersky?" http://hartwilliams.com/no1u1.htm.

2. See http://www.umc-gbcs.org/dineh-am.htm

3. Telephone conversation, Marsha Monestersky, 21 November 1999.

4. Lenora Lewis and Hopi Land Team, letter to the editor, *Tutuveni*, 22 June 1999.

5. Louise Benally, executive director of the Sovereign Dineh Nation and the Dineh Alliance, open letter to Marsha Monestersky, 1996. This letter can be found at the Hopi Project site online: http://hartwilliams.com/no1u1.htm.

6. In a 4 February 1997 press release, the assembly identified the Hopi individuals who had been working with the activists and had benefited financially from such activities.

7. Nancy Watson and Dine Bureau, *Gallup (N.Mex.) Independent*, 1–2 April 2000 (weekend edition), quoted in a story.

8. David Orton, "Rethinking Environment-First Nations Relationships," http://conbio.rice.edu/nae/docs/rethinking.html#top.

9. Chief Hector Kkailther, statement at the Umperville River Campground before the mining protest on 14 June 1985, quoted in Goldstick (1987).

10. Bill Blaikie, member of Parliament (Winnipeg-Birds Hill), *Hansard House of Commons Debates*, vol. 128, no. 126, 1st sess., 33d Parliament, 17 June 1985.

11. Sol Sanderson, Federation of Saskatchewan Indian Nations, press conference statement, Saskatoon, 20 June 1985.

12. Personal communication, Jamie Kneen, 24 February 1998.

13. Personal communication, Rita Meriwald, vice president, Human Resources, Cameco Corporation, Saskatoon, 19 July 1998.

14. Inter-Church Uranium Committee, memorandum to the premier of Saskatchewan and the Atomic Energy Control Board, Saskatoon, Saskatchewan, 14 April 1997.

15. Unlike the conventional usage of North and South in environmental discourse, "the North" in this case was used synonymously with underdevelopment and poverty while "the South" was synonymous with development and affluence.

16. Personal communication, Jamie McIntyre, Saskatoon, Saskatchewan, 22 March 1998.

17. Gerald Morin, president of the Metis Nation, interview with BBS-TV Saskatchewan, *Hunters and Trappers Say They Are Fed up with Mining in the North*, 2 March 1997.

18. Statistics in the article are compiled from defendant's exhibit nos. 116, 131, 132, 149, and 151, *Lac Courte Oreille Band of Lake Superior Chippewa Indians, et al. v. State of Wisconsin, et al.*, together with information from the Great Lakes Indian Fish and Wildlife Commission.

19. See Midwest Treaty Network Web site: http://www.alphacdc.com/treaty/.

20. *Minnesota et al. v. Mille Lacs band of Chippewa Indians et al.*, Sup. Ct. No. 97-1337, argued 2 December 1998, decided 24 March 1999.

21. Personal communication, Zoltman Grossman, Midwest Treaty Network, Madison, Wis., 18 March 2000.

22. Personal communication, Danny Kennedy, Indigenous Environmental Network Conference, Brownsville, Tex., 18 June 2000.

23. See http://www.miningwatch.ca.

24. Conference held on 10–12 September 1999 in Ottawa.

Chapter 8. Ambiguous Property

1. Field theory may be considered a branch of the linkage politics literature that posits that linkage can be understood in terms of behavior space (e.g., conflict behavior) and attribute space (e.g., economic development). It is a rather abstract formulation involving vector geometry to explain relative position of stakeholders in fields of behavior and attributes (see van Atta 1973 and Rummel 1973 in Wilkenfeld 1973).

2. Personal communication, Faye Brown, director of Honor the Earth, Minneapolis, 19 March 2000.

3. Annalee Yassi to Don Lee, chairperson of the Joint Panel on Uranium Mining, "Request for Additional Information for the MJV Project," 12 April 1996.

4. Annalee Yassi to Chief John Dantouze, Prince Albert Grand Council, 30 September 1996.

5. Annalee Yassi to Don Lee, chairperson of the Joint Panel on Uranium Mining, "Request for Additional Information for the MJV Project," 12 April 1996.

6. Personal communication, Jamie McIntyre, manager, Human Resources, Cameco Corp., 24 July 1998.

7. Vice Chief John Dantouze, press release after resignation from the panel, Prince Albert Grand Council, 3 October 1996.

8. Statement from Joint Provincial and Federal Panel on Uranium Mining, Saskatoon, Saskatchewan, 1 October 1996.

9. Government of Canada, response to the Joint Panel Recommendations on the McArthur River Uranium Mining Project, 1997.

10. Personal communication, Jamie McIntyre, 24 July 1998.

11. Personal communication, Jamie McIntyre, 23 August 1998.

Chapter 9. Resistance and Cooperation

1. For a concise, yet incisive, discussion of linkages in negotiation, see Watkins and Passow (1996).

2. It is important to keep in mind that, just as I have presented a case for why promoting resistance may be good, the flip case can also be made: certain agreements that may occur without resistance are perhaps flawed because they indicate a kind of co-optive mechanism at work. Such an argument is very difficult to evaluate empirically since it presumes that a kind of psychological game of brainwashing is being played between the stakeholders.

3. In fact, the least transparent process consisted of the interactions between the mining companies and the tribal governments—the reasons for which will be discussed in the next section.

4. This point pertaining to Best Alternative to a Negotiated Agreement (BATNA) is discussed in chapters 2 and 8.

5. The European Union has tried to focus on such an approach to capacity building, or

capacity configuration (as I call it). Much of the work in this regard is being spearheaded by the European Centre for Development Policy Management, an organization funded largely by the Dutch government. See, for example, their paper "Building the Base for Cooperation: Institutional Capacities and Partnerships," Maastricht, issue paper 3, The Netherlands, September 2000.

6. Several years hence, part of this approach has also been articulated in the dispute resolution literature as the concept of BATNA. Indeed, an article on the sources of negotiating power by Roger Fisher (1983) identifies BATNA as a source of power.

7. The phrase "who governs" is borrowed from the title of Robert Dahl's celebrated book (1961).

8. The key proponents of the utilitarian approach are Buchanan and Tullock (1962).

9. Talcott Parsons (1957) is a key proponent of the sociological approach within an economic framework.

10. Goran Therborn, "What Does the Ruling Class Do When It Rules? Some Reflections on Different Approaches to the Study of Power in Society," in Giddens and Held (1982).

11. The word *chipko* means "hugging," which refers to the practice of the adherents of embracing trees en masse as a way of preventing industrial logging.

Chapter 10. Planning for Sustainable Development

1. William Schweri and John van Willigen, "Community Resistance to Environmental Change Projects," in Millsap (1984).

2. Richard Rose (1996) is among the few political scientists who has drawn attention to important analytical ways of lesson-drawing between countries. It is important in his view to keep in mind a sense of time and place in drawing such lessons, but that being said, the potential for using such analysis as a means for introspection and policy reform is immense.

3. I am indebted to Prof. J. Edward Chamberlain of the University of Toronto for bringing Arnold's work to my attention in one of his writings.

4. The Iroquois among others had a fairly well developed political system. See Debo (1970).

5. J. Edward Chamberlain, "Culture and Anarchy in Indian Country," in Asch (1997).

6. Ibid., 6.

7. Norman Dale, "Negotiating the Future of Haida Gwaii," case chapter in Susskind et al. (1999, 924).

8. Native American Nation-Building Conference, University of Arizona, Tucson, 17–19 November 1999.

9. Kathy Brock, "Finding Answers in Difference: Canadian and American Indigenous Policy Compared," in David Thomas (2000).

10. See http://www.inac.gc.ca and http://www.doi.gov.

11. W. Ron Allen, president of National Congress of American Indians, "Testimony on the Mission and Capacity of the BIA," before the Senate Committee on Indian Affairs, 28 April 1999.

12. See the NRTEE Web site at http://www.nrtee-trnee.ca/eng/overview/overview_e.htm.

13. Ross O. Swimmer, president of the Cherokee Croup LLC, "Testimony on the Mission and Capacity of the BIA," before the Senate Committee on Indian Affairs, 28 April 1999.

14. See the Canadian Heritage Web site at http://www.pch.gc.ca.

15. In 1986, the Commonwealth of Australia commissioned a special study comparing the Australian and North American experiences vis-à-vis indigenous policy. The difference between North America and Australia is that even if title to certain land areas in Australia is granted to Aboriginals, they do not have veto power. For example, under the Northern Territories Land Rights Act, traditional Anangu owners of Ayers Rock (known to Aborigines as Uluru) and the Olgas (known as Kata Tjuta) filed a claim of ownership. They were disallowed because the land was within a national park and thus alienated. The court struggle raged for several years, and only after two acts of parliament was this region handed back to the traditional owners, with the condition that it be immediately leased back to the Australian Nature Conservation Agency (formerly the Australian National Parks and Wildlife Service). They were thus forced to grant land access to a conservation agency and had no standing for further negotiations, though monetary compensation was accorded by the lessee (the government).

16. Quoted in a statement by Paul Watson, "Response to SISIS Declaration against Racism," e-mail sent to various listservs on 9 July 1999.

17. Ibid.

18. Telephone interview, Andrew Christie, communications officer, Sea Sheppard Conservation Society, 2 June 2000.

19. Much of his theory builds upon the work of Hannah Arendt presented in her landmark work, *The Human Condition*.

Works Consulted

Achen, Christopher, and Duncan Snidal. 1989. "Rational Deterrence Theory and Comparative Case Studies." *World Politics* 41, no. 2.

Ackermann, Richard. 1999. "Is Mining Compatible with Sustainable Development? A World Bank Perspective." Memorandum circulated to mining industry.

Aggarwal, Vinod, ed. 1998. *Institutional Designs for a Complex World: Bargaining, Linkages, and Nesting.* Ithaca: Cornell University Press.

Alaska. 1998. *Commentary on the Proposal of the Governor's Task Force on Subsistence.* January.

Ali, Saleem H. 1999. "Green Alliances: Anti-mining Activism and Indigenous Communities in the New World." *Cultural Survival Quarterly* 15, no. 3.

———. 2000. "Shades of Green: Mining, NGOs and the Pursuit of Negotiating Power." Ed. Jem Bendell. *Terms for Endearment: Business, NGOs and Sustainable Development.* Sheffield, UK: Greenleaf Press and New Academy for Business.

Ali, Saleem H., and Larissa Behrendt, eds. 2001. "Mining and Indigenous Rights: Can Impacts and Benefits Be Reconciled?" Special issue of *Cultural Survival Quarterly* (April).

Ambler, Marjane. 1990. *Breaking the Iron Bonds: Indian Control of Energy Development.* Lawrence: University Press of Kansas.

Amy, Douglas. 1987. *The Politics of Environmental Mediation.* New York: Columbia University Press.

Anaya, S. James. 1996. *Indigenous Peoples in International Law.* New York: Oxford University Press.

———. 2000. "The Cultural Survival Working Group Session on Sovereignty." Lecture, 5 May, Cambridge, Mass.

Arendt, Hannah. 1998. *The Human Condition.* Chicago: University of Chicago Press. Second posthumous edition with annotation.

Arnold, Matthew. 1993. *Culture and Anarchy.* Cambridge, UK: Cambridge University Press.

Asch, Michael. 1997. *Aboriginal and Treaty Rights in Canada: Essays on Law, Equality and Respect for Difference.* Vancouver: University of British Columbia Press.

Auty, Richard M. 1995. *Patterns of Development: Resources, Policy and Economic Growth*. London: Edward Arnold.

Ayres, R. U., and U. E. Simonis, eds. 1994. *Industrial Metabolism*. Tokyo: United Nations University Press.

Barnard, Chester. 1938. *The Functions of the Executive*. Cambridge, Mass.: Harvard University Press.

Basso, Keith. 1996. *Wisdom Sits in Places: Landscape and Language among the Western Apache*. Albuquerque: University of New Mexico Press.

Benedek, Emily. 1999. *The Wind Won't Know Me: A History of the Navajo-Hopi Land Dispute*. Norman: University of Oklahoma Press.

Benedict, Jeff. 2000. *Without Reservation: The Making of America's Most Powerful Indian Tribe and Foxwoods: The World's Largest Casino*. New York: Harper Collins.

Berger, Peter, and Richard John Neauhaus. 1977. *To Empower People: The Role of Mediating Structures in Public Policy*. Washington, D.C.: American Enterprise Institute.

Blair, Roger, and Jeffrey Harrison. 1993. *Monopsony: Anti-trust Law and Economics*. Princeton: Princeton University Press.

Blunt, Peter, and D. Michael Warren. 1996. *Indigenous Organizations and Development*. New York: Intermediate Technology Publications.

Boal, William. 1995. "Testing for Employer Monopsony in Turn-of-the-Century Cola Mining." *RAND Journal of Economics* 26, no. 3:519–36.

Boal, William, and Michael Ransom. 1997. "Monopsony in the Labor Market." *Journal of Economic Literature* 35:86–112.

Bob, Clifford. 1997. "The Marketing of Rebellion in Global Civil Society." Ph.D. diss., Massachusetts Institute of Technology.

Bodley, John H. 1998. *Victims of Progress*. 4th ed. Mountain View, Calif.: Mayfield Publishing.

Boulding, Elise. 1997. "The Role of NGOs in Reducing or Preventing Violence." *Transnational Associations* 49, no. 6:317–27.

Boulding, Kenneth. 1989. *Three Faces of Power*. Newbury Park, Calif.: Sage.

Bourdieu, Pierre. 1977. *Outline of a Theory of Practice*. New York: Cambridge University Press.

Brecher, Jeremy, and Tim Costello. 1994. *Global Village or Global Pillage: Economic Reconstruction from the Bottom Up*. Boston: South End Press.

Bresette, Walter, and Rick Whaley. 1994. *Walleye Warriors: An Effective Alliance against Racism and for the Earth*. Philadelphia: New Society Publishers.

Brockener, Joel, and Jeffrey Z. Rubin. 1985. *Entrapment in Escalating Conflicts: A Social Psychological Analysis*. New York: Springer Verlag.

Buchanan, J., and G. Tullock. 1962. *The Calculus of Consent*. Ann Arbor: University of Michigan Press.

Burgess, Guy, and Heidi Burgess. 1995. "Beyond the Limits: Dispute Resolution of Intractable Environmental Conflicts." In *Mediating Environmental Conflicts*, ed. J. Walton Blackburn. London: Quorum Books.

Burrell, Gibson, and Gareth Morgan. 1973. *Sociological Paradigms and Organizational Analysis*. London: Heinemann.

Canada. 1993. Joint Federal-Provincial Panel on Uranium Mining. *McArthur River Underground Exploration Program Review*. Saskatoon: Government of Canada Publications. January.

———. 1997a. *Gathering Strength: Canada's Indigenous Action Plan*. Ottawa: Canadian Government Publishing Office.

———. 1997b. Joint Federal-Provincial Panel on Uranium Mining. *McArthur River Mining Project Review*. Saskatoon: Government of Canada Publications. February.

———. 1997c. Subcommittee of the Intergovernmental Working Group on the Mineral Industry. *Report on the Indigenous Participation in Mining: Eighth Annual Report — Increasing Knowledge*. Ottawa: Government of Canada Publications. July.

Canadian Environmental Assessment Agency. 1997. *Report of the Joint Federal-Provincial Panel on Uranium Mining in Northern Saskatchewan*. February. Web access: http://www.ceaa-acee.gc.ca/0009/0001/0001/0011/0004/mou_e.htm.

———. 1999. *Report of the Environmental Assessment Panel on the Proposed Voisey's Bay Mine and Mill Project*. March.

Canadian Institute of Resource Law. 1997. *Independent Review of the BHP Diamond Mine Process*. Calgary: University of Calgary.

Carpenter, Susan, and W.J.D. Kennedy. 1988. *Managing Public Disputes*. San Francisco: Jossey-Bass.

Chambers, David. 1998. "Comments Relating to the EIS of the Voisey's Bay Project." Bozeman, Mont.: Center for Science and the Public Interest.

Champagne, Dwayne, ed. 1996. *Chronology of Native American History*. New York: Facts on File.

Churchill, Ward. 1992. *Marxism and Native Americans*. Boston: South End Press.

———. 1997. *A Little Matter of Genocide: Holocaust and Denial in the Americas 1492 to the Present*. San Francisco: City Light Books.

Clow, Richmond, ed. 2001. *Trusteeship in Change: Toward Tribal Autonomy in Resource Management*. Boulder: University Press of Colorado.

Collier, Paul, and Anke Hoeffler. 1998. "On the Economic Causes of Civil War." *Oxford Economic Papers* 50.

Colt, Stephen. 1999. "Three Essays in Native American Economic Development." Ph.D. diss., Massachusetts Institute of Technology.

Coser, Louis. 1964. *The Functions of Social Conflict*. New York: Free Press.

Costantino, Cathy, et al. 1995. *Designing Conflict Management Systems: A Guide to Creating a Productive and Healthy Organization*. San Francisco: Jossey-Bass.

Cronon, William, ed. 1996. *Uncommon Ground: Rethinking the Human Place in Nature*. New York: Norton.

Crowfoot, James, and Julia M. Wondolleck. 1990. *Environmental Disputes: Community Involvement in Conflict Resolution*. Washington, D.C.: Island Press.

Dahl, Robert. 1961. *Who Governs? Democracy and Power in an American City*. New Haven: Yale University Press.

Dallam, H. Elizabeth. 1991. "The Growing Voice of Indigenous Peoples: Their Use of Storytelling and Rights Discourse to Transform Multilateral Development Bank Policies." *Arizona Journal of International and Comparative Law* 8, no. 2.

Dalton, Melville. 1950. "Conflicts between Staff and Line Managerial Officers." *American Sociological Review* 15:342–51.

Davis, Graham. 1995. "Learning to Love the Dutch Disease: Evidence from the Mineral Economies." *World Development* 23, no. 10.

Debo, Angie. 1970. *A History of the Indians of the United States*. Norman: University of Oklahoma Press.

Deci, Edward L. 1980. *The Psychology of Self-Determination*. Lexington: Lexington Books.

de Levis, Duc. (1764–1830). "Maxims de Politique." *Politique*.

Deloria, Vine, ed. 1985. *American Indian Policy in the Twentieth Century*. Tulsa: University of Oklahoma Press.

Deng, Francis M., et al. 1996. *Sovereignty as Responsibility: Conflict Management in Africa*. Washington, D.C.: Brookings Institution.

Denhardt, Robert B. 1993. *Theories of Public Organization*. 2d ed. Belmont, Calif.: Wadsworth.

Dillehay, Tom. 2000. *The Settlement of the Americas: A New Prehistory*. New York: Basic Books.

Dobson, Andrew. 1999a. *Justice and the Environment: Conceptions of Environmental Sustainability and Dimensions of Social Justice*. New York: Oxford University Press.

———, ed. 1999b. *Fairness and Futurity: Essays on Environmental Sustainability and Social Justice*. New York: Oxford University Press.

Domhoff, G. William. 1971. *The Higher Circles: The Governing Class in America*. New York: Random House.

Donahue, John, and Barbara Rose Johnston, eds. 1998. *Water, Culture and Power: Local Struggles in a Global Context*. Washington, D.C.: Island Press.

Durie, M. H. 1998. *Te Mana Te Kawanatanga: The Politics of Maori Self-Determination*. New York: Oxford University Press.

Durkheim, Emile. 1949. *The Rules of Sociological Method*. Trans. Sarah Solovay and John Mueller. 8th ed. New York: Free Press.

Duryea, M., et al. 1992. *Culture and Conflict: An Annotated Bibliography*. Victoria, B.C.: University of Victoria, Centre for Dispute Resolution.

Eade, Deborah. 1997. *Capacity-Building: An Approach to People-Centred Development*. Oxford: Oxfam UK and Ireland.

Eder, Klaus. 1996. *The Social Construction of Nature: A Sociology of Ecological Enlightenment*. Thousand Oaks, Calif.: Sage.

Eggert, Roderick. 1992. "Exploration." In *Competitiveness in Metals: The Impact of Public Policy*, ed. Merton J. Peck et al. London: Mining Journal Books.

———, ed. 1994. *Mining and the Environment: International Perspectives on Public Policy*. Washington, D.C.: Resources for the Future.

Ehrlich, Paul, and Anne Ehrlich. 1997. *Betrayal of Science and Reason: How Anti-environment Rhetoric Threatens Our Future*. Washington, D.C.: Island Press.

Ekrich, Arthur. 1963. *Man and Nature in America*. New York: Columbia University Press.

Emerson, Richard. 1962. "Power-Dependence Relations." *American Sociological Review* 27:31–40.

Emery, Alan R. 2000. *Integrating Indigenous Knowledge in Project Planning and Implementation*. Hull, Quebec: Canadian International Development Agency.

Enright, Michael. 2000. *This Morning Media*. CBN-AM radio transcript, St. John's, Newfoundland. 29 February. Item #0229550.

Escobar, Arturo. 1995. *Encountering Development: The Making and Unmaking of the Third World*. Princeton: Princeton University Press.

Etzioni, Amitai. 1964. *Modern Organizations*. Englewood Cliffs: Prentice Hall.

Evans, Anthony M. 1997. *An Introduction to Economic Geology and Its Environmental Impact*. Oxford: Basil Blackwell.

Evans, Brock. 1994. "An Environmental Perspective on the National and Global Mining Industry." Paper presented before the Society of Economic Geologists Symposium in Honor of Charles Meyer, Seattle, Wash., 25 October.

Evans, Geoff, et al., eds. 2001. *Moving Mountains: Communities Confront Mining and Globalization*. Sydney: Otford Press.

Evans, Peter. 1979. *Dependent Development: The Alliance of Multinational, State and Local Capital in Brazil*. Princeton N.J.: Princeton University Press.

Fischer, Frank, and Maarten A. Hajer, eds. 1999. *Living with Nature: Environmental Politics as Cultural Discourse*. New York: Oxford University Press.

Fisher, Roger. 1983. "Negotiating Power: Getting and Using Influence." *American Behavioral Scientist* 27, no. 2.

Fisher, William H. 1994. "Megadevelopment, Environmentalism and Resistance: The Institutional Context of Kayapo Indigenous Politics in Central Brazil." *Human Organization* 53, no. 3.

————. 1996. "Native Amazonians and the Making of the Amazon Wilderness: From Discourse of Riches and Sloth to Underdevelopment." In *Creating the Countryside: The Politics of Rural and Environmental Discourse*, ed. Melanie DuPuis and Peter Vandergesst. Philadelphia: Temple University Press.

————. 2000. *Rain Forest Exchanges: Industry and Community on an Amazonian Frontier*. Washington, D.C.: Smithsonian Institution Press.

Fixico, Donald. 1998. *The Invasion of Indian Country in the Twentieth Century: American Capitalism and Tribal Natural Resources*. Niwot: University of Colorado Press.

Flanagan, Thomas. 2000. *First Nations: Second Thoughts*. Montreal: McGill-Queens University Press.

Fleet, Cameron, ed. 1997. *First Nations—First Hand: A History of Five Hundred Years of Encounter, War and Peace Inspired by the Eyewitnesses*. Rowaton: Saraband Inc. and Prospero Books.

Folberg, J., and A. Taylor. 1984. *Mediation: A Comprehensive Guide to Resolving Conflicts without Litigation*. New York: Jossey-Bass.

Friends of the Earth. 1999. *Green Scissors '99 Report*. Washington, D.C.: Friends of the Earth Publications.

Gaventa, John. 1980. *Power and Powerlessness: Quiescence and Rebellion in an Appalachian Valley*. Urbana: University of Illinois Press.

Gedicks, Al. 1993. *The New Resource Wars: Native and Environmental Struggles against Multinational Corporations*. Boston: South End Press.

————. 1998. "Corporate Strategies for Overcoming Local Resistance to New Mining Projects." *Race, Gender and Class* 6, no. 1:109–23.

————. 2000. *Resource Rebels: Native Challenges to Mining and Oil Corporations.* Boston: South End Press.

Geertz, Clifford. 1973. *The Interpretation of Cultures.* New York: Basic Books.

Ghioto, Gary. 2000. "Coal Mines and Indians." *Boston Globe,* 30 January.

Giddens, Anthony, and David Held, eds. 1982. *Classes, Power and Conflict: Classical and Contemporary Debates.* Berkeley: University of California Press.

Glasbergen, P. 1998. *Co-operative Environmental Governance.* Dordrecht, Netherlands: Kluwer.

Godoy, Ricardo. 1990. *Mining and Agriculture in Highland Bolivia: Ecology, History, and Commerce among the Jukumanis.* Tucson: University of Arizona Press.

Goldstick, Miles. 1987. *Wollaston: People Resisting Genocide.* Montreal: Black Rose Publications.

Goldtooth, Tom B. K. 1995. "Indigenous Nations: Summary of Sovereignty and Its Implications for Environmental Protection." In *Environmental Justice: Issues, Policies and Solutions,* ed. Bunyan Bryant. Washington, D.C.: Island Press.

————. 2000. Presentation given at the Protecting Mother Earth Conference, Brownsville, Tex., 15 June.

Goodall, Jane. 1999. *Reason for Hope: A Spiritual Journey.* New York: Warner Books.

Gore, Al. 1992. *Earth in the Balance.* New York: Plume.

Greer, Jed, and Kenny Bruno. 1996. *Greenwash: The Reality behind Corporate Environmentalism.* New York: Apex Press; Kuala Lampur, Malaysia: Third World Network.

Grim, John, ed. 2001. *Indigenous Traditions and Ecology: The Interbeing of Cosmology and Community.* Cambridge: Harvard Divinity School, Center for World Religions.

Grinde, Donald, and Bruce Johansen. 1999. *Ecocide of Native America: Environmental Destruction of Native Lands and Peoples.* San Francisco: City Light Books.

Grossman, Zoltan. 2000. "Geographies of Inclusion: Interethnic Alliances for Rural Environmental Protection." Unpublished manuscript.

Guha, Ramachandra. 2000. *The Unquiet Woods: Ecological Change and Peasant Resistance in the Himalaya.* 2d ed. Berkeley: University of California Press.

Haas, Ernst. 1980. "Why Collaborate? Issue-Linkage and International Regimes." *World Politics* 32, no. 3.

Haas, Peter. 1990. *Saving the Mediterranean: The Politics of International Environmental Cooperation.* New York: Columbia University Press.

Hacking, Ian. 1999. *Social Construction of What?* Cambridge: Harvard University Press.

Hall, Susan E. 1993. *Conoco's "Green" Oil Strategy.* Case Study 9-394-001. Boston: Harvard Business School.

Hanna, Susan, ed. 1996. *Rights to Nature: Ecological, Economic, Cultural, and Political Principles of Institutions for the Environment.* Washington: Island Press.

Haunschild, Pamela R., and Christine Beckman. 1998. "When Do Interlocks Matter?: Alternate Sources of Information and Interlock Influence." *Administrative Science Quarterly* 43 (December): 815–44.

Hedges, Christopher. 1998. "Below It All in Kosovo, A War's Glittering Prize." *New York Times,* 8 July, A4.

Heemskerk, Marieke. 1999. "Unraveling the Choices of Gold Miners and Non-miners:

A Case Study among the Ndjuka Maroons in Suriname." Ph.D. diss., University of Florida, Gainesville.

Hester, R. E., and R. M. Harrison, eds. 1994. *Mining and Its Environmental Impact*. London: Royal Society of Chemistry.

Hine, Robert V., and John Mack Faragher. 1999. *The American West: A New Interpretive History*. New Haven: Yale University Press.

Hood, Christopher. 1984. *The Hidden Public Sector: The World of Para-Governmental Organizations*. Studies in Public Policy Number 133. Glasgow: Centre for the Study of Public Policy, University of Strathclyde.

Houck, John, and Oliver Williams. 1996. *Is the Good Corporation Dead? Social Responsibility in a Global Economy*. London: Rowman and Littlefield.

Inter Press Service. 1993. *Story Earth: Native Voices on the Environment*. San Francisco: Mercury House.

International Council on Metals and the Environment (ICME). 1999. *Mining and Indigenous Peoples*. Ottawa, Canada: ICME.

International Institute for Environment and Development (IIED). 2002. *Breaking New Ground: Mining, Minerals and Sustainable Development*. London: Earthscan.

Iverson, Peter. 1982. *Carlos Montezuma and the Changing World of American Indians*. Albuquerque: University of New Mexico Press.

Jamieson, Brian, and Stan Frost. 1997. *The McArthur River Project: High Grade Uranium Mining*. London: Proceedings of the Uranium Institute Symposium.

Jasanoff, Sheila. 1990. *The Fifth Branch: Science Advisors as Policymakers*. Cambridge: Harvard University Press.

———. 1995. *Science at the Bar: Law Science and Technology in America*. Cambridge: Harvard University Press.

Johnson, Charles. 1994. "A Sovereignty of Convenience: Native American Sovereignty and the United States Plan for Radioactive Waste on Indian Lands." *St. John's Journal of Legal Commentary* (spring).

Johnston, Barbara Rose, and John M. Donahue, eds. 1998. *Water Culture and Power: Local Struggles in a Global Context*. Washington, D.C.: Island Press.

Kalt, Joseph, and Stephen Cornell, eds. 1992. *What Can Tribes Do? Strategies and Institutions in American Indian Economic Development*. Los Angeles: UCLA American Indian Study Center.

Kanfer, Stefan. 1993. *The Last Empire: De Beers, Diamonds and the World*. New York: Farrar Straus Giroux.

Kaplan, Robert. 2000. *The Coming Anarchy*. New York: Vintage.

Kaufman, Harold. 1959. "Towards an Interactional Conception of Community." *Social Forces* 38:1, 8–17.

Keck, Margaret, and Kathryn Sikkink. 1998. *Activists beyond Borders: Advocacy Networks in International Politics*. Ithaca: Cornell University Press.

Kenny, Michael, and James Meadowcroft. 1999. *Planning Sustainability*. London and New York: Routledge.

Kerr, Alex. 2000. *Impact Benefit Agreements as Instruments for Indigenous Participation in Non-Renewable Resource Development*. Toronto and Vancouver: Compass Consulting.

King, Gary, Robert Keohane, and Sidney Verba. 1994. *Designing Social Inquiry*. Princeton: Princeton University Press.

Klare, Michael. 2001. *Resource Wars: The New Landscape of Global Conflict*. New York: Henry Holt.

Koehler, George F., and George D. Tikkanen. 1991. "Red Dog, Alaska: Discovery and Definition of a Major Zinc Lead-Silver Deposit." *Economic Geology*, monograph 8, 268–74.

Kolb, Deborah M., and Jean Bartunek, eds. 1992. *Hidden Conflicts in Organizations: Uncovering Behind-the-Scenes Disputes*. Newbury Park, Calif.: Sage.

Korten, David C. 1996. *When Corporations Rule the World*. New York: Kumarian Press.

KPMG Management Consultants. 1996. *Canadian Environmental Management Survey 1996*. Toronto.

Krech, Sheppard. 1999. *The Ecological Indian: Myth and History*. New York: Norton.

Kriesberg, Louis. 1998. *Constructive Conflicts: From Escalation to Resolution*. Oxford: Rowman and Littlefield.

Kuletz, Valerie. 1998. *The Tainted Desert: Environmental and Social Ruin in the American West*. New York: Routledge.

Labrador Inuit Association. 1996. *Mineral Development in Northern Labrador*. Nain, Newfoundland: LIA.

LaDuke, Winona. 1999. *All Our Relations: Native Struggles for Land and Life*. Boston: South End Press.

Lanning, Greg. 1979. *Africa Undermined: Mining Companies and the Underdevelopment of Africa*. New York: Penguin Books.

Latour, Bruno. 1999. *Pandora's Hope: Essays on the Reality of Science*. Cambridge: Harvard University Press.

Lee, K. 1993. *Compass and Gyroscope*. Washington, D.C.: Island Press.

Levins and Lewontin. 1985. *The Dialectical Biologist*. Cambridge, Mass.: Harvard University Press.

Libby, Ronald. 1989. *Hawke's Law: The Politics of Mining and Aboriginal Land Rights in Australia*. University Park: Penn State Press.

Limerick, Patricia Nelson. 1999. *Something in the Soil: Field-Testing the New Western History*. New York: Norton.

Litfin, Karen. 1998. *The Greening of Sovereignty in World Politics*. Cambridge: MIT Press.

Lohmann, Susanne. 1997. "Linkage Politics." *Journal of Conflict Resolution* 41, no. 1:38–67.

Loram, C. T., and T. F. McIlwraith, eds. 1943. *The North American Indian Today*. Toronto: University of Toronto Press.

Love, Frank. 1974. *Mining Camps and Ghost Towns: A History of Mining in Arizona and California along the Lower Colorado*. Los Angeles: Westernlore Press.

Lowe, Mick. 1998. *Premature Bonanza: Standoff at Voissey's Bay*. Toronto: Between the Lines Publications.

Lukes, Steven. 1975. *Power: A Radical View*. London: Macmillan.

Lund, Brishkai, and Michelle leBaron Duryea. 1994. *Conflict and Culture: Report of the*

Multiculturalism and Dispute Resolution Project. Institute for Dispute Resolution, University of Victoria, Canada.

Majone, G. 1996. *Regulating Europe*. London and New York: Routledge.

March, James, and Herbert Simon. 1993. *Organizations*. 2d ed. Oxford: Blackwell.

Marmor, Theodore. 1994. *Economic Security and Intergenerational Justice: A Look at North America*. New York: Urban Institute Press.

Martin, Calvin. 1978. *Keepers of the Game: Indian-Animal Relationships and the Fur Trade*. Berkeley: University of California Press.

———. 1998. *The Way of the Human Being*. New Haven: Yale University Press.

Masek, Steve, and Patrick Reinsborough. 1997. "Help Save the Dineh Nation at Big Mountain." *Minnesota Daily*, 20 May.

Mastenbroek, Willem. 1987. *Conflict Management and Organizational Development*. New York: Wiley.

McMaster, Gerald, and Lee-Ann Martin. 1992. *Indigena: Contemporary Native Perspectives*. Hull: Canadian Museum of Civilization.

McNish, Jacquie. 1999. *The Big Score: Robert Friedman and the Voissey's Bay Hustle*. Toronto: Doubleday Canada.

McPhail and Davy. 1998. *Integrating Social Concerns into Private Sector Decision Making: A Review of Corporate Practices in the Mining, Oil, and Gas Sectors*. Washington, D.C.: World Bank.

McPhee, John. 1971. *Encounters with the Archdruid*. New York: Farrar Straus Giroux.

Mikesell, Raymond F., and John W. Whitney. 1987. *The World Mining Industry Investment Strategy and Public Policy*. Boston: Allen and Unwin.

Miller, David. 1990. *Market, State, and Community: Theoretical Foundations of Market Socialism*. New York: Oxford University Press.

Millsap, William, ed. 1984. *Applied Social Science for Environmental Planning*. Boulder: Westview.

Milton, Kay. 1996. *Environmentalism and Cultural Theory: Exploring the Role of Anthropology in Environmental Discourse*. New York: Routledge.

Mining Watch Canada. 1999. "Mining's Toxic Orphans—Abandoned Mines Represent over $1 Billion Federal Liability." *Mining Watch Canada Newsletter*. Winter.

Minow, Martha. 1999. *Between Vengeance and Forgiveness: Facing History after Genocide and Mass Violence*. Boston: Beacon Press.

Mitchell, John. 1998. *Companies in a World of Conflict: NGOs' Sanctions and Corporate Responsibility*. London: Earthscan.

Mitchell, Lawrence. 2001. *Corporate Irresponsibility: America's Newest Export*. New Haven: Yale University Press.

Mitra, Amit. 1993. "Chipko: An Unfinished Mission." *Down to Earth* (New Delhi), 30 April.

Moodie, T. Dunbar. 1995. *Going for Gold: Men, Mines and Migration*. Berkeley: University of California Press.

Moody, Roger, ed. 1992. *The Gulliver File: Mines, People and Land: A Global Battleground*. London: Minewatch.

Moorhead, G., and Ricky Griffin. 1992. *Organizational Behavior: Managing People and Organizations*. Boston: Houghton Mifflin.

Morris, Aldon D., and Carol McClurg Mueller, eds. 1992. *Frontiers in Social Movement Theory*. New Haven: Yale University Press.

Murphree, David, et al. 1996. "Toxic Waste Siting and Community Resistance: How Co-optation of Local Citizen Opposition Failed." *Sociological Perspectives* 39, no. 4.

Murphy, Lucy Eldersveld. 2000. *A Gathering of Rivers: Indian, Metis and Mining in the Western Great Lakes: 1737–1832*. Lincoln: University of Nebraska Press.

Mutter, John H. 2002. *To Slay a Giant: The Fight to Protect the Wolf River from the Crandon Mine*. Shawano, Wis.: Burstone LLC Press.

Nash, June. 1993. *We Eat the Mines and the Mines Eat Us: Dependence in Bolivian Tin Mines*. New York: Columbia University Press.

Natural Resources Canada. 1998. *The Whitehorse Mining Initiative*. Ottawa: Canadian Government Publications.

Nichols, Roger L. 1998. *Indians in the United States and Canada: A Comparative History*. Lincoln: University of Nebraska Press.

Nies, Judith. 1998. "The Black Mesa Syndrome: Indian Lands and Black Gold." *Orion* (summer).

Novak, Steven. 1990. "The Real Takeover of the BIA: The Preferential Hiring of Indians." *Journal of Economic History* 50, no. 3.

Olson, Paul A., ed. 1990. *The Struggle for the Land: Indigenous Insight and Industrial Empire in the Semiarid World*. Lincoln: University of Nebraska Press.

O'Neill, Thomas. 2000. "New Caledonia: France's Untamed Pacific Outpost." *National Geographic*, May.

Osgood, Charles E. 1962. *An Alternative to War or Surrender*. Urbana: University of Illinois Press.

Ozawa, Connie. 1991. *Recasting Science: Consensual Procedures in Public Policy Making*. Boulder: Westview.

———. 1996. "Science in Environmental Conflicts." *Sociological Perspectives* 39, no. 2:219–30.

Parsons, Talcott. 1957. *Economy and Society*. New York: Free Press.

Peattie, Lisa R. 1994. "Symbolic Appropriation in Social Movement Work: Australian Aboriginal Rights in an Internationalized World of Ideas." Unpublished monograph, Department of Urban Studies and Planning, Massachusetts Institute of Technology.

Peet, Richard, and Michael Watts. 1997. *Liberation Ecologies: Environment, Development, Social Movements*. London: Routledge.

Peluso, Nancy Lee. 1992. *Rich Forests Poor People: Resource Control and Resistance in Java*. Berkeley: University of California Press.

Peluso, Nancy, and Michael Watts, eds. 2001. *Violent Environments*. Ithaca: Cornell University Press.

Perrow, Charles. 1986. *Complex Organizations: A Critical Essay*. 3d ed. New York: McGraw Hill.

Pfeffer, Jeffrey. 1992. *Managing with Power: Politics and Influences in Organization*. Boston: Harvard Business School Press.

Pfeffer, Jeffrey, and Gerald Salanick. 1978. *The Organizational Control of Organizations*. New York: Harper and Row.

Piven, Frances Fox, and Richard Cloward. 1979. *Poor People's Movements. Why They Succeed, How They Fail.* New York: Vintage.

Prager, S. 1997. "Changing North America's Mind-Set about Mining." *Engineering and Mining Journal* 198, no. 2:26–44.

Predelli, Line Nyhagen. 1995. "Ideological Conflict in the Radical Environmental Group Earth First!" *Environmental Politics* 4:123–29.

Pruitt, Dean, and Jeffrey Rubin. 1986. *Social Conflict: Escalation, Stalemate and Settlement.* New York: Random House.

Rabe, Barry. 1994. *Beyond Nimby: Hazardous Waste Siting in Canada and the United States.* Washington, D.C.: Brookings Institution.

Ragin, Charles. 1987. *The Comparative Method: Beyond Qualitative and Quantitative Research.* Berkeley: University of California Press.

Raiffa, Howard. 1982. *The Art and Science of Negotiation.* Cambridge: Harvard University Press.

Resnikoff, Marvin, Kim Knowlton, and Kal Island. 1996. *Comments on the Environmental Impact Assessment of the McArthur River Mine.* A report prepared for the Saskatchewan Uranium Coalition by Radioactive Waste Management Associates.

Ridley, Matt. 1996. *The Origin of Virtue: Human Instincts and the Evolution of Cooperation.* New York: Penguin.

Riley, Hannah, and James Sebenius. 1995. "Stakeholder Negotiations over Third World Natural Resource Projects." *Cultural Survival Quarterly* 19, no.3.

Rio Algom. 2000. *Environmental Health, Safety and Community Report.* April.

Ripley, Earle A., et al., eds. 1996. *Environmental Effects of Mining.* Delray Beach, Fla.: St. Lucie Press.

Roberts, Peter W., and Tim Shaw. 1982. *Mineral Resources in Regional and Strategic Planning.* London: Gower.

Robinson, Joan. 1969. *The Economics of Imperfect Competition.* London: Macmillan.

Rootes, Christopher, ed. 1999. *Environmental Movements: Local, National and Global.* London: Frank Cass.

Rose, Richard. 1996. *Lesson-Drawing in Public Policy.* London: Chatham.

Rosenau, James. 1969. *Linkage Politics.* New York: Free Press.

Ross, Marc Howard. 1992. *The Management of Conflict: Interpretations and Interests in Comparative Perspective.* New Haven, Conn.: Yale University Press.

Ross, Michael. 1999. "The Political Economy of the Resource Curse." *World Politics* 23.

Rotberg, Robert. 1996. *Vigilance and Vengeance: NGOs Preventing Ethnic Conflicts in Divided Societies.* Washington, D.C.: Brookings Institution.

Rothenberg, David. 1995. "Having a Friend for Lunch: Norwegian Radical Ecology versus Tradition." In *Environmental Resistance Movements: The Global Emergence of Radical and Popular Environmentalism,* ed. B. R. Taylor. Albany: State University of New York Press.

Said, Edward. 1987. *Beginnings: Intention and Method.* New York: Columbia University Press.

Sandole, Dennis J. D., and Hugo van der Merwe. 1993. *Conflict Resolution Theory and Practice: Integration and Application.* Manchester: University of Manchester Press.

Schelling, Thomas. 1978. *Micromotives and Macrobehavior*. New York: Norton.

———. 1960. *The Strategy of Conflict*. Cambridge: Harvard University Press.

Schlosberg, David. 1999. *Environmental Justice and the New Pluralism: The Challenge of Difference for Environmentalism*. New York: Oxford University Press.

Schoepfle, Mark, et al. 1984. "Navajo Attitudes toward Development and Change: A Unified Ethnographic and Survey Approach to an Understanding of Their Future." *American Anthropologist* 86 (December).

Schoepfle, Mark, et al. 1984. "Navajos and Energy Development: Economic Decision Making under Political Uncertainty." *Human Organization* 43, no. 3.

Schrijver, Nico. 1997. *Sovereignty over Natural Resources: Balancing Rights and Duties*. New York: Cambridge University Press.

Schumacher, E. F. 1973. *Small Is Beautiful: Economics As If People Mattered*. New York: Harper Perennial.

Schwartz, Michael, and Shuva Paul. 1992. "Resource Mobilization versus the Mobilization of People: Why Consensus Movements Cannot Be Instruments of Social Change." Ed. Aldon D. Morris and Carol McClurg Mueller. *Frontiers in Social Movement Theory*. New Haven: Yale University Press.

Scott, James. 1985. *Weapons of the Weak: Everyday Forms of Peasant Resistance*. New Haven: Yale University Press.

———. 1990. *Domination and the Arts of Resistance*. New Haven: Yale University Press.

Scott, W. Richard. 1998. *Organizations: Rational, Natural and Open System*. 4th ed. New York: Simon and Schuster.

Sebenius, James. 1983. "Negotiation Arithmetic: Adding and Subtracting Issues and Parties." *International Organization* 37 (spring).

———. 1990. *Negotiating the Law of the Sea*. Cambridge: Harvard University Press.

———. 1996. "Sequencing to Build Coalitions: With Whom Should I Talk First?" In *Wise Choices: Decisions, Games and Negotiations*, ed. Zeckhauser et al. Boston: Harvard Business School Press.

Selznick, Phillip. 1949. *TVA and the Grassroots: A Study in the Sociology of Formal Organization*. New York: Harper Collins.

———. 1996. "Institutionalism 'Old' and 'New.'" *Administrative Science Quarterly* 41:270–77.

Simon, Herbert. 1962. *Administrative Behavior*. New York: Free Press.

Simon, Julian. 1999. *The Ultimate Resource*. Princeton, N.J.: Princeton University Press. New edition with a tribute by Milton Friedman.

Sinkewicz, Paul. 1998. "Planning for Northern Development Gets Underway." *Saskatchewan Sage* (July).

Skocpol, T., P. Evans, and D. Rueshmeyer. 1985. *Bringing the State Back In*. New York: Cambridge University Press.

Smith, Christopher. 1999. "Navajos and Hopis at Odds over Remains of Anasazi." *Salt Lake Tribune*, 22 November.

Smith, David, and Louis Wells. 1975. *Negotiating Third World Mineral Agreements: Promises as Prologue*. Cambridge, Mass.: Ballinger.

Smith, Dean Howard. 1994. "The Issue of Compatibility between Cultural Integrity and

Economic Development among Native American Tribes." *American Indian Culture and Research Journal* 18, no. 2:177–205.

Smith, Duane A. 1986. *Mining America: The Industry and the Environment 1800–1980.* Lawrence: University Press of Kansas.

Smith, Keith Lewis. 1977. "The Clash of Values in Ecological Decision-Making: West Virginia Legislators and the Movement to Abolish the Strip Mining of Coal." Ph.D. diss., Johns Hopkins University, Baltimore.

Soref, Michael. 1982. "Corporate Interlocks among Mining Companies in Wisconsin." In *Land Grab: The Corporate Theft of Wisconsin's Mineral Resources.* Madison: Center for Alternative Mining Development Policy.

Spangler, G. R. 1997. "To Spear or Not to Spear, That Is Not the Question." *Minnesota-Out-of-Doors* 36, no. 4.

Spence, Mark David. 1999. *Dispossessing the Wilderness; Indian Removal and the Making of the National Parks.* New York: Oxford University Press.

Sponsel, Leslie. 1997. "Master Thief: Gold Mining and Mercury Contamination in the Amazon." In *Life and Death Matters: Human Rights and the Environment at the End of the Millennium,* ed. Barbara R. Johnston, 99–127. Thousand Oaks: Altamira Press.

Stammers, Neil. 1999. "Social Movements and the Social Construction of Human Rights." *Human Rights Quarterly* 21:980–1008.

Stitt, Allen J. 1998. *Alternative Dispute Resolution for Organizations: How to Design a System for Effective Conflict Resolution.* New York: Wiley.

Suliman, Mohamed, ed. 1999. *Ecology, Politics and Violent Conflict.* London: Zed Books.

Susskind, Lawrence. 1994. *Environmental Diplomacy.* New York: Oxford University Press.

Susskind, Lawrence E., and Jeffrey Cruikshank. 1987. *Breaking the Impasse.* New York: Basic Books.

Susskind, Lawrence, et al., eds. 1999. *The Consensus-Building Handbook.* Thousand Oaks, Calif.: Sage Publications.

Susskind, Lawrence, and Patrick Field. 1996. *Dealing with an Angry Public: The Mutual Gains Approach.* New York: Free Press.

Suzuki, David, and Peter Knudtson. 1992. *Wisdom of the Elders: Honoring Sacred Native Visions of Nature.* New York: Bantam Books.

Swartz, David. 1997. *Culture and Power: The Sociology of Pierre Bourdieu.* Chicago: University of Chicago Press.

Switzer, Maurice. 1998. "All Canadian Issues Are Indigenous Issues." *Globe and Mail,* 27 March.

Tamir, Orit. 1999. "What Happened to Navajo Relocatee Wisdom of the Elders from Hopi Partition Lands in Pinon?" *American Indian Culture and Research Journal* 23, no. 4:71–90.

Taylor, B. Raymond, ed. 1995. *Environmental Resistance Movements: The Global Emergence of Radical and Popular Environmentalism.* Albany: State University of New York Press.

Taylor, Theodore W. 1984. *The Bureau of Indian Affairs.* Boulder: Westview.

Thomas, David. 2000. *Canada and the United States; Differences That Count.* Toronto: Broadview Press.

Thorne, Eva. 1998. "The Politics of Policy Compliance: The World Bank and the Social Dimensions of Development." Ph.D. diss., Massachusetts Institute of Technology.

Thornton, Russell. 1990. *American Indian Holocaust and Survival: A Population History since 1492.* Norman: University of Oklahoma Press.

Tilly, Charles. 1978. *From Mobilization to Revolution.* Reading, Mass.: Addison-Wesley.

Tilly, Charles, Louise Tilly, and Richard Tilly. 1975. *The Rebellious Century: 1830–1930.* Cambridge: Harvard University Press.

Tinker, Irene. 1996. *Expectations of the Roles of Indigenous Non-governmental Organizations for Sustainable Development and Democracy: Myth and Reality.* Berkeley: Institute of Urban and Regional Development, University of California at Berkeley.

Torgenson, Douglas. 1999. *The Promise of Green Politics: Environmentalism and the Public Sphere.* Durham: Duke University Press.

Turner, Frederick Jackson. [1920] 1998. *The Frontier in American History.* Tucson: University of Arizona Press.

Useem, Michael. 1986. *The Inner Circle: Large Corporations and the Rise of Business-Political Activity.* New York: Oxford University Press.

U.S. Bureau of Indian Affairs. 2000. Data on Indian Mineral Development, Unpublished document retrieved from the Division of Minerals of the Bureau of Indian Affairs, Denver, Colorado.

U.S. Geological Survey. 1999. *Monitoring the Effects of Groundwater Withdrawals from the N Aquifer in the Black Mesa Area, Northeastern Arizona.* USGS Fact Sheet 064-99. Paper prepared in cooperation with the Arizona Department of Water Resources and the Bureau of Indian Affairs. USGS Fact Sheet 064-99.

U.S. Senate. 1998. Committee on Indian Affairs. *Oversight Hearing on Economic Development.* 9 April.

Vaughan, Diane. 1996. *The Challenger Launch Decision: Risky Technology, Culture and Deviance at NASA.* Chicago: University of Chicago Press.

Vecsey, Christopher, and Robert Venables. 1980. *American Indian Environments: Ecological Issues in Native American History.* Syracuse: Syracuse University Press.

Wadden, Marie. 1991. *Nitassinan: The Innu Struggle to Reclaim Their Homeland.* Toronto: Douglas and McIntyre.

Waldman, Peter. 1998. "How Suharto's Circle and a Mining Firm Did So Well Together." *Wall Street Journal,* 29 September, A1.

Walker, R.B.J. 1996. "Space/Time/Sovereignty." In *Perspectives on Third-World Sovereignty,* ed. Mark Denham and Mark Lombardi. London: Macmillan.

Wapner, Paul. 1996. *Environmental Activism and World Civic Politics.* Albany: State University of New York Press.

Warhurst, Alyson, and Ligia Noronha. 1999. *Environmental Policy in Mining: Corporate Strategy and Planning for Closure.* Boca Raton: Lewis Publishers.

Warry, Wayne. 2000. *Unfinished Dreams: Community Healing and Reality of Aboriginal Self-Government.* Toronto: University of Toronto Press.

Watkins, Michael, and Samuel Passow. 1996. "Analyzing Linked Systems of Negotiation." *Negotiation Journal* 12, no. 3.

Watkins, T. H. 2000. "Hard Rock Legacy." *National Geographic* 197, no. 3.

Weaver, Jace, ed. 1996. *Defending Mother Earth: Native Perspectives on Environmental Justice.* New York: Orbis.

Weber, Max, trans. [1924] 1947. *The Theory of Social and Economic Organization*. Ed. T. Parsons and A. H. Henderson. New York: Free Press.

Weisberg, Barry. 1970. *Ecocide in Indochina*. San Francisco: Harper and Row.

Weisbrod, Burton. 1975. "Toward a Theory of the Voluntary Non-profit Sector in a Three-Sector Economy." In *Altruism, Morality and Economic Theory*, ed. Edmund Phelps. Troy: Russell Sage Foundation.

Weller, Jack E. 1965. *Yesterday's People: Life in Contemporary Appalachia*. Lexington: University of Kentucky Press.

Westcott, Malcolm R. 1988. *The Psychology of Human Freedom: A Human Science Perspective and Critique*. New York: Springer Verlag.

Whiteley, Peter, and Vernon Masayesva. 1998. "The Use and Abuse of Aquifers: Can the Hopi Indians Survive Multinational Mining?" In *Water, Culture and Power: Local Struggles in a Global Context*, ed. John Donahue and Barbara Rose Johnston. Washington, D.C.: Island Press.

Wilkenfeld, Jonathan. 1973. *Conflict Behavior and Linkage Politics*. New York: D. McKay and Co.

Wilkinson, Charles. 1999. *Fire on the Plateau: Conflict and Endurance in the American Southwest*. Washington: Island Press.

Zartman, William. 1992. "International Environmental Negotiations: Challenges for Analysis and Practice." *Negotiation Journal* 8 (April): 112–23.

Zillman, Donald, et al., eds. 2002. Human Rights in Natural Resource Development: Public Participation in the Sustainable Development of Mining and Energy Resources. Oxford: Oxford University Press.

Index

About the Author

Saleem H. Ali is Associate Professor of Environmental Planning at the University of Vermont's Rubenstein School of Natural Resources, and on the adjunct faculty of Brown University's Watson Institute for International Studies. He is also on the visiting faculty for the United Nations–mandated University for Peace. In October 2007, the award-winning science magazine *Seed* chose him as one of eight "revolutionary minds" for his willingness to transcend disciplines for the effective study and practice of conflict resolution. Dr. Ali has authored several empirical papers on environmental conflicts in the extractive industries and has also produced two educational videos on the challenges faced by mining companies and communities in developing countries under grants from the Tiffany & Co. Foundation. He is the editor of *Peace Parks: Conservation and Conflict Resolution* (MIT Press, 2007) and the co-editor of *Earth Matters: Indigenous People, the Extractive Industries, and Corporate Social Responsibility* (Greenleaf Publications, 2008). Professor Ali received his doctorate in environmental planning from the Massachusetts Institute of Technology, a masters in environmental studies from Yale University, and his bachelors in chemistry from Tufts University (summa cum laude). Further details about his research can be found at www.saleemali.net.